D0504690

The Imaginary Autocrat

The Imaginary Autocrat

Beau Nash and the Invention of Bath

JOHN EGLIN

First published in Great Britain in 2005 by
PROFILE BOOKS LTD
58A Hatton Garden
London EC1N 8LX
www.profilebooks.com

1 3 5 7 9 10 8 6 4 2

Typeset in Poliphilus by MacGuru Ltd
info@macguru.org.uk
Printed and bound in Great Britain by
Clays, Bungay, Suffolk

A CIP catalogue record for this book is available from the British Library.

ISBN 1 86197 302 0

For
Caroline
and
Aaron
and
Mary Katherine
and
Perry
and
Nolan

Contents

Acknowledgements

This book owes its origins to the suggestion of Linda Colley, and to the encouragement as well as patience of Peter Carson. I am grateful for the support of the University of Montana, which came in the form of sabbatical leave in the autumn of 2003 and grants from the University Research and Creativity Council, as well as from the Boone and Ambrose Funds of the Department of History. An institutional grant from the National Endowment for the Humanities, administered through the Henry E. Huntington Library in San Marino, California, allowed me to spend seven productive months there.

Scholars who have worked at the Huntington will immediately appreciate its resemblance to a Georgian resort, and time I spent there as an NEH Fellow bore the analogy out in many amusing and gratifying ways. My 'Worthy Benefactor' was Roy Ritchie, who, even without a white tricorne hat, was a superb Master of Ceremonies, as well as an informed interlocutor on English and American resort culture. Research and writing were aided by the insights, observations, and questions of other members of the Company, especially Deanne Williams, David Underdown, Susan Amussen, Lois Schwoerer, John King, Walter Woodward, Thomas McLean, Paul Goring, Amanda Vickery, John Styles, Julian Hoppit, Karen Harvey, Ava Arndt, and the top toast of the spring season, Mark Canuel.

The book has also profited from numerous extended discussions with Lawrence Klein and Kenneth Lockridge, and conversations with Peter Briggs, Peter Borsay, Jim Caudle, Pamela Edwards, Philip Carter, Michèle Cohen, Thomas Kavanagh, Donna Andrew, Denis Reynaud and Jo Guldi. Susan Whyman provided invaluable assistance with the Verney Papers. John Brewer, Trevor Fawcett and Molly McClain responded helpfully to written queries. I received valuable advice from Jeff Wiltse, Anya Jabour, Paul Lauren, Linda Frey, Michael Mayer and Fred Skinner, all colleagues in the History Department at the University of Montana. Numerous archivists assisted in research queries, including Margaret Bailey, Anne Mitchell, Esyllt Jewell, Mary Robertson, Sue Hubbard, Margaret Richards, Clare Rider, Rosemary Dunhill, James Stevenson and Philip Hocking. Dianne Rapp assisted with illustrations. I am grateful to Sir Edmund Verney, Bt, and the Claydon House Trust for permission to consult and quote from the Verney family papers, of which the Trust holds copyright.

John Camacho, Mark Foley, Janet Doud, Carol and Luther Luedtke, and Howard Gaass were patient and generous hosts during research trips on both sides of the Atlantic. My erstwhile UM colleague Pamela Voekel, along with Bethany Moreton, first introduced me to the pleasures of the bath in Hot Springs, Montana. Arthur W. Lavidge III has contributed signally to this project in resembling Beau Nash in personality and disposition more closely than anyone I know.

Missoula, Montana
April 2005

Chronology

1674	Richard Nash born 18 October in Swansea, Glamorganshire, Wales
1687	Visit of Mary of Modena, consort of James II, to Bath
1691	Nash matriculates at Jesus College, Oxford
1693	Nash admitted bencher of the Inner Temple
1699	Death of Richard Nash Senior of Camrose, Pembrokeshire, Wales
1702, 1703	Visits of Queen Anne to Bath
1704–5	Conventionally received dates of Nash's arrival in Bath
1705–8	Conventionally received dates of Nash's appointment as Bath MC
1710	Earliest archival reference placing Nash in Bath
1716	Nash made honorary freeman of Bath, along with William Pulteney
1727	Death of Elizabeth Nash, widow of Richard Nash Senior of Camrose
1734	Visit of Prince and Princess of Orange to Bath
1735	Nash assumes post of MC at Tunbridge Wells
1738	Visit of Frederick and Augusta, Prince and Princess of Wales, to Bath
1755	Nash files suits against Thomas Joye and Metcalfe Ashe of Tunbridge Wells
1757	Nash files suits against Walter and William Wiltshire and Charles Simpson
1761	Richard Nash dies 3 February in his house in Saw Close, Bath

1762	Oliver Goldsmith's *Life of Richard Nash* published in October
1705	First Pump Room built
1708	Thomas Harrison opens Assembly Rooms
1720	Expansion of Harrison's Rooms
1727	John Wood begins rebuilding St John's Hospital complex for Duke of Chandos
1730	Catherine Lindsey opens Assembly Rooms
1736	Completion of Queen Square
1748	Completion of Parades
1751	First expansion of Pump Room
1758	Completion of Circus
1688	James II deposed
1689	William III and Mary II named joint monarchs
1701	Act of Settlement
1702	Accession of Queen Anne
1707	Act of Union between England and Scotland
1710	Gaming Act 9 Anne *c.* 19
1714	Accession of George I under Act of Settlement
1715	First Jacobite Rebellion
1721	South Sea Bubble
1722	Atterbury Plot exposed
1727	Accession of George II
1738	Gaming Act 12 George II *c.* 18
1739	Gaming Act 13 George II *c.* 19
1744	Gaming Act 18 George II *c.* 34
1745	Second Jacobite Rebellion
1753	Lord Hardwicke's Marriage Act
1756	Edward Braddock killed at Fort Duquesne
1759	Seizure of Quebec
1760	Accession of George III

Introduction

I would have you know, that the Genius of Bath is connected with and depends on the Genius of Britain: – Whenever, therefore, the kingdom at large is in a flourishing state, Bath is sure to be so too, and is as soon affected by the distresses ... The riches and the poverty of the whole, the virtues and the vices, meet and assemble here; and whatever man may know of either, is found here.[1]

Bath is a Georgian Pompeii preserved not by fallen volcanic ash but by the less catastrophic and more gradually shifting sands of fashion. As one of only two cities in the British Isles to be designated in its entirety as a UNESCO World Heritage Site (Edinburgh is the other), it is one of Britain's national treasures. Then again, the phrase 'national treasure' fails to do justice to a town which has achieved reliquary status in a heritage-obsessed nation. It architecturally reinforces notions of the eighteenth century as an age of (perhaps excessive) refinement and (possibly stultifying) serenity. It is a telling point that Peter Borsay, a leading historian of Georgian urban development singularly qualified to write a definitive study of eighteenth-century Bath, has written instead about the ways that *nineteenth-* and *twentieth-*century commentators *represented* the city.[2] Bath is inextricably associated with Britain's 'aristocratic century', as the historian John Cannon has described it, its status as emblem of elegance reinforced by the posh retailers that line its streets, tempting its visitors with the autoerotic thrill of upmarket consumerism. Its first real architect, John Wood, might have been pleased, even if his grand vision for

Bath failed to restore Roman civilisation along with Roman building. Not until Ruskin would anyone ascribe such transformative power to configurations of stone and brick and mortar, and with more justice.

For visitors today, Bath's unbroken vistas of classical façades wrought in warm, sensuously tawny limestone evoke the serene elegance we so easily associate with the Georgian period. It is a little disquieting, then, to see how neoclassical architecture put eighteenth-century observers like Robert Whatley in mind of ruins. Before John Wood the architect even began his first block of row houses in the city, starting the classicisation completed by his son and namesake, Whatley imagined Bath as a classical ruin resembling the ancient Roman Forum that his well-to-do contemporaries visited on their Grand Tours. In the dedicatory epistle to his *Characters at the Hot-Well* of 1724, he described Bath as he thought it might appear to an observer writing 300 years into the future, when the city's Augustan landmarks would be mouldering heaps of stone, relics of an antiquity ennobled by decrepitude:

> *the Great Pile of Building, made use of for the common Receptacle of all the Company, adjoining to the Town Wall, at the East End of the Grove, the Ruins of which are now with Difficulty perceivable ... The only real piece of ... remaining ancient Grandeur is that which is still call'd the Pump-House, built within the same happy Period; and this the Corporation have with becoming Zeal ... from time to time kept up, as a standing Memorial of what they once were.*

Bath's architectural heritage, however, was not as much the focus of this speculative and nostalgic archaeology as were the surviving memorials of Richard Nash, Bath's legendary Master of Ceremonies, the recipient of Whatley's dedication, a human monument remarkable for a large white beaver hat worn over a black wig. From the imagined perspective of a Bathonian in the year 2023, Whatley recounts

> *a Tradition among the Inhabitants, that soon after the Building of that great Pile, which I mentioned above, and of which we still see some Ruins, his Picture was set up there; and some time after that, his Statue in the fine Walk that lay between the Town Wall on that Side and the River. The Picture, in all probability, met with its Fate before or on the Fall of the Building. And through the Length of Time, the Injuries of the Weather, and Decay of the Town, this Statue has lain neglected, and little remains of it intire but the Pedastal; but of which the Inscription being worn out by Time is not legible.*

By this imagined twenty-first century, Bath has declined, and its buildings fallen into ruins, due to the discontinuation of a custom among visitors 'of voluntarily submitting themselves ... to the Direction of one Gentleman, whom they set up as the common Dictator among them in Matters of Ceremony and Order'. Nash performed this office with greater 'Prudence, Discretion, good Sense, and good Manners' than any of his predecessors or successors, inspiring visitors 'to live with each other' in 'good Humour and genteel Easiness', and drawing 'a great Concourse' to Bath 'for Entertainment, as well as ... for Cure'.[3] Whatley was soon wrenched from his dreamscape back into his own time:

> *I have so long been in my own Thoughts one of the twenty-first Century ... But taking a Turn or two in my Chamber for the Refreshment of my Mind, and accidentally casting my Eye out of my Window, I saw you this Moment go into Hays's; and the very agreeable Oddness of your Appearance, your black Wig, scarlet Countenance, and brown Beaver Habit, brought me out of the deep Reverie into which I had fallen, and I actually saw that very Man living in my Time of whom I was writing as if he had liv'd 300 Years before me.*

Now it is we who find ourselves in the third millennium, not quite

1. *William Hoare's portrait of Richard Nash depicts the Bath MC in the white hat and black wig that became the trademarks of his position*

300 years after Whatley wrote, but almost exactly three centuries after Nash's probable arrival in Bath. Harrison's Assembly Rooms, the old Pump Room and the town wall, all important landmarks when Whatley wrote in 1723, no longer stand. The site of Harrison's is now a traffic island from which bus tours leave, while the site of its counterpart, Dame Lindsey's Rooms, now houses a pub and a video store. The Orange Grove, one of the resort's key social stages in Nash's day, has been denuded of trees and reduced to a small, inconspicuous roundabout overshadowed by the acromegalic bulk of the Imperial Hotel. We do not see the ruins that Whatley would have expected – and perhaps hoped – to see. Neither he nor anyone living in his time would have comprehended our own impulse towards historical preservation, and still less that there should be government offices devoted to it.

Two important points arise from Whatley's dedication. First, all of Bath, rightly or wrongly, is Richard Nash's memorial. As Whatley very presciently guessed, Beau Nash is as much of a fixture in the Bath of twenty-first century tourists and tour guides as he was in the Georgian resort. Few tourists will visit Bath today without hearing or reading of the iconic figure who ruled the social whirl of the Georgian resort. Those who join tours, eavesdrop on them or read the relevant sections of travel guides are sure more than once to run across the story of the hapless Duchess of Queensberry, who was peremptorily divested of the lace apron she wore to a ball in open contravention of Nash's regulations; similarly, they will learn that men who appeared in the Assembly Rooms in boots were likely to have the 'King of Bath' ask loudly if they had brought their horses as well. Visitors, including quite decently educated ones, will nevertheless confuse Richard 'Beau' Nash with the Regency dandy George 'Beau' *Brummel*, or the Regency architect *John* Nash (whom they naturally but erroneously assume was the designer of the Circus and Royal Crescent).

Secondly, Whatley reminds us that the Bath shown to tourists today is not Nash's Bath. The serene and seamlessly Georgian *polis* known to us is very different from the dynamic and rapidly changing cultural centre known to its 'King', who would not even have recognised the Bath of Jane Austen's day. The Cross Bath, the most frequented of four mineral baths operating in the eighteenth century, fell off the tourist itinerary and slowly descended into disrepair. The Roman baths, now decorated with Victorian pastiche statuary, lay hidden under accretions of pavement for most of the eighteenth century. The rooming house in Saw Close which was Nash's last residence today houses a restaurant purportedly haunted by the ghost of his last mistress, Juliana Popjoy. Nash was in fact quite poor by the time he took rooms here; his house in John Court, where he lived for forty years, is mysteriously not marked. If Nash's ghost haunts any location in Bath, it is the Parades, the site of the most prestigious accommodation until the completion of the Circus in 1758, only three years before his death.[4] Nash never saw the Royal Crescent and never set foot in the Upper Assembly Rooms, or in the present Pump Room, the result of extensive remodelling in 1790. During his lifetime, and indeed long afterwards, Bath was a work in progress, a fact acknowledged about two decades ago in a production of Sheridan's *The Rivals* at the National Theatre in London in which one set design featured a half-built Royal Crescent sheathed in scaffolding.[5] We do not think of construction sites as classically serene places, and this is not the image we retain of Bath. At the same time that its architecture and infrastructure were unfinished products in development, so were the different facets of its culture. In his agelessness, and in his ability to remain fashionable while resisting fashion, Nash represented stability, but his own indifference to change did not prevent the resort from changing around him.

Bath was already a well-established spa town when Nash arrived there some time in the middle of the first decade of the eighteenth century, but it was not yet pre-eminent. There were other spas, such as Buxton and Epsom, and Tunbridge Wells was at least as fashionable as Bath, if not more so. Bath's mineral springs had long been touted as a panacea for a wide range of physical ailments when Queen Anne visited in 1702. This visit, according to the received narrative of Bath history, was the making of the resort. Bath's sudden cachet took the spa by surprise, however, and the fashionable visitors who now came in droves found a rude provincial town ill prepared to receive, house or entertain them. It was at this point, the story goes, that Nash, a gambler and man-about-town with a knack for organising entertainment, stepped into the breach, importing musicians from London to play at the weekly balls in the evening and to perform in the Pump Room during the day. By dint of his imposing physical presence and a personality as forceful as it was engaging, Nash moulded an amorphous collection of visitors into a sociable corps – the Company – and drew them into a fixed social routine which governed their every movement from the first glass of the waters in the morning to the last dance at the balls in the evening. As the quality of the amenities and entertainment at Bath improved under Nash's management, so did the quantity of visitors. Soon other resorts followed this lead, prompting Whatley to award Nash not only his accustomed title 'King of Bath' but also the suzerainty of other spas, such as Bristol Hotwells, Tunbridge and Scarborough.[6]

Such princely attributes were apposite given the social authority ultimately ascribed to Nash as Master of Ceremonies. He was credited with developing a code of conduct enjoining civil behaviour on the part of all visitors to all other visitors regardless of background, an achievement that would have reminded classically educated contemporaries of ancient Greek lawgivers such as Lycurgus or Solon. Most famously, Nash was supposed to have outlawed the wearing of swords, precluding the possibility of duels, once frequent events which purportedly claimed the life of at least one of Nash's supposed predecessors. Whether or not Nash unilaterally imposed and enforced these regulations, they were invaluable, as spas like Bath were the first public spaces to be frequented by both established landowning gentry families and those of newly affluent merchants, traders and bankers.

There were more and more of these public spaces in the first decades of the eighteenth century, a phenomenon scholars of the period describe as the expansion of the public sphere. The standards of civility which Nash sought to enforce in Bath were soon taken up by writers and journalists such as Joseph Addison and Richard Steele, who were increasingly in a position to shape public opinion, a development scholars call the project of 'politeness'.[7] 'Politeness' in its Georgian context is as difficult to translate as the Italian *virtù* in a Renaissance context in that both terms can mean several things, all of which reflect cultural values associated with dominant or emerging social groups. 'Polite' Georgians were 'civil', yes, but what did this mean? Some readers will immediately think of Oscar Wilde's definition of gentility as the avoidance of *unintentional* rudeness. Politeness also connoted sophistication, polish and urbanity, and demeanour which was pleasant, obliging and no more formal than necessary. 'Politeness' was also about appearances, and more and more men and women in Britain were concerned about the image they presented to the world. One study of middle-income families in England shows that between 1675 and 1715 the percentage of such households having at least one mirror doubled from 22 per cent to 44 per cent – and families living in the fashion-obsessed capital were excluded from the sample. Demeanour, cutting the right figure, was crucial as well, and involved displaying correct posture and gait and employing appropriate gestures, disciplines that were the province of the dancing master, together with more material attributes such as wearing suitable clothes, possessing proper accessories and using them in the right way. Sociologists today would have no difficulty recognising eighteenth-century 'politeness' as 'cultural capital'. In Britain, at the nexus of a worldwide trade network, it was increasingly possible to purchase many of the requisites of politeness – fine clothes of cotton, linen and silk, and the accoutrements of domestic entertainment, such as china and all the apparatus of tea, coffee and chocolate. In London, where 88 per cent of 'middle-class' households were equipped with mirrors as early as 1675, the percentage of such homes with tea, coffee or chocolate pots rose from 2 per cent in 1675 to 48 per cent in 1705, 78 per cent in 1715, and 96 per cent in 1725.[8] For the first time, men and women in Britain, even those from outside the landed aristocracy and gentry, were able to make themselves over using the resources and opportunities that a commercial society and a worldwide trading empire made available to them.

The emergence of 'politeness', however the term was defined, represented for contemporaries a perceptible shift in social norms, a shift discernible enough to afford Oliver Goldsmith a point of departure for a project a publisher tossed his way. Goldsmith was not yet in 1762 the author of *The Vicar of Wakefield*, *She Stoops to Conquer* and 'The Deserted Village', but a hack writer living on the margins of literary respectability, dependent on the kindness of contacts like John Newbery, best known as a publisher of the new genre of children's literature. 'Mr. Nash – the man in Bath, you know – died the other day,' we imagine Newbery dropping solicitously. 'Old fellow went off without a farthing, of course. Estate's loaded with debts. Wanted to publish his memoirs – can you imagine that? Anyway, his executor's got all his papers. Might be something in it. Interested?' Goldsmith

2. Oliver Goldsmith was still a literary unknown when his biography of Nash was published in 1762, and he remained so for some time afterward

needed the work and the money, and could not turn anything down at that stage of his career. Over the next several months, he managed to cobble together the Georgian equivalent of a genre familiar to us, the instant celebrity biography. There was a problem, however. Although Nash was a celebrity, no one was really sure why. What had he done, and why should anyone care? Goldsmith's solution was ingenious. Pressed to place his subject in a larger context and assign to him some kind of significance, he would credit Nash with introducing politeness into British society:

> *He was the first who diffused a desire of society, and an easiness of address among a whole people who were formerly censured by foreigners for a reservedness of behaviour, and an awkward timidity in their first approaches. He first taught a familiar intercourse among strangers at Bath and Tunbridge … That ease and open access first acquired there, our gentry brought back to the*

metropolis, and thus the whole kingdom by degrees became more refined by lessons originally derived from him.[9]

It helped matters, where Goldsmith was concerned, that he, like many other eighteenth-century Britons, was not certain that 'politeness' and the 'public sphere' it had emerged from were salutary developments. The new culture of consumerism and the public sphere had created a corrupting appetite for luxury. Those who catered to these desires, touted on the one hand as agents of civilisation, appeared to others as purveyors of decadence. Nash neatly and conveniently personified this ambivalence, and Bath under his ascendancy stood proxy for all of the potentialities and liabilities of the brave new world of the British eighteenth century. Politeness, refinement and innocent amusement shaded imperceptibly into luxury, vice and corruption, and nowhere more so than in Georgian Bath, where the finely dressed gentleman could be a notorious cardsharp and the elegant suitor a penniless opportunist. As the literary scholar Peter Briggs has said, Nash served to focus debate in a culture that remained deeply ambivalent about politeness and the manners that went with it.[10]

This consideration might explain why Richard Nash has fascinated and frustrated biographers since Oliver Goldsmith took up the challenge in the immediate aftermath of Nash's death. No fewer than four biographies of Nash have appeared over the course of the twentieth century;[11] every generation, it seems, has needed its own. Nash fascinates prospective biographers because his dazzling eccentricity and the unique social and cultural role he created for himself have made him an irresistible subject. He is a frustrating subject, however, because little is known of his early years, and because documentation is lacking. Nash himself admitted that he rarely picked up a pen, and most of the papers turned over to Goldsmith were printed. Only three autograph letters are known to survive. In these circumstances, one might well ask whether a biography of Nash is really possible. Those who have tried have been forced to rely on material culled from printed sources, especially Goldsmith's biography, John Wood's *Essay Toward a Description of Bath* and the anonymous *Jests of Beau Nash*.[12] This material, recapitulated so uncritically for so long as to be canonised as a narrative tradition, is still the staple of guided tours in Bath today and of existing books on Nash and eighteenth-century Bath. Most of these works were written for popular audiences by authors who, although often very capable and accomplished in other areas, were not professional scholars. They ranged from Lewis Benjamin, who hid his Jewishness under the pen name 'Melville', to Edith Sitwell of the literary family and John Walters, who was, appropriately enough, a retired tabloid journalist.[13] Their work, targeted to a stereotype of readers interested in the Georgian period, tended to be dilettantish and anecdotal. David Gadd, one of the more responsible of these writers, instructively deemed his own book 'historically accurate to the extent that it is ever sensible to make such a claim'.[14] To be fair, writers such as Alfred Barbeau and Willard Connelly did spend time off the beaten research track,[15] but for the most part authors inevitably overlooked the truly interesting story which is to be found only in letters, journals and other documents not intended for publication, or between the lines of anecdotes culled from printed sources.

That said, when approaching a subject like Nash, no scrupulous historian can ignore even the most apocryphal anecdotes, for these constitute an important part of Nash's history. Legends may be debunked; legend itself remains. Nash was as concerned for his reputation in posterity as for his image during his life. Whatley, who described the ruins of Nash's statue as he thought it would look in 2023, wrote his dedication fifteen years before Nash's portrait went up in the Long Room at Wiltshire's, and nearly thirty years before a statue of Nash was actually erected, not in the Spring Gardens but in the Pump Room. If Nash was somehow underwriting Whatley's publication (perhaps by collecting subscriptions for it, which he as dedicatee may well have done), he was already spinning a myth for posterity. In a very real sense, Nash was engaged in the project of autobiography while he still lived. He provides such a vivid and compelling instance of self-invention that, to a great degree, the anecdotal Nash *is* the historical Nash, and the story behind the story is as fascinating as the legend that Nash managed to construct around himself. Much of his story, as recapitulated in Goldsmith and Wood and by biographers over the next two centuries, was his own invention, and important details of this narrative were never challenged, even by harsh critics such as Robert Peach.[16] As tempting as it may be to the empirically minded, any attempt to nail down the facts of Nash's life in a comprehensive way would be futile. For Nash resists chronology to the same degree that he defies empirical verification. His beginning is apocryphal, and his ending may be as well, but for the decades between these terminal dates, his biographers have inevitably allowed him to stand outside of time and outside of events that certainly had an impact on Bath.

One would like to think, of course, that Oliver Goldsmith, given sufficient time and resources, would have done enough justice to his subject matter to give Nash a chronology, but time was certainly not on his hands. The *Life* appeared in the autumn of 1762, only a year and a half after its subject's death. It was written from material that Nash himself had gathered in the last several years of his life for a projected autobiography. In conspicuously advertising his intention to publish memoirs, Nash was effectively forestalling the (for him very unpleasant) necessity of ever putting pen to paper; his solicitation of subscriptions for this project was widely interpreted as generalised blackmail, and subscribers understood that their names would not be mentioned in Nash's rumoured forthcoming tell-all memoirs. 'To such ladies as have secret histories belonging to them,' Sarah Scott wrote to her sister, '[Nash] hints that he knows every ones private life & shall publish it.' As more subscriptions were raised, the greater the assurance was that no such memoir would ever appear from Nash's hand: 'The whole money, two guineas, is to be paid down at once, for he does not pretend any book is to come out.'[17] What materials Nash did assemble passed only after his death into Goldsmith's hands through Nash's executor, George Scott.

If Goldsmith knew Nash, it was only by reputation, and it is not clear that he even knew anyone in Nash's immediate circle before undertaking the biography. Neither is there any record that Goldsmith ever visited Bath before Nash's death; he did visit Bath, possibly for the first time, as the guest of Viscount Clare in 1771. There are points in the *Life of Nash* at which Goldsmith does seem to speak as an acquaintance, writing of seeing Nash one evening in Wiltshire's, or watching him wait an entire day at the Smyrna Coffee House in London 'in order to receive a bow from the Prince, or the Duchess of Marlborough'. Alfred Barbeau, a more energetic researcher than many writers about Bath, pointed out that if Sarah Churchill is meant in this passage, Goldsmith cannot have witnessed the exchange, as he was only sixteen and still in Ireland when the Duchess died in 1744. Slips like these are among the signs that the *Life* was written in haste and rushed to the presses with cursory editing. A remark that George Scott made about being misidentified as the *compiler* (rather than the author) of the *Life* is particularly revealing in this connection.[18] The *Life of Nash* was published anonymously, while Goldsmith was still an unknown, and may originally have been intended as a ghostwritten memoir by someone (such as Scott) who did know Nash.

Two and a half centuries after Goldsmith, we face the additional challenge of explaining to readers raised in post-industrial democracies of the information age what, exactly, Nash did, and why, exactly, he was significant. One of the most recent writers on Nash sees him as a prototype of modern celebrity, the first public figure famous for being famous.[19] Yet Nash's reality was more extraordinary than his myth. Whatever title was ultimately ascribed to him, and whatever authority he appropriated, he seems to have acquired it more or less on his own, with little or no support from any individual or institution. More to the point, many of Nash's contemporaries were aware of the scale of his achievement. Elizabeth Montagu wrote to her husband in 1753 of Nash's 'empire over Mankind, which in so extraordinary a manner he gained & has preserved'.[20] Observers in a position to know harboured no illusions that Nash's position was legitimated by the formal consent of the Company, the Corporation of Bath, or anyone else. They knew that Nash owed his position to little other than the sheer effrontery connoted by period usage of the term 'assurance.' He was a living illus-

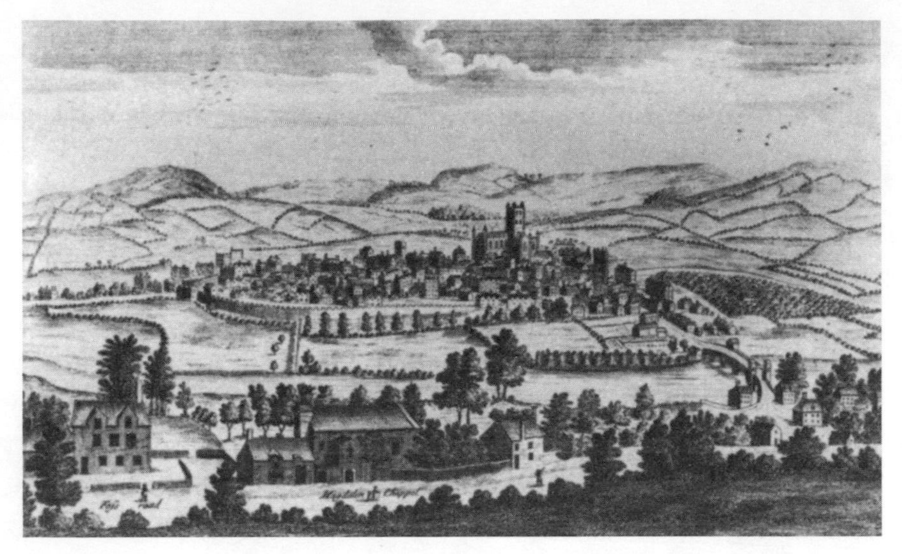

3. Bath very much as it was when Nash arrived early in the eighteenth century

tration of what could be achieved with sufficient self-confidence and self-possession, key attributes of Georgian politeness.

Consequently, this book is concerned as much with Nash's invention of himself as it is with the invention of Bath, and addresses itself not only to the world that Nash made possible, but to the world that made *him* possible. The opening chapters put Nash's rise to prominence in the wider context of Bath's history and mythology. Subsequent chapters examine the sources of Nash's cultural authority as 'King of Bath' under the headings of the subsidiary titles he claimed: Regulator of the Diversions and Moderator of Disputes at Play, to which I have added a third, Overseer of the Marriage Market. We then trace Bath's rapid expansion in the first half of the century, developments that Nash's promotion of the spa and its amusement culture helped to make possible. In fact, as the last chapters make clear, Bath was able to adapt more successfully to cultural change than its 'worthy benefactor' or any of his successors.

1

Bath and Its Kings

I profess to write the history of a man placed in the middle ranks of life; of one, whose vices and virtues were open to the eye of the most undiscerning spectator, who was placed in public view without power to repress censure, or command adulation, who had too much merit not to become remarkable, yet too much folly to arrive at greatness.

It is of very little importance who were the parents, or what was the education of a man who owed so little of his advancement to either.

We should begin his life with his own words: 'I was born October 18, 1674, in Swansea, Glamorganshire.' His father and namesake was Welsh and, Nash insisted, a gentleman, while his mother was the niece of a royalist officer, Colonel Poyer, executed after forces loyal to Parliament took Pembroke.[1] The picture that emerges of Nash's social background was one as solid and respectable as it was unremarkable. Nash Senior was partner in a bottle-making concern, and made enough money, from the factory's small output of just under a thousand quart-bottles a week, for Nash to attend grammar school in Carmarthen, as Goldsmith relates, and as a twentieth-century biographer was able to substantiate.[2] Nash boarded at Carmarthen until he turned seventeen in 1691. Nash Senior apparently sold his share of the glassworks in around 1692, moving to a small farm in the parish of

Camrose, three miles north-west of Haverfordwest, his birthplace. At his death in September 1699, he left thirty head of cattle, 100 sheep, eight pigs, twenty geese and a crop of wheat, barley, oats, peas and hay. These with his household goods (three beds and other furniture, four brass and iron pots, five pewter dishes and one pewter candlestick) and 'weareing Apparell' were valued at £46 2s. 9d. Even if the 'Goods Cattles, & Chattles' were undervalued by the two illiterate husbandmen assigned the task, Richard Nash of Camrose was a man of fairly humble circumstances, as the designation 'yeoman' indicated.[3] When his widow, Elizabeth, died in August 1727, his son and namesake inherited all of her lands, tenements, cattle and chattels according to testamentary formulae, but these were valued at a grand total of £16 7s.; an additional £9 was distributed among Elizabeth's two daughters and seven grandchildren.

No wonder, then, that Nash never discussed his parents, an omission which his contemporaries inevitably noted. When the Duchess of Marlborough made insinuations on that score, Nash answered no, he was *not* ashamed of his father, rather it was his father who had cause to be ashamed of him. He may well have been a disappointment to his father, for as little as we know about Nash *père,* or about the early life of Nash *fils,* this much is clear: the elder Nash was willing to make great sacrifices in the cause of educating his only son. His two daughters were not so fortunate, and at least one of them was left illiterate, witnessing her mother's will with a crudely drawn cross.[4] Nash Senior's decision to sell his partnership and take up sheep farming at the same time that his son was to leave Wales and enter Oxford suggests that he committed much of what he had in the world to securing his son's future. Without access to the financial intermediaries that a more substantial businessman (preferably with London contacts) would have used, he might have had no choice but to entrust a not inconsiderable sum of money to his son. Perhaps the son had done nothing in the first seventeen years of his life to create any apprehensions on his father's part.

The elder Nash may have secured for his son the patronage of the first Duke of Beaufort, whose former seat in Swansea was leased to

Nash senior and his partner, John Man, for their glassworks. It was possibly as a Beaufort client that Nash entered Oxford. In March 1692 he matriculated at Jesus College, a predictable course for a university-bound Welshman. The modesty of his father's background, although noted on the college register, where he was listed as 'pleb', was no impediment to his entry. At Oxford, however, social hierarchy was reinforced visually. Undergraduates sporting titles of nobility were not only entitled to silken gowns trimmed in gold lace but also permitted to choose the colour. Admittedly this plumage of sky blue, scarlet or forest green was worn only for full-dress occasions, but even in 'undress' the aristocratic undergraduate was distinguished by the gold tassel on his black velvet cap. Next in the food chain were gentlemen commoners in black silk gowns adorned with row upon row of black tassels. They, with the noblemen, were entitled to the most luxurious rooms their colleges could offer, and boasted the right to dine at high table with the fellows. The next rank down, that of commoners, made up the vast majority of undergraduates. Nash was a 'batteler', a rank peculiar to his college. Unlike commoners, who paid a flat fee for their board, battelers paid on an *à la carte* basis. This provision spared Nash the ignominy of becoming a servitor, obliged to wear a tell-tale round cap, which advertised that its wearer paid his way and earned his keep by performing menial tasks for his more affluent contemporaries.[5] Nash's buttery bills give the lie to the story, otherwise utterly plausible, that he was 'sent down' owing his college money. His name does not appear in the list of delinquent accounts.[6] There is no evidence that Nash's departure from Oxford was anything other than pro forma, as it was by no means unusual in the late seventeenth century or afterwards for undergraduates to depart after only one year without taking a degree. In June 1693 Nash was enrolled as a student of the Inner Temple, the occasion of a social promotion, if only in archival terms, as he and his father were recorded as 'gent'.

Perhaps in Oxford or perhaps in London, young Richard Nash came to believe that he was meant for greater things than returning to Wales, with some reading in law, and going into his father's old business. His father clearly intended a career for him along those lines. There was a future in bottles, after all. To begin with, the wine trade was taking off, and there were also medicinal waters being touted by various spas. In this way, Nash might actually have acquired the means to live as he subsequently chose, and lived and died in comfortable obscurity, appearing only on the historiographical radar screen two centuries or so later as part of the population sample in a historical demography of the eighteenth-century Welsh bourgeoisie. The elder Nash, however, failed to appreciate that his son was now in the second-largest city in Europe for the first time in his life. Perhaps the sums entrusted to him proved too great a temptation for a late adolescent to resist, and he never got around to reading for the bar. After Nash's entry into the Inns of Court, we are left alone with only anecdotes, generated by Nash himself, to cover the documentary gap of seventeen years between his appearance in the Inner Temple admissions register in 1693 and his resurfacing in Bath correspondence (throwing dice for very high stakes) in 1710.

That so little is known about Nash's early life is testimony to his success in constructing his own legend. 'Impostor' is too strong a word for Nash, who neither pretended to be someone he was not, nor claimed more august lineage than he actually possessed, unlike the poet Richard Savage, who claimed to be the natural son of adulterous aristocrats. Nash knew – perhaps from experience – that such ruses were unsustainable, and the tales he spread about himself were concocted to intrigue his hearers, not to impress them. Goldsmith admitted that Nash 'often spoke falsehoods, but never had any of his harmless tales tinctured with malice'.[7] For good measure, he larded his self-presentation with a healthy dose of self-deprecation. Until his old age, when more serious accusations of personal corruption began to fly, he might have agreed with Oscar Wilde that the only thing worse than being talked about was not being talked about, except that he revelled in public exposure. Nash, according to his executor, 'took great Pleasure in giving away printed Papers relating to Himself', so much so that papers like these 'were in every Persons hands acquainted with him'.[8] Nash assiduously circulated many of the stories that subsequently appeared in Gold-smith's biography and the *Jests of Beau Nash,* including those at his expense. Often their relative plausibility is our only guide in judging their accuracy, as must have been the case for Nash's contemporary hearers.

In most cases we must throw ourselves on the mercy of Goldsmith, who took Nash at his word too often, and manufactured anecdotes, or borrowed them from other sources. His interpretive instincts, however, were good. Read analytically, 'against the grain', the *Life* is a valuable source. The biographer knew, after all, what it was to live on the margins of respectability, and describes the expedients and exigencies of life on the edge with telling familiarity:

> *They who know the town, cannot be unacquainted with such a character as I describe; one, who though he may have dined in private from a cook's shop, shall dress at six for the side box; one of those whose wants are only known to their laundress, and tradesmen, and their fine cloaths to half the nobility; who spend more in their chair hire, than housekeeping; and prefer a bow from a Lord, to a dinner from a Commoner.*[9]

Young Nash became the hero of his own picaresque tale. A more colourful exit from Oxford would have to be arranged after the fact, of course, and inconvenient details such as that tedious punctilio with regard to debts airbrushed away. Goldsmith tells us that Nash became 'a professed admirer of the sex', meaning sex female, as if males were immune to objectification, and on the heels of the discovery of sex (quite reasonable for someone not yet eighteen) came the realisation that the life of a scholar was not conducive to the assiduous pursuit of it. Univer-sity life was abandoned, the hasty departure subsequently dressed up with the tale of a narrow brush with entrapment by a matrimonially ambitious local woman. So Goldsmith has it, seventy-odd years after the fact. A quarter of a century before Goldsmith wrote, however, a Cambridge don heard the head of his college say that while Nash had indeed been at Jesus (as a lowly servitor), and had indeed been expelled, it was for an assault on the proctor, who had since become Bishop of Bath and Wells.

A stint in the army was next – or was it the navy? Thomas Wilson, the same Cambridge fellow who heard stories of Nash around the high table at St John's in 1736, was also told that Nash went to sea, was cast away in Ireland, converted to Catholicism and commanded a French warship before being cashiered for bad behaviour.[10] One of numerous persistent unconfirmed rumours about Nash did have it that he was a Jacobite, a supporter of the exiled Stuart dynasty. The Earl of Egmont called him a 'violent' Tory and 'a perfect Jacobite'; of course, Nash had told him

> *that when a hundred thousand pound was put on the Pretender's head, he said, 'Why put the nation to that charge; is it not better to put three crowns on his head?' He added that a spy carried this to Lord Sunderland, who chid him, but that he answered, fifteen shillings is less than a hundred thousand pounds.*[11]

Stories like this one made Nash seem dangerous and daring to his contemporaries. According to Goldsmith, anyway, Nash purchased an army commission (later biographers thought it more likely that his father had purchased this for him) and was soon strutting about in an officer's scarlet. But if Oxford did not afford time and opportunity for the sexual adventurer he had become, the regiment did not afford the necessary income, and Nash was already spending much of his money on clothes, 'dressing to the edge of his finances'. Friends, worried that he was moonlighting as a highwayman, were relieved (on being shown a *billet doux* with £50 enclosed) to find that he was merely a gigolo.[12]

Nash's career at the Inns of Court provided the opportunity for a number of important character-developing anecdotes. The most important (if completely mythical) of these stories presents us with Nash's first epiphany, the discovery of a talent that would be the foundation of what passed for a career. The Inns of Court were among the corporate bodies with the privilege of receiving the monarch to congratulate him or her upon accession to the throne, and the benchers and barristers had traditionally marked the occasion with 'revels and a pageant', a custom which by Goldsmith's day had conveniently fallen into disuse. Apparently so many entities possessed this right of feasting the new monarch that it was some years before all could be satisfied, and, in the case of William III and the Inns of Court, no opportunity arose until after the death of Mary II. Why a rank-and-file 'bencher' barely into his twenties would have been selected by his elders and betters to superintend a royal entertainment would have been anyone's guess even in the seventeenth century. More incredible is the suggestion that a dour Calvinist like William of Orange would have been sufficiently pleased with a theatrical entertainment to offer its producer a knighthood. The episode is an elaborate backdrop for the first of many memorable 'jests', when Nash accepts the honour offered on the condition of being a Poor Knight of Windsor, in order to have a position in keeping with his fortune.[13] Since the King did not take the hint, leaving Nash unpensioned as well as untitled, there were no concrete details for those who heard Nash tell this story to pin their doubts on. By that time, of course, Nash had established his talents as an impresario, and if by circulating this tale he was padding the back end of his résumé, it made little difference to anyone.

At least the story of his close encounter with William of Orange was original. The same cannot be said of another Inns of Court episode that was adapted (admittedly with attribution) from Richard Steele. This story illustrated another of Nash's talents, namely his propensity to give away money, both his own and that of others. Steele recorded a tradition of the Templars in choosing one of their number as 'king' and allowing him an expense account. When the expense reports of one such 'king' were reviewed, the auditors questioned an expenditure of £10 'for making a man happy'. This particular sovereign responded that he had overheard a poor man saying to another that ten pounds would make him happy, and that he had obliged. Instead of demanding the remuneration that their king offered, the treasurers of the Temple doubled the sum of his alms. Goldsmith, in recounting this story, supplied the name that Steele had supposedly omitted. Nash was forever claiming that incidents in his life had inspired episodes in literary works, usually those from the Augustan period whose authors were long dead. Goldsmith, however, was so satisfied with the anecdote that he repeated it in another context in the *Life.* This time it is a 'gentleman of broken fortune' who sees Nash win £200 at picquet, and exclaims how happy that sum would make him, at which Nash hands him his winnings with the injunction to 'go and be happy'. Another of Goldsmith's insights into Nash's mode of philanthropy, however, was an unacknowledged adaptation of an earlier work. In 1759 Goldsmith published an essay, 'On Justice and Generosity', in which he translated an excerpt from Justus Van Effen, a Dutch writer. In this essay, a character named Lysippus receives a demand from his banker for repayment of a debt of £40, and is then asked for the same sum by 'a distressed acquaintance'. Lysippus immediately grants the second request, but rebuffs the first, as he will be performing a favour in one case, but merely doing what is required in the other. Goldsmith transformed Lysippus into Nash, and gives the story a plot complication, as the importunate acquaintance is surreptitiously the agent of the creditor, who had otherwise given up hope of ever retrieving his £20. The ruse succeeds, and Nash, apprised of the deception, is incensed at his creditor, since payment of his £20 'would not increase our friendship', while the loan of the same sum 'was procuring a new friend, by conferring a new obligation'.[14]

The veneer of gentility that Nash maintained was very thin but nevertheless costly to keep up, and another 'tale type' (to use the jargon of the anthropological study of folklore) shows Nash reconciling his personal dignity with his willingness to do almost anything for money – such as riding through a village naked on the back of a cow. It was said, for example, that to win a wager for fifty guineas, he stood at the west door of York Minster wearing only a blanket as the congregation left at the end of services. When the Dean of York recognised him and asked for an explanation, Nash pointed to the friends who had put him up to the wager and said that he was performing penance 'for keeping bad company'. This story, at least, bears some of the verisimilitude that other anecdotes lack. The specificity of location, the fact of its being off the beaten track for someone supposedly based in London and the conversation with the Dean do not sound like invented details. Furthermore, the Dean of York from 1697 until 1702 was Thomas Gale; in June 1705 his 23-year-old son, Samuel, visited Bath and wrote an account of it. Whether or not Nash was actually Master of Ceremonies at this time (as he later claimed), he was possibly already living in Bath. He may have known Samuel Gale, and it is tempting to think that Gale was one of Nash's companions in York.

At this point, it is Thomas Wilson's turn to be plausible in saying that Nash, after washing ashore again either literally or figuratively, 'Turned Gamester'. It was as a gamester no different from any number of others that flocked to the spas that he first appeared in Bath some time in the early years of Queen Anne's reign. It is here that Nash's story ends for the time being, so that the longer story of Bath may begin.

> *Let this then suffice for the Antiquity of the Waters ... doubtless they were known, and made use of too, long before any Author writ of them: So that to trace their Original, is to unravel the Creation, and to make enquiry for their commencement, little different than to seek after the Head of the Nile.*[15]

The history of Bath does not begin with Richard Nash, but we find in it the same mixture of fact and legend. It made sense, of course, for Bath to be ruled by a metaphorical king, for it had long been associated with kings of one sort or another, whether these kings or their kingship was mythical, symbolic or entirely too palpable and real. From the miasmic haze of antiquity came the legend, potentially provocative in the political climate of Augustan England, of Bladud, the prince exiled from his father's court some time in the ninth century BC after contracting leprosy. Turned out of the palace and reduced to herding pigs for a living, Bladud infected his porcine charges, only to find that they were cured after wallowing in some vaguely foul-smelling hot

4. Bladud, Bath's mythical founder, in an engraving from John Wood's Description of Bath

springs that swine and swineherd had run across in their meanderings over what became the Somerset countryside. Restored to health and wholeness by following the example of his pigs, Bladud returned to court and to his rightful place in the line of succession. Upon acceding to the throne, the grateful King Bladud built cisterns to contain the hot springs at the place he called Caerbadus, followed closely by a palace to which he moved his court. Bath's resulting status as a capital of the ancient British kings was a considerable source of civic pride, according to John Wood, until the seventeenth century at least.[16] Even those who accepted the verdict of antiquarian scholars that the stories of Bladud and all of the other ancient British kings were 'at best, uncertain' had a healthy respect for historical myth.[17]

An ancient royal capital it may not have been, but Celtic coins found in the King's Bath spring suggest that the springs were known in pre-Roman times, and one archaeologist suggests that the area of the three springs, prominent features of the landscape for at least 10,000 years, may have been sacred space.[18] It was hardly the pastoral setting that Bladud encountered in legend, but a thickly wooded hillside from which the steaming water ran in rivulets. Those who penetrated the ground cover, with or without pigs in tow, would have come upon what looked like the scene of some grotesque natural disaster, with the springs themselves bubbling noxiously from pools of black quicksand, surrounded by dead vegetation, rocks and boulders, all turned blood red from the mineral content – in this case oxidised iron salts – of the water. The prehistoric inhabitants of the area (traces of Iron Age settlements have been found nearby) kept clear of the springs. They may have been terrified of their appearance or put off by their odour.

For the Romans who arrived in the middle of the first century AD, the discovery of hot springs must have been a godsend in the grey, chilly and damp climate of a remote hardship post. What the native Celts avoided in fear or disgust the Romans transformed into an outpost of civilisation, a settlement they called 'the waters of Sulis' after a local Celtic deity which they grafted on to their own Minerva. The Roman baths were part of the temple complex of Minerva Sulis begun in the 60s. The largest of the springs was reinforced with masonry and fitted with a conduit that fed water into the three pools typically found at other Roman healing shrines. Aquae Sulis, with its temple and adjoining baths, and its site near the intersection of two major Roman roads, became an important religious centre. Pilgrims from all over the Roman world tossed over 12,000 coins into the springs as offerings, as well as petitions to the goddess engraved on lead and pewter tablets. Although far smaller than other Roman settlements in Britain, its wealth was out of all proportion to its size, as the number of mosaic floors found in the area, together with the continuing expansion and improvement of the temple complex, indicates. For all of its evident success, the Roman shrine was not immune to the fragmentation of the empire, and the construction of a wall around the settlement in the fourth century was perhaps the first sign of trouble. A century later, the Romans were gone, having made little effort in over three centuries of occupation towards culturally integrating Britain into their empire. The imposing temple slowly collapsed, its decorations made into paving stones as the magnificent roofs over the baths fell piece by piece into the water. Centuries passed as layer upon layer of earth and rock accumulated over the temple precinct.

Strategic considerations contributed to the gradual re-emergence of Bath beginning in the eighth century. Its proximity to the Roman roads that were still major thoroughfares was one important factor in its resurgence, as was its position on the frontier of the Anglo-Saxon kingdoms of Mercia and Wessex. The monastery of St Peter, the antecedent of the Abbey, was established by this time, and in May 973 Edgar, the first king of all the English, was crowned there, a fact that later contributed to Bath's 'royal' stature. Medieval Bath, in addition to being a market town and centre of cloth manufacture, was a seat of the compound diocese of Bath and Wells, and also the site of a Benedictine priory. When John of Tours, a physician as well as an ecclesiast, became bishop early in the twelfth century, his promotion of the thaumaturgic property of the water soon turned Bath into the pilgrimage site it had not been since Roman times. The King's Bath, Cross Bath and Hot Bath were built under the jurisdiction of the bishop and administered by the prior. When the priory fell victim to the Reformation in the Dissolution of 1539, control of the baths gradually passed through the hands of the bishop to the Corporation, which had completely taken over the baths by the 1580s. The city fathers smelt opportunity as well as sulphur in the water, and by 1569 they were committing an extraordinary sum in excess of £4,000 to new residential construction. A new bath, later to be known as the Queen's Bath, had already been built directly adjacent to the King's Bath two years earlier.[19]

Of the five baths operating at the spa by the later sixteenth century, the King's Bath was the oldest and the most extensively used, but with a water temperature of 120 degrees Fahrenheit, it was too hot for many bathers to endure. The Queen's Bath, directly adjacent and with access to the King's Bath through covered passageways, was four or five degrees cooler. The Hot Bath was the preserve of the seriously ill, who could be 'pumped' there, and the Leper's Bath was reserved for those

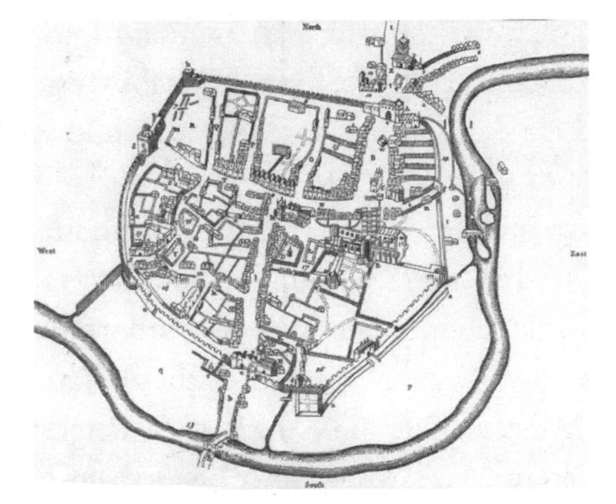

5. John Speed's map of Elizabethan Bath shows the five baths in use by that time

with infectious diseases, since care was taken that water from this bath did not circulate into any of the others. The smaller and relatively cool Cross Bath was some distance to the west of these; because it afforded *relative* privacy, it ultimately became the bath of choice for the 'better sort' of visitors. These last included royalty, buttressing the resort's claimed association with the ancient and modern monarchs of Britain. Elizabeth I visited Bath in 1574 and again in 1591, and her courtiers – the Cecils in particular – were fond of it, but it was the Stuarts, the last of Britain's *rois thaumaturges* to touch for the 'king's evil', who were particularly and even provocatively associated with Bath. It was the visit in 1613 of James I and Anne of Denmark, his queen, that the rechristening of the erstwhile 'New Bath' as the 'Queen's Bath' commemorated; she visited again in 1615, and he again in 1618. Charles I came in 1628 and 1634. It was also under the Stuarts that Bath's already thriving resort economy largely supplanted its cloth industry as the major source of income. After the Civil War wiped out whatever was left of this deteriorating trade, Bath was completely dependent on its spa.[20]

Thus the 1663 visit of Catherine of Braganza, consort of Charles II, was a near disaster. Observers would easily have assumed that she was visiting with a view to curing her infertility, as this property was, and continued to be, attributed to the water. The evident ill-success of this mission may explain why Tunbridge Wells overtook Bath as the preferred courtly spa for a time in the decades after the Restoration. A quarter of a century later, however, the visit of another royal consort restored the reputation of the water in spectacular fashion. Mary of Modena, wife of James II, having endured a series of miscarriages and stillbirths since her marriage, arrived in Bath late in the summer of 1687 in the hope of restoring her fertility. The stakes were high; without a male heir, James's throne would devolve on one of his daughters by his first marriage. In June of the next year, she gave birth to a healthy male infant. The thrones of England and Scotland had an heir apparent and Bath was vindicated. James's Secretary of State, the Earl of Melfort, erected an appropriately grand monument to the blessed event in the Cross Bath. The monument, in place by September 1688, featured a dome supported by three columns (for the three kingdoms) and surmounted by a cross and crown of thorns as well as cherubim holding a crown, orb and sceptre. The dove of the Holy Ghost descended from the centre of the dome and inscriptions made explicit the role of the water in enabling the Queen to produce an heir, securing the succession and saving Bath. The spa did not have long to enjoy its triumph, due to the inconvenient detail that James, Mary of Modena, the Earl of Melfort and the infant Prince of Wales either were or were to be staunch Roman Catholics. By the end of that year, all of them had fled to France.

Historians continue to debate the repercussions of the palace coup that Macaulay and Trevelyan dubbed the 'Glorious Revolution', but for Bath one set of consequences was already clear. The Cross Bath, the most genteel and fashionable of the baths, had been turned into a potent, and potently embarrassing, symbol of the now exiled dynasty. The Melfort monument was scarcely unveiled in the Cross Bath before it was subjected to ideological cosmetic surgery. The dove, crown of thorns and inscriptions were removed immediately after James II's flight in 1688, although Celia Fiennes noted a decade later that the 'saints and cupids according to the phancye and religion of ... Queen Mary of Modina' remained in 'thanks and acknowledgements to the Saints or Virgin Mary for the Welsh Prince she imposed on us'.[21] In

6. Bath, perhaps protesting too much, advertises its loyalty to the new regime in 1689

addition to hastily hacking at masonry, the Corporation took great and immediate pains to greet the *new* dynasty, and to publicise the efforts of 'A Great number of the best Quality of the City of *Bath*' to commemorate the coronation of William and Mary and express 'Gratitude for their happy deliverance from *POPERY* and *SLAVERY*'. The procession they staged included a 100 young men marching in formation with swords, followed by 200 'Virgins, with Crowns on their Heads, and Sceptres in their Hands'. Twenty-five women followed, costumed as Amazons with 'their right Paps so artificially concealed, [that] the Spectators thought them cut off, to compleat the similitude'. Should any contemporaries have failed to take the point, a broadside with an engraving of the procession appeared.[22]

The intractable Jacobite associations that dogged Bath in spite of these demonstrations explain the near obsession of local authorities with procuring royal patronage for the resort. In subsequent accounts of the spa's history, much more credit was given to the visits of Anne as Princess and Queen as pivotal in the emergence of Bath as a fashionable centre. This is not to say, of course, that her visits in 1702 and 1703 were not highly beneficial to the spa. They fell close to her accession and presented an opportunity for local elites, including the Bath Corporation, to demonstrate their loyalty. In addition, a royal visit to Bath or anywhere else entailed a concourse of high-ranking visitors. Anne was accompanied, for example, by the Lord Treasurer, Sidney Godolphin, and by Charles Hedges, one of the Secretaries of State; Hedges's colleague, the Earl of Nottingham, held down the fort in Whitehall. Neither Godolphin nor Hedges, nor any other member of the Queen's entourage, was permitted to leave Bath before her, even on official business, without her permission.[23] For the duration of the monarch's stay, Bath had a captive market. Once she left, however, it was to be over eighty years before another sitting sovereign would visit the spa. The importance of this royal visit to Wood, Goldsmith and other writers stemmed from its having been the last of its kind.

Clearly something more than the endorsement that came with a royal visit was needed for the growing resort to recast itself and shed its problematic associations. The passage of the baths from priory to Corporation might have secularised their day-to-day management, but it had not purged the distinctly popish odour of the miraculous from the water itself. It was already enough that the Gothic buildings of the city's fabric, especially the Abbey, were architectural reminders of its old identity as a pilgrimage site. At the same time that control of the baths passed from ecclesiastical to civil authority, the thaumaturgic properties of the water touted by ecclesiasts were supplanted by therapeutic qualities promoted by medical professionals. Initially, the medical strand in the lore of Bath's water did not supplant the thaumaturgic strand as much as intertwine with it. Thomas Ken, Bishop of Bath and Wells until unseated as a non-juror in 1691, was reluctant to banish the aura of sacred mystery from the water completely and, hearkening to his medieval predecessors, clung to whatever vestiges of authority over the water he could claim for his see. 'Good Christian Brother or Sister,' he addressed those he clearly still thought of as pilgrims, 'Whatsoever the Calamity ... which brings you to this place, I am sensible how tender a regard I ought to have for you; since you are come within my

7. This image of the Cross Bath curiously has Melfort's monument largely intact. Note the spectator's gallery

Fold.' Ken would defer to the medical community only up to a point, and advised his 'flock' to

> *observe the advices of your spiritual Physitians, as you are wont to do those of your Corporal. Do not think the Baths can do you any good, without Gods immediate blessing on them; for it is God that must first heal the waters, before they can have any virtue to heal you.*[24]

Likewise, medical practitioners saw nothing wrong with even politically provocative miracles if these augmented their client base. While the Bath physician Thomas Guidott tactfully omitted Mary of Modena from his list of 200 remarkable Bath cures, he twice mentioned 'the new *marble* Cross, erected by *JOHN* Earl of *Melfort*', knowing that no explanation of the events that had occasioned the monument would be necessary. He also carefully noted the decorations, akin to votive offerings, that the grateful cured left, from the engraved brass rings that lined all of the baths, to the crutch that Elizabeth Booth left on the Melfort Cross, to the lead bench a Northamptonshire gentleman donated to render the Cross Bath more 'convenient' (and more poisonous) to the bathers, until this was removed for Melfort's monument.[25]

Ultimately Guidott and other doctors recognised that the water's reputation would be best grounded on a foundation of empirical proof in the form of mutiple case histories. The water had now to draw its power from neoclassical reason rather than Gothic superstition; its properties had to leave the realm of religious miracle for that of scientific fact. Another practitioner, Robert Pierce, echoed Guidott's suggestion that 'for the Benefit of the City ... a Catalogue of Eminent Cures should every Year be printed'. And since 'to put out a Rehearsal of Cures, without naming the Persons on whom they were wrought ... might be looked on as a Deceit', Pierce, who was seventy-five and at the end of his career, was willing to throw doctor–patient confidentiality to the wind and name names, including those of peers of the realm, although he preserved anonymity 'in those Distempers that carry with them any Shew of Scandal'. Pierce hoped that the health and happiness of future patients, as well as the prosperity of the spa, would earn him the 'Pardon of those that take it amiss that they (or any of their Relations or Friends) are named in these Recitals', and he cited scruples over patient privacy to explain why no medical practitioner had yet written to endorse the curative faculty of the water.[26] In fact, the water had always enjoyed a higher reputation than the medical professionals who prescribed it, and until late in the seventeenth century the physicians needed Bath much more than Bath needed them. But as scientific rationalism increasingly came to be seen as consonant with the principles of 1688, scientific authority became the logical medium through which to promote the water and enhance its reputation.

The endorsement of medical science was a two-edged sword, however, as the scientific community was as riven with internal politics and rivalries in the seventeenth century as now, and the same medical authority which could cement reputations could also undermine them,

8. Dr John Radcliffe, physician to Queen Anne, slighted the efficacy of Bath's water and suffered attacks from the spa's medical community

especially when professional standing and ego were at stake. Bath, basking in the glow of a second consecutive royal visit in 1703, received a rude shock when one of the Queen's doctors, John Radcliffe, asserted that the active ingredients in the water quickly evaporated, and that the water was completely ineffectual if not drunk hot from the pump. The next year the Bath physician William Oliver, writing to recommend the ingestion of Bath water, not only took issue with Radcliffe but delivered a ten-page *ad hominem* attack.[27] Radcliffe was reportedly so incensed that he threatened to use the full force of his professional status to defame the spa enough to reduce the price of lodgings at Bath to half a crown per week.[28]

~

For Wood and Goldsmith, Radcliffe's threat to 'cast a toad into the waters' was a critical episode. It was Nash's entrée into the good graces of the resort community, his opportunity to become their Pied Piper.

'Like the hero of myth and romance,' one literary scholar has written of this anecdote in the *Life,* 'Nash establishes his authority ... by resolving a crisis as he enters the city.'[29] Goldsmith, largely parroting Wood, related

> *that it was in this situation of things ... that Mr. Nash first came into that city, and hearing the threat of this Physician, he humorously assured the people that if they would give him leave, he would charm away the poisons of the Doctor's toad, as they usually charmed the venom of the Tarantula, by music. He therefore was immediately empowered to set up the force of a band of music, against the Doctor's reptile; the company very sensibly encreased, Nash triumphed, and the sovereignty of the city was declared to him by every rank of people.*[30]

This story, like the others in the Nash cycle, raises more questions than it answers, but they are important questions. The story poses a relationship between the spa's therapeutic culture and its amusement culture, a relationship that puzzled Goldsmith, who wondered how it was that the sick were able to entice the well to follow them to Bath, as much as it puzzles us. Goldsmith could never satisfactorily answer his own question, but it did give him grounds for crediting Nash with turning a healing spa into a playground. As it happened, healing and amusement had coexisted in Bath for some years before Nash arrived.

2

The Stewards of the Feast

There are more sporting Gentlemen Here then ever I saw and Mr Nash who is as Great as any of them throwes att 40 Ginnyes A Maine and Ile assure you there is nothing like want of mony to bee scene Here …

Although Richard Nash probably arrived in Bath by the summer of 1705 (possibly in the company of Samuel Gale), he does not appear in documents until 1710, when the author of the extract above named Nash among the most notable 'sporting Gentlemen' (i.e. gamblers) there.[1] Alexander Pope mentioned him in 1714, but only as one among his many acquaintances in Bath.[2] Even after he was generally recognised as a sort of master of the revels, he was still known primarily as a gambler. It was only in 1716 that Nash was noted as anything more than a regular visitor. In this, the same year that the Corporation awarded Nash the freedom of Bath, the 24-year-old barrister Dudley Ryder proclaimed him 'the life and soul of all their diversions', so much so that 'without him there is no play nor assembly nor ball and everybody seems not to know what to do if he is absent'.[3] Apart from recognising his influence over visitors, however, Ryder did not know what to call Nash. As it happened, it took as long for Nash to establish his authority as it took to find language to denominate that authority.

Robert Whatley dated his dedication to Nash in the eighteenth year of his 'reign' as King of Bath, indicating that the date of 1705 was being claimed for the beginning of his tenure as Master of Ceremonies as early as 1723. As for the circumstances of his elevation, Goldsmith and Wood tell straightforwardly of an apostolic succession. Nash, very simply, was chosen to succeed Captain Webster, who had been killed in a duel, and who presumably had been chosen to succeed *his* predecessor in his turn.

There is no archival evidence, however, that any such office ever existed at Bath before Nash occupied it. There is no record, for example, that the Corporation of Bath made any such appointment, although the Council Book lists appointments of all manner of major and minor posts connected with the baths and the Pump Room. The only mention of a Master of Ceremonies at any English spa in this period is fictitious, appearing in a comedy of manners set in Tunbridge Wells. This was Thomas Baker's *Tunbridge-Walks* of 1703, in which the position is not made to seem very prestigious or even desirable. Its occupant, the outrageously epicene Mr Maiden, is self-appointed. One character declares that 'Mr. *Maiden* is the most useful Person in such a publick Place, and distinguishes himself so obligingly by promoting ev'ry Diversion'. 'Oh, Madam,' Maiden replies, 'I am Master of the Ceremonies here, appoint all the Dancing, Summon the Ladies, and Manage the Musick.' He is also a transvestite: 'I was dress'd up last Winter in my Lady *Fussock's* Cherry-colour'd Damask, sat a whole Play in the Front-Seat of the Box, and was taken for a *Dutch* Woman of Quality.' When confronted with allegations of bedding his landlady's chambermaid, he protests, ''tis well known I have more Modesty, and never lay with a Woman in my Life.' Ultimately, Maiden is 'outed': for all his pretensions to gentility and refinement, he has no estate, and is found to have worked as a haberdasher in the Exchange.[4] It is worth noting that Maiden is a cultural broker at the same time that he is a despised parvenu. Perhaps those non-fictional cultural entrepreneurs that Maiden represented (Nash, the operatic impresario John Joseph Heidegger and the art collector and bibliophile Joseph Smith come to mind) were successful precisely because their social marginality gave them a clearer sense of the value of the commodities, tangible and otherwise, that they trafficked in. This consideration would help to explain how and why it was that Nash came to be not only a fixture of social life at the resort but its undisputed leader. As it happened, Nash arrived in Bath at a critical juncture in its history, as the town and its spa were undergoing a series of fundamental transformations. His first decade there saw important changes in the structure of its amusement culture that allowed the spa to expand on a scale undreamt of by other resorts. Nash was well placed to advance himself socially by associating himself with and even exploiting these changes, even if he had little if anything to do with initiating them.

~

The city in which Nash arrived was an established spa with an already thriving amusement culture. The pride that its citizens took in their town is evident from Joseph Gilmore's 1694 map, an extraordinary piece of topography well worth a moment of our attention. Even in the twenty-first century, maps are never objective depictions of geographic 'reality', but are instead selective representations of physical space which are conditioned by assumptions about and aspirations for that space. Accordingly, Gilmore produced an iconic representation of civic space that does not represent a place as much as an attitude about that place. It is a 'map' only in the sense that any of the paintings done of Elizabeth I in the sixteenth century are 'portraits'. It would have been of very little use to contemporaries trying to locate the lodging house they had engaged, as representation of the street pattern is seriously compromised by the pains taken to render the city's architectural profile.

In any case, the street plan is not what catches our eye. Instead, it is the border, decorated with the front elevations of all the major buildings in town, that holds our attention. Most of these are inns and lodging houses, often the property of aldermen or other prominent townspeople. Although these were scattered through the town, on Gilmore's border they present a solid architectural front of the unabashed Tudor and

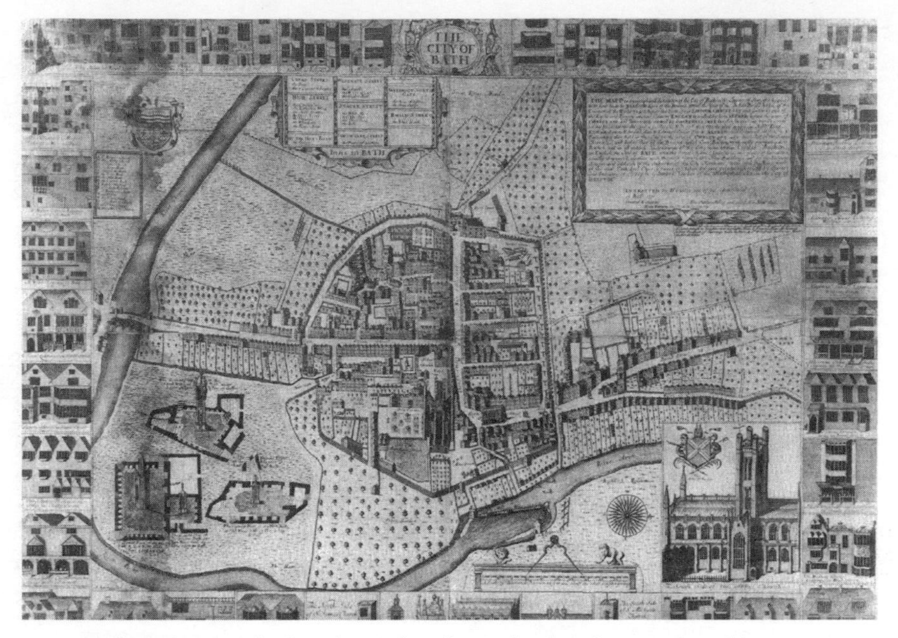

9. Gilmore's map of 1694 shows that the spa by then dominated Bath's economy

Jacobean splendour that the classicising taste of the next century would find so jarring. The baths, including the Cross Bath with the Melfort monument (complete with confessionally suspect cherubim and dove), are shown in insets. Gilmore's map was published to reflect that Bath had risen in public regard, that its inhabitants had begun 'to make their houses more commodious', with the result that the city had become 'famous for its buildings and company'.[5] Celia Fiennes was favourably impressed with the building she saw in the late-seventeenth-century city, much of which was new and well furnished.[6] Even John Wood, otherwise eager to denigrate late Stuart and early Hanoverian Bath, admitted that, under the auspices of prominent townsmen, Bath's architecture had steadily improved in the twenty years from the late 1680s. Thatched roofs were changed to tile, 'low and obscure Lights were turned into elegant Sash Windows; ... Houses were raised to five and more Stories' with 'lavish' exterior decoration. In 1707 the Bath alderman George Trim began a new street in the north-west corner of Bath, just outside the city wall, which prompted a complementary

10. Thomas Johnson's raucous scene of the King's Bath, drawn in 1672, was far from the decorous atmosphere that later promoters sought

development in the south-east corner of the city, so that Bath 'began to shew graceful Suburbs'. By 1710 it was possible for one visitor to write that Bath 'Improves much Dayly for their fine new Buildings and Beautifying the old by sashing'.[7]

Around the turn of the century, Bath's resort interests were highly satisfied with their city as it stood and took enormous pride in the fabric of the town. Were they as secure about the tenor of resort life? Some answers are suggested in another image, Thomas Johnson's 1672 engraving of the King's and Queen's Baths. This scene conveys much of the ambience of the late-seventeenth-century spa. The elegant stone balustrade encircling both baths forms an important demarcation which separates well-dressed onlookers from the chaotic scene below. Or does it? The naked boys who clamber on to the railing no doubt intend to dive into the bath, splashing the warm, sulphurous and by this point very dirty water on the genteel spectators, one of whom, perhaps in apprehension of this result, raises his hand in reproach or warning (unless he, like Samuel Pepys in 1668, is offering them money to dive into the bath).[8] The irregular buildings that hem the baths in contribute to the sense of claustrophobia and impending disorder. This is a setting in which we can well imagine disturbances of the kind related in Thomas D'Urfey's 1701 play, *The Bath,* in which the character Harebrain is known to 'sowse into the Bath stark naked as ever he was abore, and if there e're a plump *Londoner* there, a fat-shoulder'd Lass or so, ... he's on the back of her in a trice, and tabering her Buttocks round the Bath as if he were beating a Drum'.[9]

The spa's amusements manifested the same awkward coexistence of polite and popular culture, and continued to do so for decades. While at the beginning of the eighteenth century there was 'aboundance of devercion at Bath', as Elizabeth Verney assured her husband, many of them were distinctly plebeian pastimes that John Verney and his peers could only enjoy as spectators at a safe distance. He found that in addition to polite pastimes like 'Playes' and 'Balles', the amusements of Bath included 'Cudgel-playing for a silver Cupp, Maids dancing for a furbeload smock ... Men Whistling for a Gold Ring, and Boyes hunting the Pigg which was to be catcht by the tale, and by it held upp'.[10] The old Abbey Orchard was the site of 'Smock Racing and Pig Racing, playing at Foot-Ball and running with the Feet in Bags' until the end of the 1720s.[11] Even after the spa was thoroughly gentrified, popular amusements would resurface, such as the donkey race held on the town common in 1748, at the beginning of August, the off-season by then, at least two weeks before the Company began to arrive. The *Bath Journal,* not wishing to pass over 'the Diversions of *so polite a Place as this*', wrote of local boys astride suggestively named animals like 'Merry Pintle', 'Morecock', and 'Spanking Roger'. The paper took note of 'near Six Thousand Persons on the Course, *and some of Distinction too*'.[12] Such an egregiously impolite entertainment was outlandish enough to be treated facetiously by the middle of the century. Fifty years earlier the line between polite urbanity and plebeian rusticity was less sharp. In the first decades of that new century, the raucous and libertine atmosphere that lingered from the Restoration spa diminished, if it did not necessarily disappear, as a result of initiatives by both local authorities and participants in the resort trade.

~

Before Nash arrived, and indeed for some time afterwards, visitors were in a very real sense left to their own devices to entertain themselves. The irregular availability of social opportunities in these circumstances could lead to unpleasant episodes. The Countess of Strafford wrote to her husband about 'a perticular set of company six men and six women', including Lady Mary Gore and her husband, 'that mett two or three times a week to dance' at Bath in the autumn of 1711. At one of these gatherings 'all the candles was blown out, and the men was very rude, upon which Mr. Gore desired to goe no more into that company, but she told him she would and if citizens pretend'd to marry Quality they must take it for their pains'.[13]

Raising the tone of Bath's resort culture depended on competing successfully with rival spas for the patronage of established elites as well as affluent, socially mobile conspicuous consumers from London and other commercial centres. The provision of polite amusements required the presence of polite company. Fortunately, by the end of the seventeenth century there was already a critical mass of visitors to the assemblies, with their opportunities for dancing and gaming, for which Bath became famous. Beginning in the 1690s, balls were given at the Guildhall, 'a very spacious Room, and fitted up for that Purpose'. Well into the first decade of the eighteenth century, these were private, ad hoc entertainments given at irregular intervals by wealthy and distinguished visitors. Dances were still held on the bowling green when the weather was fair, or seemed so; one such ball held early in May 1706 'ended soon after it began as the weather grew cold'.[14] If a satire of 1700 is any guide, guests at the Guildhall dances could expect 'A Consort of Delicate Musick, Vocal and Instrumental, performs by good Masters: A Noble Collation of dry Sweat-Meats, Rich Wine, and Large Attendance', as well as 'Extraordinary Fine Dancing'. They

11. The Guildhall, where balls were held until 1720

could also be assured of a socially exclusive night out, thanks to the presence of 'Brawny Beadles' who guarded the door, 'looking as fierce as the Uncouth Figures at [London's] Guildhall'. These entertainments would not have gone forward without private sponsorship and the ball of this fictitious example was 'given by a Lady of Quality' who 'wore an Extraordinary Rich Favour, to distinguish her from the rest, which is always the Custome'.[15] Wealthy visitors, customarily men, took turns underwriting balls at the Guildhall in much the same way (as we shall see later) that they paid for the music played at the Cross Bath. Local tradition named the Dukes of Beaufort as the first patrons of the Guildhall assemblies.[16] It was supposedly the rakish second Duke who engaged Captain Webster, a notorious gamester later killed in a duel, to superintend these entertainments in 1703. [17] Goldsmith suggested that Webster introduced admission charges at the Guildhall in 1704, 'each man paying half-a-guinea each ball.'[18]

On particularly noteworthy occasions, such as royal anniversaries or military victories, there was understandable concern (especially given Bath's lingering Jacobite associations) that celebrations at the resort should be appropriately splendid. To this end, the organisers of a ball given in May 1706 to celebrate Marlborough's victory at Ramillies opened a subscription to cover the cost. Forty male guests paid two guineas apiece to attend, and were each given six tickets to distribute to women of their choosing. The ball must have been spectacular, as under Nash's management two guineas was the subscription for an *entire season* until the middle of the century. While the cost was covered by subscriptions, 'the stewards of ye feast' (in this case the Marquis of Annandale, Viscount Shannon, Brigadier Mordaunt and Colonel Sutton) had still to superintend complex and elaborate arrangements, such as the illumination of the Guildhall with 700 candles, and the provision of cold chickens, hams, tongues, jellies and ices, lemonade, chocolate, punch and wine. Musicians, preferably performers from London who came up for the season, had to be hired and eventually paid; the going rate for much of the century was half a guinea per musician per ball. Nothing about the ball itself could be left to chance either. Balls in the eighteenth century were ritualised and hierarchical affairs, especially when begun with highly formal and stylised 'French' dances like the minuet. Partners would have to be found for women of the Company who wished to dance, and couples would have to be led out to dance in order of social precedence. The success of a ball was measured in terms of the number of guests and their social profile, as indicated by their dress and the number of titled attendees. Less predictable but equally important criteria were the number of dancers and their skill, critical indices of the social composition of the ball. The relative social mobility and egalitarianism for which the eighteenth century was noted (in England, at least) halted abruptly at the edge of the dance floor. The observer of the Ramillies fête noted in puzzlement that while there were 'many Ladies and Gentlemen' present, 'there were not but seven pair of dancers'. Fortunately in this case, Lord Annandale 'performed very well the honors of the feast by the gracious care he took of the Ladies, and by the pleasure he had of leading the dance with Lady Betty Barclay'.[19]

In 1708 the London entrepreneur Thomas Harrison, who was already running a successful gaming house in Bath, opened new and expanded assembly rooms in Bath, with facilities for serving tea, coffee and chocolate, card rooms for gaming and sociable play, and garden walks. It is not clear that balls were held at Harrison's Rooms in 1708 or at any time before a new ballroom was built there in 1720. Once Harrison's was open for dancing, it became possible for entertainment at Bath, particularly balls and assemblies, to occur at regular and frequent intervals. Harrison could supply the staff and other requisites, such as lighting and refreshments, that hosts would once have had to arrange. At some point it occurred to someone – perhaps Nash, perhaps Harrison, or another interested party who remembered the precedent of the Ramillies ball – that a subcription book might be kept open at Harrison's for any and all balls that might be held during a season. If balls were now held by subscription and there was no 'host' as such, someone would have to step into the role. If this same person could engage the musicians, so much the better. Those who had not yet discovered an inclination towards gaming had no reason to go to Harrison's Rooms before, but those who now came to the new rooms to dance would stay to gamble, and might even return to the tables on nights when there was no ball. Some figure of the sort that became the Master of Ceremonies would have been socially and commercially useful in the increasingly commodified leisure culture emerging in Bath.

~

Another critical development in the culture of the resort began not long after the opening of Harrison's Rooms, as Bath's season was reconfigured, an ingenious strategic shift which circumvented competition and ultimately allowed the spa to operate nine months a year. Well into the first decade of the eighteenth century, Bath, in common with other watering places, ordinarily expected to receive visitors in the summer. Accordingly, the season at Bath ran from May to early October. At some point, it must have occurred to influential participants in the resort trade that any season *except* summer was more appropriate for drinking and bathing in hot mineral water. Moreover, during the hottest months of the year, London physicians increasingly preferred to send patients to cold-water spas like Tunbridge and Epsom, which were also closer at hand.[20] Bath in summer can be oppressively hot even to tourists in

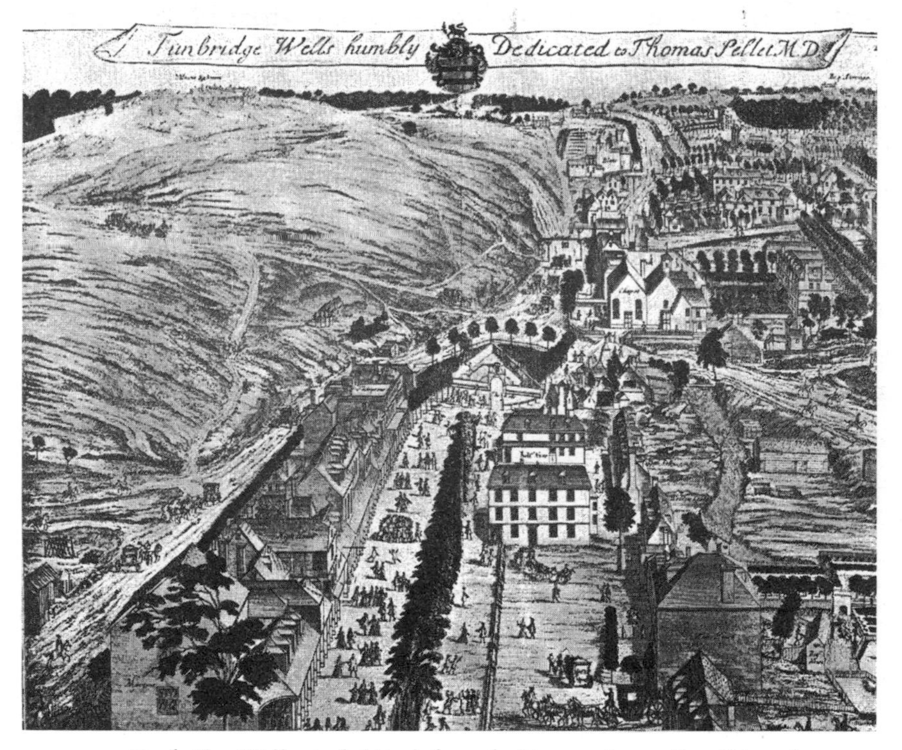

12. Tunbridge Wells rivaled Bath from the Restoration until well into the eighteenth century

the T-shirts, shorts and sandals of the compulsorily casual twenty-first century. In the non-air-conditioned eighteenth century, polite men and women were obliged to be fully covered in public or in private even during the hottest part of the day.

In the 1690s high season in Bath could continue well into June. 'I hear ye Bath is extremly full of companey & now fuller yn it ues to be, at this time of year,' wrote Anne Nicholas in June 1693. Two years later, also in June, she reported hearing 'at this time their is more people of quality at ye Bath yn euer has bin this maney years'.[21] In high summer – that is, mid-season – the resort thinned out. Roger Townshend 'found but little company' when he arrived around 10 August in 1698, although the town had filled up by the beginning of September.[22] By the next decade, fashionable visitors generally preferred what was already known (by at least 1705) as the 'latter season'. Visitors began arriving after about the third week in August, many of them turning up, coincidentally or not, around 24 August, the Feast of St Bartholomew. They began leaving from the end of September to the first week in October. Queen Anne began both of her visits in late August, staying until late September 1702 and early October 1703. Where the Queen went – and when – court and Company followed, but she, rather than setting a trend, was following one already established.

If visitors generally preferred to come later in the season, the pattern would surely be noticed by inn- and lodging-house keepers, if no one else. Peter Le Neve arrived at what should have been the very end of the season in October 1701 but as late as 22 November pronounced that both Bath's water and its Company placed it 'far before Tunbridge'.[23] Resort interests might also have realised that a summer season put Bath in needless competition with other spas, Tunbridge in particular. When the change came, it came quickly. As late as 1709 Richard Steele related in the *Tatler* that the Bath season had hardly begun in the middle of May, but in the *Spectator* only two years on, he has Simon Honeycomb make his appearance at Bath in the autumn.[24] It is tempting on the basis of this evidence to pinpoint the date of the rescheduling of the Bath season to the year 1710. A letter written to the Hampshire gentleman Thomas Jervoise that year indeed refers to 'the seasons', including a 'latter season' in the autumn, at Bath.[25] Other sources point to a gradual development over the course of the decade. The Countess of Strafford found Bath still very lively in December 1711, indicating a lengthening autumn season, yet John Gay still spoke of visiting Bath in summer as late as 1715.[26] The more important but intractable question, of course, is not when this change was effected, but how. The relative speed with which the season was restructured suggests the possibility that persuasive individuals, perhaps even charismatic figures, convinced resort interests that altering the season made good business sense.

As Johnson's engraving suggested to us earlier, healing and amusement were not necessarily at cross-purposes in late-seventeenth-century Bath. Bathing, the spa's *raison d'être,* was recreational, in many different senses, as often as it was therapeutic. Genteel visitors might watch the crowd in the King's Bath (perhaps, like Samuel Pepys, giving a child sixpence or a shilling to dive in), but otherwise they avoided its raucous atmosphere, preferring the Cross Bath.[27] Initially, it was the relative privacy of this bath, surrounded as it was by a high wall, that made it the preferred bath for elite visitors, such as Catherine of Braganza in 1663 and Pepys in 1668. This seclusion was compromised in 1674, when a covered gallery was built over the north wall, ostensibly to shelter those who drank from the pump that was installed at the same time. Two years later another gallery was built over the south side. Ultimately this gallery was occupied by musicians who entertained bathers and drinkers both, making the Cross Bath a prototypical Pump Room and possibly the social centre of the spa.[28]

The reconfigured Cross Bath afforded opportunities for voyeurism that were not available at drinking spas like Tunbridge, and this aspect of Bath attracted visitors, such as the notorious Earl of Rochester, who did not come to Bath for their health. '[T]o see a nasty old Satyr in the Cross Bath,' one of Thomas D'Urfey's characters complains, 'laving within a quarter of a yard of a beautiful young Creature, with Snowy Neck, and Breasts that shew like a Lilly in a Glass, always gave a loathsome Idea to me.' The playwright believed that it had been customary from the 1670s at least for male spectators to engage musicians to serenade the female bathers during the season, and for the visitor who ordered the music on a particular day to have the prerogative of presenting a bouquet to the bather of his choice. '[T]he Bouquet will be dispos'd of before you get to the Cross Bath, if you don't make haste,' one of his characters is warned. 'Pretty Mrs *Doll Trippet* will have it to day, my Lord *Peagoose* gives it and the Musick.' One of the contributors to Richard Steele's *Tatler* also believed that the custom of toasting individual women bathers in the Cross Bath was well established from the days of Restoration libertines.[29]

The Cross Bath posed a sore temptation to male spectators to let their imaginations run riot. At the turn of the eighteenth century, mixed bathing was still permitted even at the Cross Bath, which was already 'more Fam'd for *Pleasure* than Cures', and the scene, the same observer claimed, of

> *all the Wanton Dalliancies imaginable; Celebrated Beauties, Panting Breasts, and Curious Shapes, almost Expos'd to Publick View; Languishing Eyes, Darting Killing Glances, Tempting Amorous Postures, attended by soft Musick, enough to provoke a Vestal to forbidden Pleasure ... The Ladies ... Wade about like Neptun's Courtiers, suppling their Industrious Joynts. The Vigorous Sparks, presenting them with several Antick Postures ... and by Accidental Design, thrust a stretch'd Arm; but where the Water Conceal'd so ought my Pen.*[30]

There were male bathers as well, although convention dictated that men and women would keep to different sides of the bath. Thomas Gale witnessed no misbehaviour at the Cross Bath on the June day he spent at the spa in 1705, noting that the sexes kept to their respective corners 'with the greatest order and decency'. Men who violated this stricture were subject to fines levied by the Serjeant of the Baths; women, on the other hand, were 'supposed to be so modest as not to come near the gentlemen'.[31] Celia Fiennes left nothing to chance, using a full complement of four guides, two women and two men, when she bathed around 1687. The women served to steady her, 'for the water is so strong it will quickly tumble you down', and the men 'to cleare the way' of unspecified obstacles, possibly potentially obstreperous male bathers. As decorous as the Cross Bath seemed to her, the need for such an official as the Serjeant of the Baths advertised the ever-present threat of disorder. This official was the closest equivalent office to a Master of Ceremonies in the gift of the Corporation. According to Celia Fiennes, he patrolled the galleries, keeping order and chastising 'rude' spectators or bathers. '[M]ost people of fashion sends to

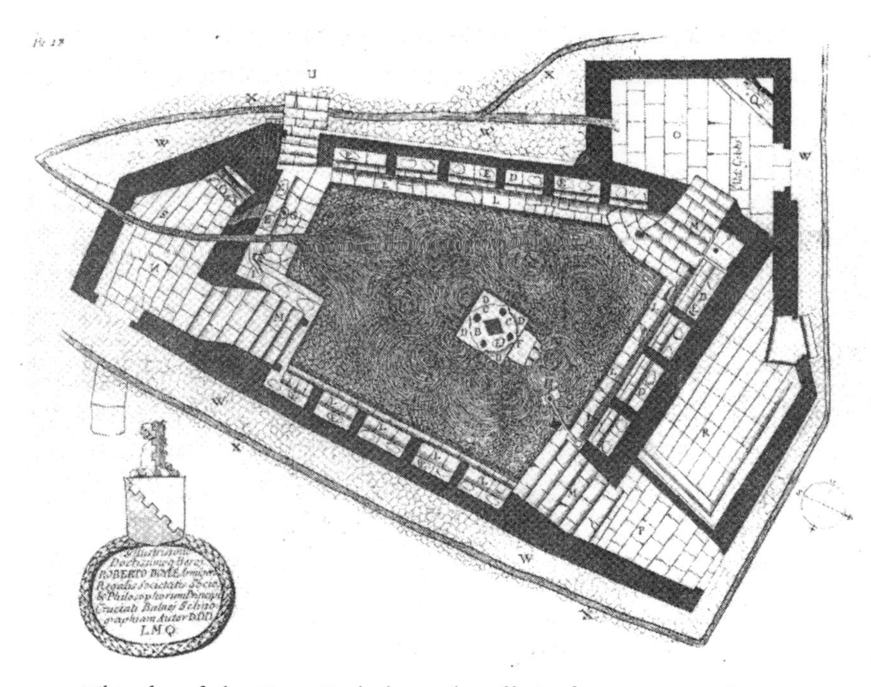

13. This plan of the Cross Bath shows the galleries for spectators and musicians, as well as the conduit from which visitors could drink

him when they begin to bathe,' she related, and he was particularly solicitous of them, in anticipation of a suitable gratuity 'at the end of the Season'.[32] The Serjeant of the Baths was the apex of a hierarchy of service sector workers appointed by the Corporation to what were essentially lucrative concessions over every aspect of getting bathers from their lodgings to the baths, out of their clothes, into the prescribed bathing costumes, into and around the baths, and out and back again. One of D'Urfey's characters avers that 'a Serjeant of the Bath us'd to be as much respected here during the season, as at London a Serjeant at Law during the Term'.[33]

Women in Celia Fiennes's day dressed for bathing in gowns made of canvas, which in the eighteenth century gave way to linen that was either unbleached or dyed yellow to disguise the natural discoloration resulting from the water. They were brought from their lodgings in sedan chairs to the bath, and presented with a bowl that held flowers, or a perfumed hankerchief, or perhaps snuff, all intended to counteract the odour of the water. A 'young Lady so Amuseing herself,' John Wood suggested, 'seldom failed of becoming an Object of Admiration to some young Gentleman in the Gallery by the Side of the Bath'.[34] Observers often suggested that younger women bathed not for their health but to display themselves to advantage in surroundings seemingly designed with heterosexual male voyeurs in mind:

> *In finest Dress each Female Head attir'd,*
> *All equal Care still take to be admir'd;*
> *Plump heaving Breasts are in their Beauty seen,*
> *More white than Snow, beneath the Waters clean;*
> *Each Face with Blush the Sulph'rous Heat inspires:*
> *No ruddy Paint the Female here requires.*[35]

Few Cross Bath spectators could equal the enthusiasm of the unapologetic fetishist of Thomas D'Urfey's lines 'on a Lady's going into the Bath':

> *Each day I provide too,*
> *A bribe for her Guide too,*
> *And gave her a Crown,*
> *To bring me the Water where she sat down ...* [36]

By the 1720s printed descriptions of bathing suggest that men were subtly or otherwise discouraged from bathing at the same time as women, at least in the Cross Bath. Dudley Ryder saw both sexes bathing on different sides of this bath in 1716, but three undergraduates who visited a decade later believed that only women bathed there.[37] Daniel Defoe's *Tour* focuses entirely on female bathers in its treatment of the Cross Bath, as if this bath were an entirely feminine preserve. By 1714 there were twice as many women (eight) as men employed as guides to conduct novice bathers through the Cross and Hot Baths; at the King's and Queen's Baths, eight men and six women served as guides. These held their employment on condition of their decent and orderly behaviour,[38] and their presence probably served also to deter misbehaviour among the bathers, as the office of Serjeant of the Baths had fallen into abeyance. The number of bathers at all of the baths had most likely outstripped the capacity of any single appointee to supervise them. Ultimately, there were limits to the efficacy of either formal or informal regulations or sanctions. There was nothing but convention to stop men and women bathing together, a practice that continued to raise eyebrows, as well as prurient speculation. In 1734, however, Mary Chandler defended the Cross Bath as 'a safe Retreat / From Sights indecent, and from Speeches lewd, / Which dare not there, with Satyr-Face, intrude'.[39] One widely circulated anecdote had Nash shoving a male visitor into the bath fully dressed for the indiscretion of admiring his own wife *viva voce* as she bathed.[40] It was informal conventions observed among the Company rather than any regulations imposed by the Corporation that governed who bathed and who watched, and when, where, and how. Jonathan Swift wrote of the young wife of a wealthy prelate who 'in the Cross Bath, seeks an heir /Since others oft have found one there', safe from the oversight of her husband, since

> *... if the Dean by chance appears*
> *It shames his cassock and his years.*
> *He keeps his distance in the gallery*
> *Till banished by some coxcomb's raillery;*
> *For, it would his character expose*
> *To bathe among the belles and beaux.*[41]

In 1737 the Corporation imposed standards for bathing costumes – no male over the age of ten would be allowed into any bath without drawers and waistcoat, or any female 'by day or night without a decent shift'.[42] The Corporation's effort in January 1753 to impose different days for male and female bathers at all four publicly accessible baths failed after only one season.[43]

More effective than any of these regulatory initiatives were changes in the structure of amusements. Goldsmith was not wildly off the mark in positing Nash's riposte to Radcliffe as the beginning of the reign of politeness in Bath. If catastrophe was ever in the offing from Dr Radcliffe's ruffled feathers, it was averted by a rapid rear-guard action on the part of the Corporation that brought about the construction of the first Pump Room in 1706, which allowed larger numbers of patients to drink the water hot from the source, as Radcliffe recommended. (In fact, Radcliffe was never as averse to Bath as the pamphlet literature suggested and was still sending his patients there nearly a decade after the contretemps with Oliver.[44]) Physicians, if their confidence had ever wavered, could now prescribe the water in good conscience to be drunk and topically applied (or 'pumped') as well as bathed in, and the spa's client base could continue to expand. Moreover, ingestion was a more socially decorous therapeutic option than immersion, and avoided the numerous improprieties that the intimate activity of bathing inevitably threatened. After the new and improved Harrison's opened its doors for dances as well as rattling dice, someone – possibly Nash or possibly Harrison himself – hit upon the brilliant marketing idea of having musicians for the balls play in the Pump Room for the two hours in the morning that the Company assembled to drink the water. This advance publicity would infallibly draw visitors to the balls – and thus to the gaming tables. This alteration also shifted the focus of the spa and its visitors from bathing to drinking. While many visitors might still begin their day with 'Bathing in the Hot Waters for Health or Pleasure', the Pump Room was the scene of Bath's *levée du roi,* the first assemblage of the Company, as often as not paying court to its king.

~

With Nash's agency or without it, then, the period roughly corresponding to the reign of Queen Anne witnessed crucial transitions in the structure of Bath's amusement culture. The most important of these changes was the institution of public subscriptions as the primary means of financing public entertainment. Subscriptions not only made

14. A typical eighteenth-century coffeehouse

it possible for entertainments to be held at regular intervals (for example, the balls held twice a week), but also gave visitors a corporate identity. Members of 'the Company' were entitled to privileges and immunities which expanded as time passed. Most importantly, they had the right to be treated as equals by other members of the Company, and the obligation to extend the same courtesy, *while at Bath* (acquaintanceships begun there and at other spas were notoriously ephemeral). They were listed in the subscription book (kept in the Pump Room, where visitors could peruse it) and received tickets to the balls. Once Bath had a regular newspaper, their names would be listed there. They could expect a visit from the Master of Ceremonies, once there was such a thing, and by the time he passed from the scene, they had acquired the time-honoured customary right of electing his successor. Nash, who ultimately if not initially administered the subscriptions, created and controlled a public that was regenerated every season.

The first defining moment for this new corporate entity, the Company, came quickly. In order to build his Rooms, Harrison had audaciously torn down a portion of the borough walls. The Corporation was so incensed that in June of 1710, armed with a Chancery Writ and with the Company safely decamped, they unanimously ordered the wall rebuilt 'up against Mr. Harrison's house ... as high as the top of Mr. Harrison's windows'. When visitors arrived in the autumn, they found that the assembly rooms – which they were, upon their subscription, encouraged to think of as *their* assembly rooms – did not look out on the Terrace Walk but instead faced a stone wall. Somehow, the Corporation's action galvanised the Company. In May 1711 the Corporation heard it 'reported for a certainty that the persons of Quality & Gentry now residing in this City have threatened & are resolved to pull down or cause to be pull'd down' the offending wall. In the face of this threat, the Corporation essentially capitulated, resolving that '(to oblige the Nobility and Gentry) a Committee shall be appointed to be chosen out of the Corporation to treat with the sd Mr. Harrison for accommodating all matters relating to that suit'. Who rallied the visitors to take such effective, concerted action? This crisis, rather than Dr Radcliffe's fit of pique, may have been the occasion of Nash's rising to the leadership of the Company. Five years later, the Corporation took the extraordinary step of granting Nash the freedom of the city, along with no lesser figure than William Pulteney, the Secretary at War.[45] As Ryder put it in 1716, and as any other 24-year-old might put it today, Nash was 'the man'. His precipitate rise to social ascendancy at Bath coincided with various efforts to redefine the resort, and even if he did not instigate the changes described in this chapter, he appeared to be the right person in the right place at the right time. We have still to explain how he was able to sustain his position over the next four decades, an exploration that will take us further into the life of the resort.

3

Regulator of the Diversions

It is ... as difficult to avoid making one in this mad Company, as it is easy to despise what they are doing: The Course of Things is as mechanical as if it went by Clockwork, and you cannot well be a free Agent, where the whole Turn is to do as other People do: It is a Sort of Fairy Circle, if you do not run round in it, you either cannot move at all, or are in every Body's Way.[1]

What a round of silly Amusements, what a giddy Circle of nothing, do these Children of a larger size run every day![2]

The pleasures of Bath had as their price the nagging suspicion that one's time might be better employed. No one truly enjoyed pleasures who did not earn them by previous application to business, Lord Chesterfield admonished his son, but how was one to attend to business in such an unbusinesslike place? It helped, of course, to be ill. Some infirmity, any infirmity, preferably conspicuous but not unsightly or otherwise noisome, would preserve a visitor from feeling the need to explain his or her presence. Otherwise, it was necessary to affect ennui, and project frivolity on to others, if one were to retain any self-respect. 'I do from my soul most sincerely pity you, to be so long doomed to a Place so delightfully tiresome,' sympathised the poet James Thomson to a correspondent in Bath. 'Delightfully, did I say? No; it is merely a scene of waking Dreams, where nothing but the Phantoms of Pleasure fly about, without any substance or Reality.'[3] This pose of boredom might plausibly have stemmed from the received wisdom that Bath's frivolities ran on a strict schedule. High season at Bath could seem like a grandiose game of musical chairs. Music, which before Thomas Edison had to be performed live if it was to be heard at all, had a power to command attention, and in this case attendance, that it simply does not have today in the age of recorded and amplified sound. Nash's control of the Pump and Assembly musicians was undisputable – 'No Nash; no music in the pump!' wrote Mrs Delany in 1757[4] – and a key source of his social suzerainty. Francis Fleming, who taught music at Bath and played in the Pump and Assembly ensemble for many years, asserted that the orchestra 'was considered as Mr Nash's', since he paid each musician two guineas a week from the subscriptions collected during the autumn and spring seasons. It was no matter to the musicians that their overlord paid them with others' money:

> They *were* his *servants;* he *was* their *patron; nor would he suffer any of them to enter into articles with those who had diversions out of the rooms. Yet he never restrained them for pursuing any business that might be to their advantage, and which did not interfere with the amusements of the rooms.*[5]

If, as Fleming suggests, most of the professional musicians working in Bath were beholden to Nash, then anyone wishing to hire musicians for a private social function would have to do so through his agency. Nash's control of subscriptions, and his resulting control of musical entertainment, contributed to the establishment of a routinised social round at the spa, much as John Wood and other writers were describing by the late 1730s and 1740s, and which Pope seemed to acknowledge as early as 1714 in writing of 'the manner of life which all people are obliged to here'.[6] Of course, it is possible that Nash noticed that most of the better class of visitors drank water between eight and ten in the morning, soon after rising, and therefore those were established as the hours that the orchestra would play at the Pump Room. Similarly, Nash may have observed that balls began to wind down after eleven at night, and thought it best that the band quit before the Company tired and left of their own accord. It is quite plausible, then, that without anyone, including Nash, intending this result, what was merely customary became obligatory. Thomas Goulding insisted that 'because he took the opportunity always to come at the Season of the Year, when most of the Company came, ... they thought it was owing to his bringing them'.[7] Just as it would be a mistake to ascribe as much importance to Nash's authority as Wood and others did, it would be misleading to accept uncritically similar accounts of the round of amusements.

For Nash, the appearance of power *was* power, and appearance itself transcended reality. Nash's collusion with Thomas Harrison, his appropriation of the subscriptions, his control of the musicians and therefore of entertainment at Bath formed the structural basis of his authority. The substance of that authority, whether real or perceived, grew as the result of his personal charisma. If it had not, Goldsmith would not have been able to credit Nash with anything beyond the routinisation of social relations at Bath. He exploited his position to acquire relational capital which extended his suzerainty over other aspects of the spa's leisure culture. Nash's personality cult was sustained in part on the presupposition of visitors that a routine, a round of leisure activities as immutable as the canonical hours, actually existed. Whether or not visitors kept the schedule as scrupulously as Wood and other observers indicated, we shall attempt to follow it, from arrival to departure.

~

Getting to Bath became steadily less arduous as roads in its vicinity were improved, developments which the Corporation was empowered to undertake in successive private acts of Parliament. It was often claimed that the near accident Queen Anne met with as she and her entourage rode over Lansdown was instrumental in procuring this legislation. If the roads were in better shape, other more exciting hazards lay in store. The road between London and Bath was understood to be crawling

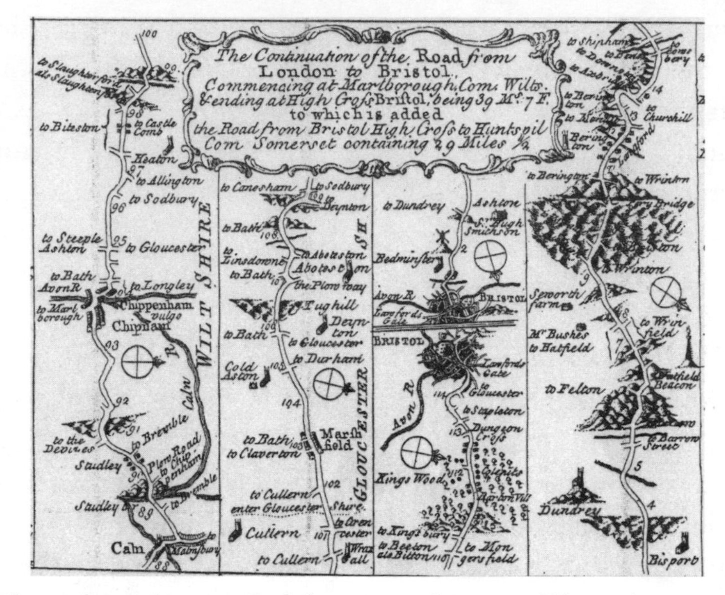

15. *This road map shows much of the route Londoners would have taken to Bath*

with highwaymen, who were an accepted threat to travellers. In preparation for his own journey to Bath, John Verney arranged with his banker to draw money on account 'if I should be robbd goeing or want money when there'.[8] The *Bath Journal* melodramatically warned its readers in September 1751 'that no less than Seven Highwaymen ... now infest the Road to Bath, expecting, as is supposed on the Occasion of the approaching Season, to meet with extraordinary Booty'.[9] Highwaymen, if they posed greater danger, were better conversational fodder, and we can more easily imagine George Scott dining out on his close encounters with 'collectors' than on bad road conditions. As he and his wife were leaving their inn at Newbury,

> *the Landlady told my Wife that an Highwayman waited for us at the Top of the Hill beyond the Town. A man certainly crossed the Common towards us when we came to the Spot just mentioned, but I suppose did not like our Appearance and so returned back the same Way he before had rode.*

Having made the most of his brush with danger, Scott then admitted that the highwaymen operating between Newbury and Marlborough were targeting 'the poorer sort of People, and Others who travel without Fire Arms under Contribution'.[10] Then as now, the poor were as disproportionately the victims of crime as they were the perpetrators. In this case, they were softer targets. Scott's coachman was as armed and dangerous as any of the two or three highwaymen that they may have come across.

The highwaymen who in reality or hyperbole patrolled the approaches to Bath were the last reminders visitors were to have of the world they were escaping, and their presence reinforced the notion of Bath as a retreat from an uncertain environment. Like novices entering the cloister, visitors were encouraged to believe that they had entered a sacred zone, precincts consecrated to the pursuit of polite leisure. Similarly, the bells that signalled the entry of distinguished visitors, but whose din accompanied the arrival and settling in of humbler spa-goers, contributed to the charmed atmosphere.[11]

The humblest visitors made the journey on the public stage services that increased in number over the period. By 1740 fifteen stages ran between London and Bath per week during the seasons.[12] More affluent visitors came in coaches hired for the trip. The grandest arrived in their own carriages, a mark of great distinction which caused considerable stir at the city gates.[13] The weary occupants of these prestige conveyances had escaped highwaymen only to fall into the clutches of the Abbey ringers, who pealed the bells to announce their arrival, and the city musicians, who turned up at their lodgings to serenade them. Both groups expected liberal gratuities. Wood tells us that the customary donation was anywhere from a crown to a guinea, according to the status of the new arrivals,[14] although one suspects that inverse proportions applied according to the visitors' social aspirations. The doggedly unpretentious John Penrose thought his wife extravagant for throwing a few coins when musicians visited them in Abbey Green.[15] Ringers, singers and bandsmen may have employed an alert system similar to that Baron von Pöllnitz observed at Spa. The Capuchin friars who

16. Sarah Porter, who kept the subscription book at the Pump Room

descended upon visitors there kept 'in their Pay a cunning Boy, whose Office it is, during the Season, to observe the Arrival of Strangers', follow the coach to the visitors' lodgings, read the labels on cases and query coachmen, postilions and other servants.[16] Thomas Goulding warned visitors of 'Runners' who lay waiting

> *like Hawkes of Prey; and as soon as a Family comes to Town, by their Assurance, introduce Themselves: Then they give Characters of all Sorts of Shop-Keepers, and set Prices to Provisions; making the Gentry believe by false Insinuations, they can buy cheaper than Prime-Cost. Such base Proceedings give a Supposition, that the Towns-People are all Sharpers, and their Servants all Cheats.*[17]

The initial outlay continued, as the head of a visiting family was then expected to make the rounds to pay subscriptions. His first stop would be the Pump Room, where the redoubtable Sarah Porter kept the subscription book. Until the names of the Company were reported

17. The Pump Room from the Abbey Churchyard, as it appeared in Nash's day

in the Bath newspapers, the subscription book was the best means of informing oneself of the other visitors present. If a head of household for any reason failed to report to Mrs Porter, not to worry, as she was notorious for her ability to ambush new arrivals. The two guineas he paid for balls at the assembly rooms and for music at the Pump Room procured him three tickets to the twice-weekly balls. Subscriptions for access to Bath's other sociable venues – the coffeehouses, the walks, the bookshop – were often assessed on the same socially calibrated 'sliding scale' of one crown to one guinea as the gratuities to the musicians. The social psychology which operated in those situations was probably similar to the pressure on today's museum visitor to make an 'optional' donation of a 'suggested' amount.

Women of the Company subscribed in their own right to the 'Ladies Coffee House' by the Pump Room, where, like the men, for a (minimum) contribution of a crown per season they had access to newpapers, as well as pen and ink. They also subscribed to James Leake's bookshop. James Leake the Elder, whose shop occupied a privileged position between the assembly rooms on Terrace Walk, dominated the book trade in Bath soon after he opened for business in the early 1720s. By the next decade he was dubbed 'Prince of all the coxcombical Fraternity of Booksellers', who, 'not having any Learning himself, ... seems resolved to sell it as dear as possible to Others'.[18] As books were expensive articles that short-term visitors were less likely than affluent residents to purchase, Leake's shop operated as a circulation library which lent books to seasonal visitors who paid a five-shilling subscription fee. Samuel Richardson, updating Defoe's *Tour,* called Leake's 'one of the finest Bookseller's Shops in *Europe*', so much so that 'Persons of Quality' would 'generally subscribe a Guinea', which to Richardson was 'the very best Money laid out in the Place, for those who go for Pleasure or Amusement only'.[19] Leake, in common with other booksellers of the period, was involved in publishing books as well as selling them. His shop was an oasis for those who relished at least the appearance of intellectual seriousness. It was certainly so for Elizabeth Anson, who, in the best Bath epistolary tradition, found the resort 'odious' and its amusements 'disagreeable employments'. Thanks to Leake, however, even in Bath she could feel herself on the cutting edge of European intellectual life – or at least as close as her own powers of application would bring her. 'I have no Literary intelligence for Mr Yorke yet,' she incriminatingly wrote to Lady Grey, 'for Mr Leake sends me word that somebody is reading Rousseau's Works (if I can find out who, I will get their Character of them for him, wch will save me the the trouble of giving one).'[20]

Leake's reputation among the last generation of Bath historians has been made by two titles in particular, Thomas Stretzer's *Description of Merryland,* published in 1740, and its sequel, *Merryland Displayed.* The character of these works may be guessed from their pseudonymous authorship by 'Roger Phuquewell' (i.e. Fuckwell). That a prominent figure in Bath's cultural life, and what passed for its intellectual life, should be a covert pornographer has proved too tempting for some historians to heed warnings from the English Short Title Catalogue, as well as that of the British Library, that the imprint is false (as is often the case with early modern erotica), and that the books were actually published in London by Edmund Curll. The choice of Bath for the imprint is nevertheless indicative of contemporary perceptions of the resort's atmosphere (continental pornographers often used Venice as an imprint for the same reason), and the choice of Leake – no doubt for the sake of verisimilitude – testifies to his pre-eminence in Bath's corner of the Republic of Letters.

~

By the height of Nash's ascendancy in the 1720s and 1730s, the Pump Room had supplanted the Cross Bath as the centre of social interaction in the morning, and the baths were much less of a social focus than they had been in the late seventeenth century. Nash, as far as we can tell, seldom or never appeared in the baths or at them. The Master of Ceremonies preferred to make his first public appearance of the day at the Pump, open from seven in the morning, the first opportunity that most of the Company took of being seen in public as well. It was the clearing house of information about other members of the Company, and the point where visitors established their membership of it. Accordingly, 'The Pump' was the first stop for the fifth Earl of Orrery, a young Irish peer just come into his title. '[A]s soon as the circling Whisper had taken air that the Earl of Orrery was present,' he related breathlessly, 'all Eyes were fixed upon me.'[21] The Pump Room was also the point at which newly inducted members of the Company were acquainted with the rules governing their behaviour. Nash's legal code, in which he followed every epochal ruler from Hammurabi to Solon to Justinian, was displayed in the Pump Room at least by the early 1720s. Whatley recorded seven regulations in 1723 (of the eleven that John Wood listed two decades later):

> *I. That a Visit of Ceremony at coming to Bath, and another at going away, is all that is expected or desired by Ladies of Quality and Fashion: – Except Impertinents.*

> *II. That Ladies, coming to the Ball, appoint a Time for their Footmen's coming to wait on them Home; to prevent Disturbances and Inconveniencies to Themselves and Others.*
>
> *III. That Gentlemen of Fashion never appearing in a Morning before the Ladies in Gowns and Caps, shew Breeding and Respect.*
>
> *IV. That no Person take it ill that any one goes to another's Play, or Breakfast, and not to theirs: – Except Captious by Nature.*
>
> *V. That no Gentleman give his Tickets for the Balls to any but Gentlewomen. – N.B. Unless he has none of his Acquaintance.*
>
> *VI. That all Whisperers of Lies and Scandal be taken for their Authors.*
>
> *VII. That all Repeaters of such Lies and Scandal be shun'd by all Company: – Except such as have been guilty of the same Crime.*[22]

In addition to his written regulations, a number of Nash's verbal decrees were circulated and celebrated in oral tradition. Nash outlawed the wearing of swords in Bath, it was said, by forbidding this traditional prerogative of gentlemen to all except those who, because of their lack of social standing were not ordinarily entitled to the privilege.

Goldsmith made much of Nash's regulation of dress, quoting admonitory verses addressed to gentlemen who wore boots in the assembly rooms, such as the Earl of Peterborough, who, according to Lady Hervey, wore 'boots all day' in 1725, 'having brought no shooes with him'.[23] That many of Nash's strictures, written and otherwise, concerned correct dress can only have increased the anxiety of the sartorially insecure. Visitors often spent their first days in Bath in a kind of social quarantine, for their heavier cases, including their finer clothes, were often sent up by carrier and would only arrive some days later. '[N]o fashionable Place can be approached, without much form,' John Penrose reported, 'and we had not our Box from the Carrier till this morning.' James Thomson's concern that friends at the resort had 'at last got their cloaths' was well placed; 'to be at Bath, yet debarred from the Rooms,' he commiserated, 'must have been a cruel situation to such as knew less how to converse with, and enjoy themselves'.[24] Walter Wiltshire, ultimately proprietor of one of the assembly rooms, accordingly carried on a brisk and lucrative business ferrying baggage to Bath and back, a trade over which his family enjoyed a monopoly until near the end of the century.[25] Certain essential items could be purchased locally from haberdashers, lacemen and other Bath retailers in this consumer mecca. Even Mercy Doddridge, the wife of a nonconformist divine, went shopping for suitable accessories in Bath.[26]

~

> *When the Hour of Dinner draws near, and People return from Walking, Riding, Playing, and their other Amusements, they are sure to find their Tables covered with the best of Provisions of all Kinds. ... no City in the World can be furnished with better and cleaner Cook Maids to dress them.*[27]

> *Our Cooks fit only for Lycaon's Feast,*
> *Combine to vitiate and deceive our Taste. . . .*
> *Here Elder-berry's prest for Lisbon Grape;*
> *A Norway Rat assumes a Rabbit's Shape;*
> *Horse-flesh turns Ven'son, and a Cat a Hare;*
> *And none, by seeing, guess their Bill o'fare ...*

Fashionable Georgians breakfasted at ten, generally on nothing more substantial than 'butter'd rolls and tea'.[28] 'Supper' was late in the evening, and light, taking a cue from its etymology in the French 'souper'. Dinner, at around three in the afternoon, was the main meal of the day and, for

John Wood, enjoyed particular pride of place in Bath. Bath cooks, he claimed, were in high reputation and much sought after, and were hired away all over the country, including London.[29] Provisions may have been plentiful and of high quality, since, according to John Penrose, they were certainly expensive. 'All Poultry is excessive dear,' he particularly complained. 'You cannot have a Turkey here under 7s. 6d. and about a fortnight ago 15s. was asked for a Green Goose, not a meal for one Man.' High prices for foodstuffs were only to be expected in a resort with a captive market of affluent visitors. It cannot have been an encouraging sign that keepers of stalls in Bath's market showed in their own speech and dress their keen awareness of the social profile of their customers. '[T]hey all, even the very Butchers, mince their Words,' Elizabeth Penrose reported, and one morning 'a Woman went by' very presentably dressed 'in a white shag Hat and an Habit' while leading 'a Horse loaden with Muffins'. Wood's verdict on Bath cooks notwithstanding, the Penroses' Abbey Green landlady was in no danger of losing hers to Cornwall, as Penrose found the cooking there execrable.[30]

Cooking for such a clientele in the eighteenth century more often than not involved roasting meat on a spit, and if the quality of the final product was indifferent, it was possibly due to the labour-saving device of the dogwheel. A small dog was shut inside a contraption resembling a pet hamster's exercise wheel, and by means of pulleys and belts the helpless animal's flight instinct turned the joint of meat. Bath's culinary establishment had for one reason or another resisted the introduction of the smokejack, which replaced canine legwork with inanimate clockwork. The smokejack turned the joint at a uniform speed, however, and it was necessary to decrease the velocity of the turn as the meat cooked, as would result when a turnspit dog fatigued. Consequently, cooks were inured to their animal labour, and by the middle of the century there were said to be in excess of 3,000 turnspit dogs in Bath, readily identifiable by their 'exceeding long Backs' and 'short bandy Legs' – indicating that they were possibly bred for the purpose.

Some observers jokingly regarded turnspits as one of the city's liveried companies and described sophisticated organisational behaviour.

Wood described daily convocations of turnspits 'in one Part of the City or another', meetings 'which seem to indicate something between them more than a bare Assembly'. Bath's chairmen persecuted them mercilessly, 'as though those robust People were determined to Fright the little Animals out of the superior Understanding they appear to be endowed with'.[31] Bishop Warburton claimed to have seen an entire pack of turnspit dogs, who had turned up to services with their cooks, flee the Abbey in a body when passages from the prophecy of Ezekiel describing the vision of the wheel were read.[32] More than one writer related the apocryphal story of a practical joker locking up all the turnspits in the city for three hours on Sunday afternoon, when the dogs were needed to turn the Sunday roast. Smollett had Peregrine Pickle pull off this prank, but Philip Thicknesse asserted that one of the Spencers, a waggish kinsman of the Duke of Marlborough, had enlisted chairmen to corral turnspits to the same end.[33] Turnspit lore was one more aspect of Bath that, like its Master of Ceremonies, lent the spa a welcome element of endearing eccentricity.

How true those Cards Life represent!
'Tis all in Tricks, and Honours spent:
We Shuffle, Cut, and deal about,
Till all the Stock of Life runs out ... [34]

The fourteen to sixteen waking hours that visitors had somehow to fill could not be completely polished off drinking the water or bathing in it, walking, riding, visiting or even reading (as light would fail in this world *still* lit only by fire). Fortunately, sociable play at cards was a highly effective means of killing time, and was an essential element of the Bath routine as John Wood and other commentators described it (so, too, was gambling – so much so that it is treated in a separate chapter). Some members of the Company seemed to spend every waking moment with cards in hand, which also seemed to constitute their sole topic of conversation. '"How d'ye do?" is all one hears in the morning, and "What's trumps?" in the afternoon,' Elizabeth Montagu complained from Bath in 1739.[35] Committed gamesters, the Warwickshire gentleman George Lucy wrote, uttered no sounds from morning until night except 'a few phrases related to the Game', which he thought might usefully be printed on a chart and laid on the table so that players could simply point, saving them 'the trouble of [putting] thoughts into words'. Lucy knew whereof he spoke – his particular game was whist, and he played it incessantly during successive seasons at Bath in the 1750s.[36] For those inclined to justify their preoocupation, whist and other sociable games such as quadrille, hombre, commerce and picquet provided a framework for social relations, and validated important cultural values. A polite card game was a medium of meeting others and cementing acquaintance, and the partnerships involved in many of these games paralleled the connections and alliances that provided social cohesion. At the same time, sociable card play, especially in bidding and trick-taking games, reinforced notions of precedence and deference. In the course of a hand, the hierarchically arranged deck was first thrown into disarray by shuffling, much as the social order was destabilized by the exigencies of an increasingly urban and commercial culture. As the hand was played, however, hierarchy reasserted itself, not in absolute terms, but in the context of an interaction represented by a 'trick'. A game of this sort was a reminder that it was only through social interaction that social status had any meaning at all. These reflections of social relations become clearer when we reconstruct, to the degree that we can, the experience of play.

It is nearly impossible to reconstitute completely how hombre and quadrille, the ancestors of bridge, were played, and it would have been impossible for a contemporary to acquire this socially useful knowledge from available printed descriptions of these games, even those purportedly written 'in Favour of those who have no Notion at all of the Game'. It would never have occurred to Edmund Hoyle, whose name is now associated with books detailing the rules of card games from contract bridge to gin rummy to 'go fish', to publish a book under his name explaining to novices exactly how one played whist, or quadrille, or ombre, or picquet. He assumed that his readers would already know the basic rules of these games, having acquired this knowledge informally through observation and practice as one of the social skills necessary for entry into polite society. Indeed, one of Hoyle's predecessors, Richard Seymour, declared that anyone 'who in Company should appear ignorant of the Games in Vogue, would be reckon'd low bred, and hardly fit for Conversation'. One factor complicating reconstruction of these games was that rules could vary 'according to the Humours of the Company'.[37] Critical points of procedure had to be negotiated and settled beforehand, a necessity which reinforced card playing as a polite exercise. Would players, for example, be allowed to examine discarded tricks? If by inadvertent omission these questions were not settled beforehand, they would have to be pressed or yielded in the course of play, presenting additional opportunities for the display of social agility. A game of cards, then, was a social obstacle course. The initially unsettled nature of procedure in these games was very much part of the larger 'game' in which the polite world involved its members.

The rules of these games, as much as we can know of them, were byzantine, full of 'complex idiosyncrasies' that make them 'too baroque for modern tastes'.[38] To complicate play further, until the later nineteenth century, playing cards were marked only with figures (in the case of face cards) or the approriate number of 'pips' (on the lower cards). The seven of spades, then, had only its seven 'spades' to identify it, and lacked the helpful numeral index on the left corner. It is easy to see why the works of authorities like Hoyle and Seymour are full of provisions for what we might otherwise consider very careless errors in play. Much is made, for example, of players inadvertently receiving too few or too many cards. This circumstance did not result in a misdeal, as long as the player reported the error and corrected it in the exchange of cards. Rules also governed speaking or playing out of turn, inadvertently 'facing' cards (i.e. turning them face up) and, more incredibly, failing to claim winnings.

Although money changed hands at hombre, quadrille, picquet and other largely sociable games, the worst criticism levelled at them was that they were dull and occasioned dullness in others. 'Cards,' asserted one critic, ' ... make People easy, by allowing them to be dull, and superseding the Necessity of their being entertaining.'[39] They also diverted attention from matters of more consequence. George Lucy's whist partner Mrs Wright told him of 'a Gent a few Nights before' who forfeited 'two hundred and fforty fish', referring to game counters equivalent to blue chips in poker. Mrs Wright added only as an afterthought that her daughter-in-law had just suffered her second miscarriage. Eliza Haywood wrote of a nobleman who forgot his effort to seduce a young woman as soon as he began to win her money at picquet.[40] After tremors from the London earthquake of 1750 were felt in Bath, a satirist imagined the response of a woman in the assembly rooms asked if she had felt the quake:

> *O, yes indeed, replied She, I was horribly fright'ned. Pray, whose Club is that? I can assure you, the House where I lodge, mov'd several Times. Lord, Sir, you have trumpt my Queen, which is the best Card. My Maid said, that the Pewter in the Kitchen rattled together, and some Spoons fell from the Dresser. You never follow my Lead Sir, I threw away that Suit an Hour ago; well, they have got the odd Trick against the best Hand I ever had; I thought the Earthquake praesaged me no Good, so Heaven defend us.*[41]

Ombre, quadrille and whist were taken seriously enough at the resorts to absorb the attention of even a workaholic like the Duke of Chandos, whose nightly whist game at Mrs Lindsey's occupied 'most of our thoughts' during his visit to Bath in the autumn of 1726.[42] No one, perhaps, took cards as seriously as the Countess of Bristol. Chandos related 'a great quarrel between Lady Orkney and Lady Bristol at Quadrille', in which the combatants 'publickly declared they would never play with each other again, nor would either play with any one who should ever play with the other, but next day they were reconciled & plaid as lovingly together as ever they had done before'.[43] The Duchess of Dorset was reportedly brought to Tunbridge in 1730 'by force of Arms' just to partner Lady Bristol at quadrille and thereby 'defye the rest of the world'.[44]

For the most part, sociable gaming was represented as a 'polite and innocent' amusement and escaped serious criticism, because ombre, quadrille, whist and games like it required skill and could thus be distinguished from pure games of chance, and also because stakes were comparatively low. The 'two hundred and fforty fish' allegedly lost at 'double tour' whist was exceptional, if not apocryphal, and George Lucy's loss of half a guinea after two hours of play was more typical; when Sir Armine Woodhouse lost three times that amount in half the time, he 'abused all the Company and retired'.[45] The seven guineas that Lady Vere Beauclerk won playing quadrille against the Countess of Bristol at Tunbridge Wells in 1730 would have fed a working family for several months, but it was petty cash for Lady Bristol, who judged members of the Company by their ability and willingness to 'play deep' – that is, for high stakes.[46] We will meet her again, and other committed gamblers like her, in another chapter.

~

Say – Dancing can we name such frantick Whims?
'Tis shewing Postures: 'tis distorting Limbs:
'Tis a lewd Riot of capricious Bears:
An ill conducted Hop of Wappineers.
Think then, if such mad Freaks can give me Sport,
Who hate Noise or Mob of any Sort.[47]

Card play, as well as serious gambling, helped to occupy the Company in the assembly rooms on the five nights of the week (including Sunday, which shocked the pious no end) that balls were not held. The balls, held Tuesday and Friday during the seasons and on special occasions like royal commemorations, were the defining rituals for members of the Company where the peculiar and ephemeral social order created in a Bath season was performed.

Dance *was* a performance, and the Company flocked to balls in the assembly rooms in Bath, as well as those in London and elsewhere, to act as spectators as well as participants. In fact, the first hour of the ball, modelling French courtly practice, was taken up with minuets, in which only one couple danced at a time, watched attentively by the rest of the Company. When the first minuet had finished, the man retired and Nash, as Master of Ceremonies, would bring the woman a second partner. The minuets would continue until each woman who stood up for them had danced with two men. The function of the minuet was particularly important at Bath, for it was a strictly regimented and hierarchical dance given pride of place in a resort culture which valued itself on its willingness to relax social boundaries. The succession of dancers was governed by precedence and consequently, the services of a Master of Ceremonies were invaluable. Nash was noted for how 'methodically' he took 'the Ladies out to dance', meaning that distinctions of rank were strictly observed.[48]

Elite society in Georgian England worshipped itself not as much through organised religion, as Emile Durkheim would have it, as through the minuet. It was almost a penitential rite less about pleasure than about display. This ritual character was reinforced aurally as a single tune was played monotonously over and again for each pair of dancers:

> *... [W]hy should I mention a Hundred or more,*
> *Who went the same Circle as others before,*
> *To a Tune that they play'd us a hundred Times o'er?*[49]

Before the age of recorded sound, it seemed less monotonous for the same tune to be played over again, but apparently there were limits even then. Contemporary accounts of the minuet do not describe a pleasurable pastime as much as a social sacrament which reminded the Company twice a week of the existence of a social hierarchy.

A young woman's first minuet was not only her first appearance in 'society', but an acknowledgement of her particular niche within it.

Lady Elizabeth Hervey did exceptionally well to hold her own through four minuets.[50] Elizabeth Montagu took steps to ensure that her charge Miss Carter would make the right impression when her time came. 'I did not think it right she should dance minuets at the Ball till she was quite perfect in it,' she wrote to her husband in 1753,

> *but Mr West, Mr Pitt all their family & some other company were here the other day, & I made her dance a minuet with Master West by way of using her to do it in company that her apprehension & confusion may be less when she is to dance in a full assembly, she acquitted herself so well as to get great commendation & indeed I think will make a fine dancer.*[51]

The West Indian historian (and cricket enthusiast) C. L. R. James once famously remarked that no one knew cricket who *only* knew cricket. The same was true of dancing in the eighteenth century. Knowing how to dance entailed knowing a great deal else. Dancing, and the process of learning to dance, was critical cultural capital for actual and aspiring elites in the European eighteenth century. One member of the Company impressed with Nash's social confidence naturally asked who his dancing master was. Instruction was begun as early as possible, as the pupil had to learn again how to stand and how to walk. The dancing master's pupil had to master the niceties of posture, gesture and gait before learning even the most basic dance steps. Pupils also learned etiquette and essential social skills under his tutelage. In Bath as elsewhere, skills acquired from a dancing master could be put to use taking a turn on the public walks, before a pupil so much as set foot in a ballroom. Even a seemingly simple stroll in the Orange Grove was as hierarchical and ritualised as the minuet, as rules governed who was to walk before or behind whom. Moreover, encounters on the walks were occasions for displaying knowledge of the vernacular of gesture, slightly different in outdoor settings, where men could not slide their feet and women could not curtsy. Nash held court here as well. As the autumn season of 1726 flagged, Lady Glenorchy reported that some of the Company were still 'Gay enough to go & play with Mr Nash upon the walks'.[52]

Lessons begun in childhood, before bad habits became ingrained, were best, although this caveat did not deter some dancing masters from tapping into the social-mobility market and giving lessons to adults. Dudley Ryder began lessons at twenty-four, too late to instil the self-confidence he was too well aware he lacked.[53] In one contemporary print, entitled *Grown Ladies Taught to Dance*, the satire implicit in the title is belied by the concentration and determination shown in the face of the socially ambitious matron practising her curtsy. The parvenu market was also serviced with printed manuals purportedly aimed at those who would try to teach themselves. Published guides such as Rameau's *Dancing Master* and Tomlinson's *Art of Dancing* are invaluable sources for cultural historians, but for contemporary readers they would only have served to reinforce the notion that these skills could never be 'book-learned'. Basic motor skills learned in infancy had to be taught to pupils again with a view to proper deportment rather than just coordinated movement. First they would learn to stand:

> *The Head must be upright, without being stiff; the Shoulders falling back, which extends the Breast, and gives a greater Grace to the Body; the Arms hanging by the Side, the Hands neither quite open nor shut, the Waste steady, the Legs extended, and the Feet turned outwards.*

Once they had mastered standing, along with the five permissible positions for the feet, walking was next. The proper length of a step was the length of one's foot, which would prevent the speed of walking from being too fast or too slow. Aside from standing and walking, there were additional niceties, such as the right way for a man to remove his hat and the correct way to enter a room (taking a few steps into the room to ensure that the entrance was clear for others). The important business of paying honours – bows and curtsys – was next. Men were to master the 'bow forward' with the 'bow behind', which in combination allowed a number of bows to be made in graceful sequence. For women, the equivalents, the full and half-curtsy, were made easier by the fact of long skirts.[54]

The dress code mandated for the minuet reinforced its ritual aspect. Women were required to wear court dress, with the skirts of the petticoat and overdress protruding sideways over an elliptical 'hoop' worn around the waist. Their hair was to be dressed with lappets, strips of fabric which hung down on either side. Nash's enforcement of his sartorial strictures gave rise to the most famous of all Nash anecdotes, which every Bath tour guide will tell at least once in the course of a working day. Goldsmith told the tale in the voice of an eyewitness. Nash, he related,

> *had the strongest aversion to a white apron and absolutely excluded all who ventured to come to the assembly dressed in that manner. I have known him on a ball night to strip even the Duchess of Q[ueensberry] and throw her apron at one of the higher benches among the ladies' women, observing that none but abigails appeared in white aprons.*[55]

The Duchess of Queensberry was the celebrated Kitty Hyde, who visited Bath in 1721, not long after her marriage. Her picture, of which Charles Jervas is thought to have painted three versions in the later 1720s, hangs in the National Portrait Gallery in London, Petworth House in Sussex and Stanford University in California. She is costumed as a dairymaid, complete with milk pail, and wears the item that captures our attention, a white lace apron. One cannot help thinking that the anecdote would not have come into existence without the portrait. As one of the great glamorous figures of her day, the Augustan equivalent of a supermodel, Catherine Hyde had the power to set trends, often unintentionally. Any number of women of her generation might as a result have turned up on full-dress occasions decked out as dairy-maids, or shepherdesses, or in some other prettified pastoral guise. Nash may indeed have established his power of judicial review as *arbiter elegantiarum* by illustrating for his constituency the fine line separating a

18. Katherine Hyde had only recently married the Duke of Queensberry when she sat for Charles Jervas. Is the apron she wears the one that so incensed Nash?

fashion from a fad. The incident as Goldsmith describes it also parallels Pope's reference to the Duchess in his *Epistle to a Lady:*

> *If QUEENSBERRY to strip there's no compelling*
> *Tis from a handmaid we must take a Helen.*[56]

Given Nash's taste for adapting literary texts to the reconstruction of his own past and Goldsmith's tendency to follow that precedent in order to pad out Nash's biography, the 'apron incident' may be an invention of the order of any of the Inns of Court episodes. Then again, the predilection for aprons as an article of ball dress was a documented nuisance elsewhere. The governors of the Ladies' Assembly of Derby stipulated in the 1740s that 'No Lady shall be allowed to dance in a long white apron.'[57] Ronald Neale suggests that the objection to white aprons stemmed from prostitutes wearing them to signal their availability.[58] If this was established practice at resorts, and was generally recognised as such, surely prohibitions should have been unnecessary, as no woman of the Company, however august, would then dare to wear one.

If 'French' dances like the minuet were performances of hierarchy, the English country dances that followed were demonstrations of social aplomb. Women who had danced minuets briefly retired to remove their hoops for these less formal but still decorous dances. In important respects country dances were diametrically opposed to the minuet. The term for us conjures up images of rustic folk dancing, but 'country dance' was a corruption of *contre danse,* which referred to the dancers standing in parallel lines facing 'against' each other. Several couples took the floor at once rather than just one, and after a brief acknowledgement of precedence as the dancers stood in lines in order of social rank, dancers frequently changed partners (same-sex pairings, however brief, were not unusual). Furthermore, the names of the dance tunes (well over 300 in one compilation), each with its distinctive set of steps, were redolent with the earthiness of the countryside. Polite ladies and gentlemen might dance to tunes like 'Cuckolds all arow', 'Lady of Pleasure', 'Punk's Delight', 'Rub Her Down with Straw', and 'Johnny Cock thy Beaver', just as they might dance to 'Epsom Wells', 'Tunbridge Walks', and 'New Bath'. It is easy to imagine a ball ending with the exuberant 'Joan Sanderson', which required the dancers to engage in a sung dialogue with the musicians, and a ritualised greeting and parting:

This Dance is begun by a single Person, (either Man or Woman)

19. Country or 'English' dances were less formal than 'French' minuets, as Hogarth's engraving from The Analysis of Beauty *suggests*

> *who taking a Cushion in their hand dances about the Room, and at the end of the Tune they stop and sing,* This dance *it will no farther go. The musicians answer, I pray you good Sir, who say you so? Man,* Because *Joan Sanderson* will not come too. *Music.* She must come too, and she shall come too, and she must come whether she will or no. *Then he lays down the Cushion before a Woman, on which she kneels, and he Kisses her, singing,* Welcome *Joan Sanderson,* welcome, welcome. *Then she rises, takes up the Cushion, and both dance singing,* Prinkum-prankum is a fine Dance, and shall we go dance it once again, once again, and once again, and shall we go dance it once again?

The woman then repeated the cycle, choosing a partner through the same formula, 'and thus they do till the whole Company are taken into the Ring', whereupon the cycle reversed, with farewells replacing welcomes, 'and so they go out one by one as they came in'.[59]

Whether or not Georgian Britons saw their relationship with their sovereign in Lockean contractarian terms, there could be little doubt that the King of Bath ruled by the consent of the governed, for they were known to withdraw their consent when it suited them. Affronts could be quite pointed, especially in the 1720s, relatively early in Nash's ascendancy. According to Goldsmith, Nash's command of the ball schedule was absolute, with the music ending promptly at eleven, and reportedly not even Princess Amelia was allowed as much as one dance after Nash lifted his finger to signal the band. In 1723, however, the Earl and Countess of Grantham successfully insisted that the balls begin an hour earlier than Nash stipulated.[60] A satirist in 1725 found Nash 'Hardly secure in all his right divine':

> *For lo! unsummon'd beaux (how strange to tell,)*
> *Presumptuous durst elect the favourite* Bell,
> *And with emboldened front, uncall'd advance*
> *To dance* French *dances they ne'er saw in* France.[61]

If the occasional visitor chose not to take Nash's authority seriously, there was little he could do – or needed to – except look forward to their departure.

~

> *[T]he Gentry runs the Gauntlet the Second Time when they leave the Town. First of all, there's a Guinea to the Pumper: Second, a Crown to the Boy at the Pump-handle: Third, Half-a-Guinea to the Serjeant: Fourth, a Crown to the Cloth-Woman: Fifth, a Crown to the Bath-Guide: Sixth, a Crown to the Chair-Men: Seventh, a Guinea to the Cook-Maid, where you lodge: Eighth, two Guineas to the Chamber-Maids: Ninth, half-a-Guinea to the Scullion: Tenth, a Crown to each Porter at the Long-Room Doors: Eleventh, to the Ostlers and Boot-Catchers one Guinea: The last of all, is a Present to the Strip-*

> *my-Coach-Beggars ... they had need have good Estates that come ... for amongst us all, we try whether they will stand the Test, or not.*[62]

Bath's social routine was for those who had 'good Estates' or could otherwise afford to lavish the necessary expenditure on their self-presentation, and to appear on the walks, at the Pump or in the Assembly Rooms when everyone else did was the most effective means of making one's consumption conspicuous. It was certainly possible for visitors to live outside of the 'fairy circle', and there is circumstantial evidence that the resort's economy was bolstered by the presence of large numbers of visitors who could not afford to live in the style of the Company. Thomas Cox heard in the late 1720s that 8,000 families came to Bath in any given season; by the 1740s, John Wood claimed that Bath could accommodate 12,000 visitors.[63] If we take these figures with the knowledge that only 500 or 600 visitors were ever listed in the Company during the 1740s, we can only conclude that even if the estimates are exaggerated, many more visitors came to Bath than had the resources to cut a figure in the assembly rooms. The London solicitor Arthur Collier was too humble to be listed in the *Bath Journal* during any of the five visits he made to Bath in 1745 and 1746, unlike Sir Oswald Mosley, the Staffordshire baronet (and ancestor of the British fascist leader), with whose daughter Collier was romantically entangled.[64] The presence of large numbers of plebeian visitors had been acknowledged for some time. 'The Bath was never fuller and never less Quallity in it,' Sir Thomas Cave complained to his father-in-law in 1709.[65] The Countess of Bristol indicated as much to her husband in 1723. '[T]hey pretend to calculate that there is near 7,000 strangers here,' she wrote, 'and out of 100, 99 that never were seen before.'[66]

If the 'middling sort' were so numerous at Bath, why, then, did they leave so little trace of themselves in the archives? The absence of archival evidence reflects the political economy of writing in the eighteenth century. While women and men of this amorphous category were certainly literate – it was one of the attributes that marked them off from the lower orders – pen, ink, paper and postage were still too costly for letters to be written and dispatched except for particularly important business. Even among elites, the purely sociable letter – full of the observations, commentary and gossip that cultural historians relish – is comparatively rare, and not solely because such correspondence was often destroyed by descendants concerned to preserve reputations or simply to clear out clutter. Postage was expensive, amounting to three to four pence for a single-sheet letter, which was roughly comparable to what it costs today to send a book manuscript by courier. This expense could be justified in the service of managing a business, estate or household *in absentia*, but made sociable correspondence a luxury. While visitors to Bath had the leisure to write letters, ill health also prevented them from corresponding, and it is reasonable to assume that fewer affluent visitors were likely to be legitimately ill, or at least apprehensive about their health. Many of the 'middling sort' may have come to Bath in the summer, a possibility suggested by the slight *increase* in weekly stage services between London and Bath during what was supposed to be the off-season.[67] These visitors, several of whom in any given week rated a mention in the arrivals column, could take advantage of cheaper accommodation, and avoid the expense and nuisance of putting in appearances at balls, plays and concerts.

The Company had been able to consolidate enough to assert its interest in confronting the Bath Corporation over the expansion of Harrison's Rooms in 1711. If such a moment arrived for those less privileged visitors outside the Company, it was towards the end of the 1720s, and came as a challenge not to the officially constituted local authorities but to Nash, the semi-official overlord of the spa's amusement culture. This attempted *coup d'état* was the project of 'Captain' Thomas Goulding, a colourful local businessman. Goulding was partner in a local brewery and dabbled in agriculture, keeping orchards and livestock on his small estate at Freshford five miles south-east of Bath. Visitors to the resort would have known him primarily as a 'toyman' who sold small luxury articles such as snuffboxes, fans, rings, shoe buckles and costume jewellery.[68] Goulding sought to upstage and overthrow Nash, and institute a new home-grown Bath monarchy that would champion honest local tradesmen and retailers and look after the interests of visitors who genuinely came to the resort for their health. In publicising himself, Goulding gave vent to local dismay over the prevailing direction of the spa's economy and culture under Nash and his ally Harrison. The assembly rooms, Goulding charged, swallowed 'all the Money that the Gentry brought to Town', while '[t]he Inhabitants of the Town got nothing but a little Money for their Lodgings and Provisions; what was spent in the Town, would scarce maintain the People that lived in it'.[69] He appealed to the resentment that the local business community felt towards the Company's perceived hauteur. In a parody of Nash's regulations, a character in his play *The Fortune-Hunter* stipulates 'That all Tradesmens Wives and Daughters that have Tickets, may appear at the Ball, without giving Offence to the New-Made and Upstart Gentry'.[70]

Goulding further suggested that visitors rather than locals were responsible for Bath's lingering reputation as a Jacobite enclave. The spa's continuing Jacobite association was a serious public-relations problem, a source of tension between visitors and locals, and among visitors themselves. Bath was known to have an active Jacobite underground at least until the rebellion of 1715, and possibly afterwards. In November 1713 the Duchess of Kent was told that toasts were drunk in Bath to the health of the 'Pretender and of his glorious restauration'.[71] 'They say here are Caballs held under pretence of drinking Waters,' wrote Alexander Pope from Bath in 1714, 'and this Scandal, like others, refreshes me & elevates my Spirits.'[72] During the uprising itself two years later, General George Wade seized 200 horses and a large cache of weapons that Jacobites had stockpiled in Bath, their base of operations in the West Country. Lord Stanhope, the Secretary of State, upbraided magistrates there for their obtuseness in the face of a perceptible Jacobite threat, and it did not help Bath's reputation when the Corporation pleaded for clemency for three Roman Catholics who had been arrested.[73] 'This is certainly a most hellish hole,' Gustavus Hume wrote in 1716 with reference to Jacobitism in Bath, 'and I believe the neighbouring county is but little better.'[74] Dudley Ryder reported a very large crowd at the ball for the King's birthday that year, 'but few gentlemen that cared to dance', among whom was Lord Conway, 'a great Tory' who purportedly 'appeared there on purpose to clear himself from suspicion of being concerned in the rebellion which he lies under'.[75] Bath lay under suspicion and may have been under surveillance. John Macky, who had served William of Orange as a covert operative at the Jacobite Court of St Germain before becoming a counter-intelligence officer of sorts, was in Bath in 1722, ostensibly writing a travel narrative. His entries read suspiciously like field reports and it is very possible that he was still working in espionage. This was the year of the Atterbury Plot, and it was also in October that the Duke of Norfolk was arrested in Bath as a suspected Jacobite conspirator.[76] If Bath was a Jacobite stronghold, then from the point of view of the ministry in Whitehall, it could not be more dangerous. The Company at any given time could include high-ranking officials, and much government business was dispatched in letters dated from Bath during the season. The potential for espionage was very high. Goulding, exploiting strained relations between Company and townsfolk, defended the City and Corporation from the imputation of disloyalty by accusing visitors. It was misguided, he pleaded, 'to think that the Gentry ever let the Town's-people into their Plots or Intrigues'.[77]

Goulding's best opportunity to displace Nash may have come in August 1727, when Elizabeth Nash of Camrose died, leaving the bulk of her estate to her only surviving son. If this Richard Nash, who was also named as executor, was *our* Richard Nash, he may have gone to Wales more out of concern to keep his humble origins quiet than to collect his tiny legacy, or to see that his illiterate sister's seven children received theirs. This bothersome but necessary business may have kept Nash away from Bath for much if not all of the autumn season that year. For Nash, this would have been bad timing. The new king, George II, had acceded in June, and over that summer and autumn Goulding raised a parade regiment, captained by himself, to march and fire salutes on royal anniversaries. Goulding launched his insurgency on the King's birthday in November, when in addition to a parade, an ox, which he provided, was roasted in the marketplace adjacent to the Guildhall and served on an enormous dish made for the occasion. Catastrophe struck, however, as a result of Goulding's decision to lard the ox with 'about 100 rich Stones', as well as 'a great deal of Money',

> *which made the Populace eager to come into the cutting of it up, that they jump'd over the Gentlemen's Shoulders, some whereof got into the very Dish, and were over Shoos in Gravey; one of them being more eager than the rest, was thrust into the Belly of the Ox, and almost smother'd, and the Fat flew about in such a plentiful manner, that the Gentlemen were obliged to quit the Table.*

Goulding made a better show when Princess Amelia visited Bath the next June in conjunction with the opening of the Avon Navigation. His ox was successfully roasted and eaten, and his speech, following the parade and salute, was acknowledged by the Princess from her window. Nash, if Bristol's newspaper was to be believed, had been upstaged: 'The Honour of this Day was so successful, that 'tis modestly computed, this City was never so Populous since built before; so that numerous Concourse and Advantage must accrue from the generous Undertaking of Capt. Goulding.' For good measure, Goulding published *The Whole Lives and Proceedings of Sancho and Peepo* to expose Nash, his pretensions, his collusion with Harrison and what Goulding viewed as the parasitic character of the resort economy. On Coronation Day that October, however, 'Captain Goulding had the Misfortune to loose one of his best Oxen; and what was worse, he thought it most for his Safety, to abandon his Engagement with the British Champion', a prizefighter, 'and asked his Pardon at the Brink of the Stage.' Goulding lamented for years afterwards that 'there was no Notice taken' of any of the celebrations he had sponsored.[78]

Meanwhile, Nash had recovered his due prominence. Nash had

20. Frederick, Prince of Wales, who visited Bath in 1738 with his equally attractive and popular consort, scoring a triumph for Nash

the judgement to sponsor entertainments that were less messy and more exclusive, and expanded the range of amusements available to the Company. When the opportunity arose to entertain royalty, he had the good sense to erect monuments in stone to mark the occasion and his role in it. Princess Amelia visited again in 1734, preceded closely by her sister and brother-in-law, the Prince and Princess of Orange, whose obelisk – raised by Nash – still stands, its inscription badly worn, in the centre of the Orange Grove, which was renamed in their honour. Four years later came a bigger prize in the form of Frederick and Augusta, the Prince and Princess of Wales. Their obelisk decorated the newly completed Queen Square, named for the recently deceased consort of George II. So that the honour might be augmented to accord with the rank of the recipient, Nash at length prevailed upon an exasperated Alexander Pope to compose lines for the inscription.

It also helped that John Wood, who considered Nash a crucial

21. The Orange Grove, named not for citrus trees but for its obelisk commemorating the visit of the Prince of Orange, was one of the principal walks

supporter, built Bath its second set of assembly rooms, which opened in April 1730 under the management of Catherine Lindsey, a retired singer. A spirit of competition flared but briefly. When Thomas Harrison died the next year, Mrs Lindsey's sister, Elizabeth Hayes, opportunely took over the lease on his establishment, giving them a corner on the market that they proceeded to exploit, until Nash intervened.[79] Perhaps he threatened to carry the balls back to the Guildhall, where they had been held for nearly thirty years, very probably, until 1720. It certainly helped his case that he chose to cooperate in the sisters' dividing their custom, so that the two sets of assembly rooms were open on alternate nights, and the weekly balls alternated between them as well. At some point in this period Nash also introduced a new public subscription, this one for regular concert breakfasts, another entertainment previously held under private sponsorship as balls had once been. By this means musical entertainment could be continued past the hour when music in the Pump Room ceased. These concerts were highly successful, often featuring internationally celebrated performers visiting from London, as well as the occasional amateur musician among

22. James Vertue's drawing of the Long Room at Wilshire's. Nash's portrait, between busts of Newton and Pope, is visible on the right

the Company. They were so well subscribed by the 1740s that they produced large surpluses.[80]

Nash was secure enough at Bath by 1735 to attempt to annex Tunbridge Wells as a satellite 'kingdom'. Improbably (or appropriately), his predecessor there was Bell Causey, a London fruit vendor who sold refreshments at Tunbridge during the season. Mrs Causey expertly flattered the social pretensions of her customers by persuading them to give entertainments, which she catered as a matter of course. Her style of social entrepreneurship was more apposite to Tunbridge's more intimate and bucolic atmosphere than Nash's effort to introduce grand and courtly assemblies there after her death in 1735. Although Nash gamely positioned himself at 'the Wells' summer after summer for the next twenty-five years, Tunbridge somehow eluded him and he was never as supreme there as at Bath. Its proximity to London, and thus to St James, Westminster and the City, created a different, and more multicultural, demographic, with continental nobility from the diplomatic corps sharing walks and assembly rooms with the families of Sephardi merchants. Bath's Master of Ceremonies would not shine in such a setting. Any stereotypically Tory xenophobia would handicap him, as would his inability to speak any language other than English. Nash lacked even French, the courtly *lingua franca,* which may have been one reason he ultimately employed Jacques Caulet, a French dancing master, as his assistant. Fortunately for Nash, Bath's Company (for the time being) contained the right mix of the established and the ambitious.

It was in the year 1738, Goldsmith asserted, that Nash achieved 'the meridian of his glory ... [H]e arrived at such a pitch of authority, that I really believe Alexander was not greater at Persepolis.'[81] Nash, having put up monuments to others, now erected his own. He presented his portrait to be hung in the Long Room at Wiltshire's between busts of Newton and Pope, as recorded in James Vertue's contemporary drawing, and in waspish lines that appeared shortly afterwards:

Immortal Newton, never spoke
More truth, than here you'll find;
Nor Pope himself, e'er penned a joke
More cruel on mankind.
This picture plac'd the busts between,
Gives satyr all his strength,
Wisdom and Wit are little seen,
But Folly at full length.[82]

The portrait, placed as it was, may have looked foolish to some observers, but to others the effect of Nash's image in the assembly rooms, together with his regulations in the Pump Room, might have been reminiscent of the royal arms above the Ten Commandments at the east end of parish churches, with the sole exception that sovereign and lawgiver were one and the same.

4

Overseer of the Marriage Market

[T]here is no place in the world so fit for the necessary and honourable business of making alliances ... [1]

Considering numbers, instances of marriage are very rare. Here people are so continually imployed in trifles, that they hardly have a moment to spare on serious thought. Dissipation prevents real impressions of friendship or love.[2]

For observers like Richard Pococke, author of the first quotation above, Bath was to matrimony what Newmarket was to horses or Billingsgate was to fish. From the early eighteenth century at least, visitors viewed Bath as a natural venue for hunting spouses either for themselves or for members of their family. In 1706 a wealthy Londoner at Bath approached John Verney, Viscount Fermanagh, and offered his daughter in marriage to Fermanagh's son 'with 7000l. downe and 8000 More at her ffathers Death ... But Mr Verney being Indispos'd and at Bath for his health, My Lord did not think it seasonable to treat at that time'. The same season, Fermanagh himself twitted a friend whose father was on an extended visit to the spa: 'Surely your father is courting some young Woman to keep his Old Back warme, or he wou'd neuer stay so long in such a nasty Towne as is Bath, which by the heate of the Waters we may conclude Hell is not far under it.'[3] George Lucy noted during a visit later in the century that at least one man of the Company left Bath with a new bride in tow, and he had heard that 'many more are upon the same plan'.[4] The Master of Ceremonies, who counted 'Protector of the Fair' among his numerous honorifics, included the marriage market under his purview, and if his surviving correspondence is any guide, Nash was a highly sought-after matrimonial consultant. In two of his three surviving autograph letters, he advises no less a figure than the sixth Duke of Somerset about which of the two Finch sisters he should marry (in the third, significantly, he apologises for bad behaviour at the gaming table). At Bath and elsewhere, love (whatever that meant) was a sociable game akin to whist or quadrille, while sex, denominated in the eighteenth century by euphemisms such as 'gallantry', was a competitive and risky enterprise analogous to hazard or faro. Marriage, on the other hand, was serious business. Was it too serious, then, as Alexander Sutherland suggested, to flourish in the giddy atmosphere of Bath?

The experience of Elizabeth Brydges allows us to reconcile Pococke and Sutherland to a degree. Sir Charles Lloyd, a young Welsh baronet, made a proposal for her hand in Bath in October 1726, a proposal made not to her but to her uncle, the first Duke of Chandos. Chandos was putting up her portion of £3,500, and asked in return a jointure of £400 per year (payable on her widowhood), £60 per year in 'pin money' and suitable provision for elder and younger children; once these particulars had been agreed upon, Chandos declared, 'I dont see any thing else can happen to give any interruption to the Conclusion of this Treaty.'[5] The Duke and Duchess agreed that the courtship could proceed to the next step: Elizabeth would actually be informed that she had a suitor. Chandos was astonished to discover that his niece did not care for her prospective husband at all. Admittedly, Lloyd had 'seen so little of the World that his carriage is awkward, and his manner of speaking not so polite', but Chandos found him 'perfectly good natur'd'; his only real failing was 'being too apt to disorder himself with Drink'. When Elizabeth would not agree to the match, she was threatened. Her uncle would wash his hands of her and her portion would go to her younger sister instead. Chandos even proposed, as the disconsolate Elizabeth shut herself in her room and wept, that Arabella Brydges come up from her father's seat (in the same coach that brought Elizabeth ignominiously down from Chandos's house) to be offered to Lloyd in her elder sister's place.[6] It was only after this emotional havoc had been unleashed, and damaging words written and spoken, that Lloyd turned out to be up to his elegantly curled wig in debt. Chandos wrote the poor Welshman off – as matrimonial fodder anyway – without another thought, or, as far as we know, a word of apology to his niece.[7] More timely intelligence about the state of Charles Lloyd's finances would certainly have saved Elizabeth Brydges a great deal of emotional distress, but such was the consequence of recruiting spouses outside of local networks of kinship and association.

For this reason, while matrimonial overtures and initial negotiations might be undertaken in Bath, the deal would usually be closed elsewhere. Thus Sutherland could write in 1763 that marriages contracted between members of the Company were comparatively rare at Bath, a defect that he attributed to the resort's ambience of superficiality. By the time that Sutherland wrote, of course, Lord Hardwicke's Marriage Act had been in force for ten years. This legislation, aimed at preventing elopements, stipulated that impending marriages be announced in the parishes in which bride and groom were resident at least three weeks prior to the event, and thus predisposed the couple to be wed in their local communities. Bath was served by its own weekly newspaper for four years before any marriages were announced in it at all. The few notices which appear in the Bath papers prior to 1753 tend to advertise the weddings not of members of the Company but of Bath residents (the relatives of local apothecaries figure prominently). The relative paucity of Bath betrothals did not lessen the resort's importance to the marriage market, however. A successful season in Bath could supply a young woman with the self-confidence necessary to making a figure in other venues in the matrimonial sweepstakes, and presented an opportunity for a single young woman to demonstrate the discretion and propriety expected of an upper-class wife. 'Bath is a good place for the initiation of a young Lady,' wrote Samuel Johnson to Hester

Thrale. 'She can neither become negligent for want of observers, as in the country; nor by the imagination that she is concealed in the croud, as in London.'[8] Johnson's advice would have been as valid sixty years earlier.

Even at relatively humble social levels, marriage had always involved the transfer of property, and was inevitably spoken of in unapologetically mercenary terms. Single women were crassly commodified, like the heiress, 'a Twenty-thousand pounder', who was George Lucy's neighbour in Bath.[9] But by the second half of the seventeenth century, traditional forms of both real and movable property had been joined by new and seemingly less stable forms such as paper securities and the introduction of concepts of credit – the by-products of an already global economy. New language made available by the financial revolution inevitably found its way into matrimonial discourse. In fact, as one scholar has recently argued, the ease with which the language of commerce, credit and finance was adapted to courtship and matrimony alarmed and discouraged contemporary observers.[10] In May 1726, months before the débâcle of Sir Charles Lloyd, the Duchess of Chandos wrote out of anxiety for her niece Elizabeth, 'whose Merit Chiefly Consists in her Person, & more yn Comon sweetness of Temper, wch according to ye general judgement of ye World have but very little Weight against Money'.[11] Contemplating the engagement of Lord Noel Somerset in Bath in 1740, Elizabeth Montagu wrote even more cynically:

> *a Man of Merit & a younger Brother is a purchase only for a great fortune; as for those who have more merit than wealth, they must turn the penny by disposing of their worthless virtues for Riches, the exchange may sometimes be difficult, virtues not being Sterling, nor merit the Current coin of the Nation, however it is possible to bring about the exchange, Men of Estates loving to buy curiosities they don't understand, [and] fools every day buy sensible wives.*[12]

23. Elizabeth Montagu, shown later in her life, was a frequent visitor to Bath during Nash's ascendancy, and was a trenchant observer of its marriage market

Contemporaries were concerned with reason about the increasingly mercenary tone of courtship, for by 1700 the marriage market (if the traffic is understood in patriarchal terms as consisting of commodified prospective brides) was a bear market, as reflected by the increasing ratio of portions paid by the bride's family with respect to jointures promised by the groom's family.[13] Where before, in keeping with metaphors drawn from property in land or specie or durable goods, a bride, commodified as she might be, had a stable intrinsic value, now her value could fluctuate due to forces not entirely within her or her family's control.

The public culture through which women were marketed was itself a minefield in which a single false step, real or perceived, could result in disaster. The marriage market necessitated that young women of established or socially ambitious families, who throughout childhood and early adolescence had been carefully sequestered from the morally perilous public amusement culture, were suddenly thrust into the centre of it. Such a woman would usually be buffered by a thicket of older relatives and friends of her family – that is, members of her kinship network.[14] With this expectation in mind, Elizabeth Anson advised the host of a breakfast at Tunbridge that 'he must invite the Mothers as well as the Misses, or he may go without Company, there having been a great fracas lately about a private Ball, to wch Lord Eglington invited the young & Fair, without the Old and Wise to guard them'.[15] Older members of the kinship network had a crucial role as chaperones, but if well chosen they also provided entry into the requisite social circles. Writing from Bath in 1748, Elizabeth Montagu reminded the Duchess of Portland of 'the infinite consequence you are of to your children as well as to the happiness of yr friends; indeed I see here sad examples of young people who want proper persons to introduce them into ye World'.[16] One immediately thinks of Catherine Morland in *Northanger Abbey,* compelled to wander aimlessly through the assembly rooms with her socially unconnected chaperone Mrs Allen, through whose agency she later falls into the clutches of the treacherous Thorpes. Both the chaperone and entrée functions were less complicated in Bath because of its small size and relative intimacy, but also because of the carefully cultivated ambience for which its Master of Ceremonies was responsible. Nash's relentless self-promotion and self-mythography created the expectation of an atmosphere at Bath of relative social openness, wholesomeness and safety. Such an atmosphere made it an ideal venue for a young woman's entry into 'the world'.

The corporate identity which Nash helped to establish among the Company engendered a *relatively* egalitarian atmosphere in Bath. Those who could afford the subscription fees and suitable clothes had the right, regardless of the source of their affluence, to expect at least civil behaviour from any other member of the Company – while at Bath. More than one commentator observed that an acquaintance made and received in Bath could not expect the same reception elsewhere. Still, as superficial and as ephemeral as this egalitarianism may have been, the expectation was created that the more egregious forms of snobbery would not be met with in Bath. Thus Sally Marshall of Highgate, the daughter of a tailor, was nevertheless 'extremely taken notice of' at Bath 'and admired as the most celebrated beauty there'.[17]

Another important consideration where marriageable young women were concerned was the *comparative* safety of Bath from the dangers of moral corruption. John Macky, in Bath very possibly to spy on Jacobite conspirators in 1722, noted, for example, that prostitutes (who might otherwise have been useful informants) were 'not to be met with' at Bath, in contrast to Tunbridge Wells and Epsom.[18] Public solicitation was clearly discouraged, although houses of prostitution existed to serve male visitors. In January 1727 a husband and wife were pilloried in Bath for keeping a brothel 'and procuring young Women to be debauch'd'. They were caught when their maid turned informant and alleged among other things that her mistress, Mrs Lewes, had 'danced N[ake]d before a Number of Gentlemen; and for her Agility, had Half a Crown of each'.[19] Avon Street, built by the Bristol architect John Strahan in the 1730s, was lined with brothels by the 1760s, including 'Mother Addams's', which Henry Penruddocke Wyndham visited and wrote of fondly in 1762.[20] John Penrose and his family took great pains to avoid even setting foot in this 'street of ill fame'.[21] Fortunately, Avon Street was easy for the Company to avoid (assuming, of course, that they wished to) as it ran south to the river from Westgate, outside of and away from the centres of fashionable amusement and accommodation. In Nash's Bath, only those who went looking for sex workers would encounter them.

Marital fraud posed a more immediate peril at the spa, a centre of upper-income spouse hunting (if not always spouse *finding*). The presence of a Master of Ceremonies ameliorated one liability of resorts, which was that the Company changed very quickly as visitors came and went, creating opportunities for impostors of all types, especially cardsharps and fortune hunters (Irishmen were stereotypically suspect). Nash spent most of the year in Bath, and ultimately the autumn and spring seasons were understood to begin and end on his arrival and departure. During the season, Nash made an effort to visit every family who subscribed at the assembly rooms. As the regulator of the balls, it was thought, he had to inform himself of the relative social standing of visitors to determine who danced before whom in the minuet, or who stood above whom in country dances. Those who loitered with intent over the course of a season or several seasons – either to fleece punters or to ensnare heiresses – would ultimately be known to Nash, who could transmit this knowledge when necessary. Thus it was, according to Macky, that everything that passed at Bath, including 'the Characters of Persons' was 'known on the Walks'.[22] This transparency posed interesting implications for social life at the spa, especially for gender relations.

~

Although Nash's position in Bath had yet to be denominated by any distinctive title, male visitors like Dudley Ryder immediately recognised his potential utility in matters of courtship. Ryder, twenty-four and a bencher of the Middle Temple, was infatuated to the point of obsession with Sally Marshall, a 'top toast' of the 1716 season. There is an air of calculation in Ryder's remarks about Nash, such that these few pregnant sentences convey as much useful information as all of the *Jests of Beau Nash*:

> *He has the privilege of saying what he pleases and talking to the ladies as his fancy leads him and no affront is to be taken, though he sometimes puts modest women to the blush. His conversation and sayings seem to make a great part of the conversation of others and the repeating of what he does or says helps to fill up the conversation very much. Upon this account, though he is a very ugly man in his face, yet he is very much beloved and esteemed by the ladies as a witty and genteel man.*[23]

Nash was well placed to serve as either matchmaker or panderer-in-chief. Ryder and others believed that he enjoyed the particular confidence of women of the Company, and Nash cultivated this perception of privileged access. A detractor wrote in 1717 that Nash 'raps at my Lady's Bed Chamber, and enters it as freely as if he was to dress her ... [he] kisses the Wife and cocks at the Husband [and] lives with the Women as Horner did [a character in Wycherley's *Country Wife*] because the Husbands are in hopes that he'll be contented with cheating them [at cards]'.[24] John Macky more objectively wrote that Nash 'is not of any Birth, nor Estate, but by a good Address and Assurance ingratiates himself into the good Graces of the Ladies, and the best Company in the Place'.[25] Beginning in the 1740s, his influence over women of the Company was advertised at regular intervals in the collections for the General Hospital, when almost all of the (quite considerable) sums collected through Nash came from women, and almost all women whose donations were recorded contributed through Nash.

For their part, women of the Company valued Nash as a confidante. They felt they could confide in him as they could in no other man (lest they compromise themselves) and no other woman (lest they betray themselves to a rival). Nash had numerous detractors who laid many charges at his door, but significantly none of them accuse him of originating or repeating any of the gossip which was a conversational staple at the resort. His discretion could be relied upon, and this fact alone was enough to gain him access to the most prestigious boudoirs in Bath. He fitted very well, by all accounts, into the role of a 'walker' – a man, generally unmarried, who serves as an escort for upper-class women whose husbands are (for whatever reason) unavailable. This social custom was well established elsewhere in Europe in the eighteenth century, especially in Spain and Italy, where such men went under the name of *cicisbeo,* or 'whisperer'. The institution did not easily translate into either the language or the culture of the British Isles, and was frequently misunderstood. Husbands among the Company were reassured, however, by Nash's keeping a series of mistresses. His serial concubinage was well known among visitors. An early printed attack on Nash told the story of one visitor, the wife of a prominent attorney, who lost £100 to Nash at the gaming table.

Nash 'had the Gallantry to take her Necklace in pawn for it; and at the next Assembly, his own dirty Mistress appear'd with it, to the terrible Mortification' of Nash's debtor 'and the wonderful Delight of the whole Company'.[26] Another visitor reportedly confronted him in public for being a 'whoremonger'. 'I have a Woman lives in my House, and that may have occasioned the Mistakes;' Nash protested, 'but if I did keep her, a Man can no more be deemed a Whore-monger, from having one Whore in his House, than a Cheesemonger, for having one Cheese.'[27]

At least four of these women have left some traces in the sources. There was Fanny Murray, the daughter of one of Nash's musicians. She was the sole survivor of triplets and was orphaned at age twelve, upon which she earned her keep selling flowers in the assembly rooms. There, her story ran, she was seduced, possibly by a kinsman of the Duke of Marlborough, and abandoned after a few weeks. She became Nash's mistress not long after she returned to the sale of nosegays, when, according to her salacious and sensationalist biography, she was all of fourteen years old. Ultimately, she threw Nash over for a more socially august lover, whereupon he took up with a Mrs Stevens, a divorcée who claimed that her ex-husband had defrauded her of a dowry of £20,000.[28] Fanny Murray, according to Lewis Melville, later married a man named Ross, and merited a mention in John Wilkes's pornographic *Essay on Woman* before her death in 1770.[29] Most colourful and mythical of all these women was Juliana Popjoy (variously spelled Papjoy and Pobjoy). She was a dressmaker, and earned the nickname 'Lady Betty Besom' for her habit of riding out in public carrying a whip with so many thongs it resembled a fly-whisk. Her eccentricities probably contributed to Nash's ending their relationship, and her decision (if her obituary is to be believed) to live in a hollow tree for the next thirty to forty years of her life does not argue for the most stable condition of mental health. She died in 1777 and is purported (by, among others, the owners of a restaurant bearing her name) to haunt Saw Close. Writers as various as Robert Peach and David Gadd claim that Juliana Popjoy returned to Nash to nurse him in his dotage, which we might have thought fortunate for Nash, did we not know from George Scott that for the last twenty years of his life he lived with one Mrs Hill. '[P]oor Nash had no small Degree of Punishment in living with this termagant Woman,' Scott related, 'Solomon could not describe a worse.'[30]

Nash never married, although it must have been tempting, given his habits, to marry into the means of supporting them, in the manner of Hogarth's Tom Rakewell. Such a marriage during the yawning documentary gap of seventeen years would serve to explain how the young man who left Oxford with very limited means in 1693 turned up in Bath in 1710, staking on a few rolls of the dice a sum nearly equal to the value of his father's estate. For a man living in that period there was no quicker way to wealth than to marry it. The ideal candidate was a suitably wealthy widow, preferably without living issue or bothersome relations. Upon remarriage, she once again became a *femme couverte* whose property automatically devolved upon her new husband. For the dedicated marital opportunist, widows were better and more vulnerable game, and thicker on the ground than unmarried heiresses. Nash nevertheless established a reputation for protecting single young women of the Company from the fortune hunters who reportedly circled like sharks to snare them, but this supposition had more to do with parental paranoia than fact.

Prospective grooms and their parents believed, reasonably or not, that Nash enjoyed the particular confidence of prospective brides and *their* parents, who likewise believed that Nash's contacts among the Company made him a formidable matrimonial impresario in the service of those who secured his favour. His letters to the Duke of Somerset present such a jaundiced view of marriage, however, that we have to wonder if Nash was really interested in brokering matrimony at all. While Charlotte and Harriet Finch were daughters of an earl, Nash agreed with his informant, Elizabeth Southwell, that they were 'fitter ... for brood than to run a race in the world, and ... good for nothing but good Wives'.[31] Significantly, in becoming 'good wives' and then 'breeding', Charlotte and Harriet would be conforming to conventionally accepted gender roles. Nash preferred Harriet for her 'vivacity' and 'good humour' over Charlotte, whom he callously dismissed as 'an old maid', finding her 'Dull and flegmatick', although she was clearly 'the better Domestick'. Nash implicitly argued for a wider social compass for women, as socially engaged women were for him the axes around which polite sociability revolved, not to mention his belief, as he advised Somerset, that 'a cheerful companion is the chiefest pleasure of Life'.[32] His vigilance on their behalf was informed by an assumption that women ought to be able to be interesting without being morally suspect.

In contrast, Nash could be merciless to women he found unattractive, dull or in any way disengaged from the world of polite heterosociability. In fact, it often seemed that Nash, who, according to Goldsmith, had taught polite and civil behaviour to a nation, badly needed lessons himself. Many of Nash's *bon mots* were aimed low, and he was not above ridiculing women for their physical appearance. Hearing that a visitor with osteoporosis had come 'straight from London', he supposedly remarked that she had 'been damnably warped by the way'.[33] Pope noted the 'impudent' attitude that Nash assumed towards women of the Company, which did not prevent Nash standing among those 'who are most in favor with the Fair'.[34] Twenty years later, his behaviour had improved somewhat, if Thomas Wilson is to be believed. 'He was formerly Rude and Saucy to strangers and especially Country Ladies that had not secrets to keep,' Wilson was informed. 'At present he is much civiler.'[35] Nash, according to Goldsmith, was aware that standards of polite heterosociability were continuously subject to change. While the Restoration suitor of his adolescence 'was solemn, majestic, and formal, ... visited his mistress in state, anguished for the favour' and 'kneeled when he toasted his goddess', the 'pert, smart and lively' Augustan beau of his maturity 'was disgusted with so much formality', and 'persuaded his lady to become as ridiculous as himself'. Nash modifed his behaviour accordingly, although he was nonplussed towards his old age that the 'whole secret in intrigue consisted in perfect indifference', as mid-century suitors took 'no manner of notice of the lady, which method was found the surest way to secure her affections'.[36]

By that point, with the life of the resort spinning out of his control, Nash needed to explain to himself and others why suitors no longer sought his assistance. For a long time, however, he appeared to be an indispensable intermediary between the sexes, and further asserted his jurisdiction over their interactions.

~

> *Every moment presents suspicion of gallantry. A Lady of fashion, on her leaving this place, is said to have looked back, uttering these words,* Farewel, Dear Bath, No where is so much scandal, no where so little sin![37]

Alexander Sutherland's commentary exposes the degree to which gossip permeated and shaped the boundaries of the resort's culture of courtship, matrimony and sex. Nash directed the most strongly worded of his regulations to the gossip that floated in the whirl of the Pump and Assembly Rooms. In stipulating 'that all Whisperers of Lies and Scandal be taken for their Authors', Nash was insisting that members of the Company take responsibility for what they said, and implicitly that they consider the veracity of the information, and perhaps examine their own motivations for repeating it. If habitués of the Pump, coffeehouses and assembly rooms had taken Nash's strictures to heart, it should not have been necessary for him to decree further 'That all Repeaters of such Lies and Scandal be shun'd by all Company', and to note that 'Several Old Women and Young Ones, of questioned Reputation, are great Authors of Lies in this Place.'[38] Nash did his best to discourage malicious innuendo, particularly important in a milieu where many visitors, namely those in search of husbands for themselves or their daughters, were obliged to put themselves on display, and in fact much of the gossip of which accounts survive tends to target women who were already married rather than those who were still single.

On the surface, it must puzzle us that families would send their unmarried daughters to what contemporary oral and written culture presented as a hotbed of sexual misconduct. Even the annals of jurisprudence supported this perception from time to time, as Bath was occasionally featured in actions for divorce 'as presenting opportunities for adulterous liaisons'.[39] Contemporaries seem to have understood, however, that adultery and fornication were more often discussed than committed at Bath. The penalty for merely falling under suspicion of 'criminal conversation' was to be the subject of a different kind of conversation, and this price was too high. 'Scandal,' Goldsmith observed, ' … fixed her throne at Bath, preferable to any other part of the kingdom.'[40] A visitor had only to give 'a willing Ear to Scandal', Eliza Haywood warned, 'and a thousand Tongues are ready to oblige you … If a person has a mind to have his Character, Humour, Circumstances … repeated, let him come to the Bath'. The targets of gossip and of printed verse were one and the same, and the more conspicuous a woman was due to her appearance, the more publicity she would suffer from. Haywood made an object lesson of one 'toast' who had the bad luck to be 'devoutly celebrated' at Bath. '[W]henever she appears, she sweeps the Walks, and all the rival Charmers are left neglected to lament their own want of Power, and contrive which way to lessen hers.' They suggest maliciously that her looks are the product of cosmetics, that her hair isn't her own, that she wears false teeth, that she contracted venereal disease from her husband before spreading it to her lover. Others contend that she is a secret and heavy drinker.

> *In this manner did they take the poor Lady to pieces, forgetting, all the while they were endeavouring to make her be thought less worthy of Esteem, their own Charms lost more by the visible Malice that sat upon their Features, than all they could say could cast on hers.*[41]

Gossip, often masked by the euphemism 'news', was a crucial form of social currency. It was, for example, 'a vital part of visiting, and had to be tolerated'.[42] Discussing third parties without their knowledge, furthermore, was itself a necessary and even honourable business, as

Charlotte Lennox has Lady Arabella, her *Female Quixote,* recognise. Arabella, noting that the fop Tinsel is 'acquainted with the greatest Part of the Assembly', naïvely asks him to recount some of their 'Adventures', to which he agrees enthusiastically, adverting that 'my Intelligence ... is generally the earliest, and may always be depended on'. When her cousin Mr Glanville warns that she is entering on 'a less innocent Amusement than Dancing', Arabella protests that

> *it is not an indiscreet Curiosity which prompts me to a desire of hearing the Histories Mr* Tinsel *has promis'd to entertain me with; but rather a Hope of hearing something which may at once improve and delight me; something which may excite my Admiration, engage my esteem, or influence my Practice.*

Naturally, she is disappointed by what she hears, and is nonplussed by the 'deal of Scandal ... utter'd in the Compass of a few Minutes'. To her, Tinsel's 'Histories ... do not deserve that Name, and are rather detached Pieces of Satire on particular Persons, than a serious Relation of Facts'.[43] This episode illustrates, however, that the distinction between 'intelligence' and 'scandal' largely depended on the utility of the information to any given observer. Tinsel's anecdotes point not to sexual improprieties but to social impostures, and in the commercialised zone of social relations represented by the marriage market, what appears to us as harmless if annoying pretension was tantamount to fraud. The marriage market would have ground to a halt without the exchange of information, and 'was heavily laced with gossip and scandal, as narrators assigned monetary and moral value to proposed unions'. Moreover, 'gossip had power when it drove up prices and produced financial offers'.[44] Prospective grooms had less to fear from the perpetual whirring of innuendo than marriageable young women, for observers thought there were too many of the latter in search of too few of the former.

Visitors to Bath who chose to be part of 'the Company', and had the wherewithal to do so, were electing to live their lives in public. The social whirl of the resort could be a claustrophobia-inducing fishbowl and for no visitor was this more true than the marriageable woman. The sudden murmur of *sotto voce* commentary that accompanies the entry of Miss Snapper in Smollett's *Roderick Random,* or Arabella, Charlotte Lennox's *Female Quixote,* into Bath's public spaces may be only a plot device, but if fiction writers could imagine such a collective response, so too could a late adolescent. It was for good reason that Nash's regulation number nine (added to the existing list by the 1740s) stipulated 'that the younger ladies take notice how many eyes observe them'. They would be put on display at the assemblies, where the front row of seats was reserved for them and where they would be expected to dance, and they would be ogled in the Cross Bath, which was equipped with galleries for (usually male) spectators. They, and their chances of securing a suitable husband, would be discussed in the Pump Room, in the coffeehouses, on the gravel walks, and handicapping contestants in the bridal sweepstakes was a favourite Bath pastime. George Lucy, for example, sent his correspondent 'a few lines made upon One of Our beauties here, … her Name is Goddard, but Alass! … She is intituled to no fortune, I'm told, till after the death of her Father, When 'tis said she will have £7000.'[45] This unprecedented exposure might have been exhilarating for many young women, but must have been stressful for others. Their sense of social claustrophobia was reinforced by the more literal kind, as the social spaces in which they were obliged to appear were actually very intimate. Neither Wood nor Nash considered any of Bath's public interiors to be adequate for the size of the Company, and the largest of these rooms, the ballroom that passed from Catherine Lindsey to Walter Wiltshire, was eighty-seven feet long by thirty wide.[46] Much available space, as Richard Steele noted, was taken up by the wide skirts of half the Company's obligatory full dress.[47]

Lampoons posed an additional hazard to the unmarried Bath *ingénue* who might otherwise escape the blades of the rumour mill. Anything she did or said could be celebrated or condemned in these amateur verses that were a staple of Bathonian print culture. A sampling appears in the commonplace book of Colonel Gabriel Lepipre who, like many

24. The interior of the Pump Room, where the marriageable were expected to make the first of many appearances over the course of a typical day

military officers, made the rounds of the resorts in their proper seasons – Tunbridge, Bristol Hotwells and especially Bath. In these three surviving volumes, he collected verses (including erotic and scatalogical pieces later excised by scandalised descendants), among them specimens of the 'water poetry' associated with the spas. Those that circulated in Bath in 1736 re-create some of the tensions that surrounded a typical Bath season. We wonder, for example, if the young woman named 'Miss Talbot' *meant* to create the psychological havoc that the water poets describe. What, for example, could the Bishop of Bristol, the venerable Thomas Secker, have said to her to earn the reproach of one irate versifier:

Why will you strive to make the Fair
Insensible of every Charm
Alone unknowing of their Power
Which every Bosom warm ...

We also wonder if the young attorney seen in conversation with Miss Talbot realised how closely he was being watched, or anticipated that verses would appear announcing his breathless infatuation with her. We could ask the same about the naval officer seen bowing to Miss

Buncomb. We begin to wonder if Miss Talbot and Miss Buncomb ever envied the invalids wrapped in blankets and confined to their rooms, and this before we are subjected to the song cycle that whirled around the Jeffreys sisters, Frances and Elizabeth. An acrostic on Frances's name was quickly followed by verses by another admirer, with responding verses 'by a Lady' suggesting that Frances just might be interested. Then verses appeared 'on Miss Betty Jeffreys on seeing her Dance wrote in ye Ball Room', with Elizabeth's 'supposed Answer', and an answer to that, followed by a final set of verses warning Betty not to attempt to outshine her sister.[48] The high dramatic pitch of all of this versifying was enough, one suspects, to make its subjects look forward to a prolonged soak in the Cross Bath, were that venue not ringed with male spectators.

Until they were safely betrothed, young women of the Company were the favoured prey of literary stalkers, who seemed to lurk behind every tree, rock and ruthlessly manicured bush in Bath, waiting to dramatise their every move in doggerel, especially if they were a 'top toast'. We, with our twenty-first-century notions of privacy and personal space, think we can imagine the feelings of a young woman of perhaps seventeen making her obligatory afternoon promenade only to discover verses about her plastered on the trunks of the sycamores in the Orange Grove. Even more disconcerting was that the verses, as often as not, addressed some specific aspect of her appearance or behaviour – what she wore or whom she spoke to or danced with.

An awful realisation arises in the reader's mind: who, and who worse, would write such verses but an envious suitor? One Miss Reade, a South Sea Company heiress, found herself the target of just such a poison pen at Bath in 1741:

The Laws of Naure then subverted, show
That Gold will each deficient Charm bestow
For Gold alone, Worth, Wit, and Sense outweighs
Hence 'tis that Reade coquettish Airs displays.

A well-prepared Bath *ingénue* would therefore have friends who could wield the pen in her defence, if she could not do so herself. Miss Reade's defenders had very good aim: 'Go, silly Fop, go learn thy self to scan[;] She's far too bright for thee, thou empty Man.'[49] Printed satires, lampoons, panegyrics and other literary ephemera might annoy and alarm those they did not charm and ingratiate, but rebuttals could and did circulate as easily.

Not all water poets were mean-spirited, and many felt that they were only offering their subjects encouragement. Contemporaries hinted that the subjects of lampoons often relished the attention, even if it was unfavourable, on the principle that no publicity was bad publicity. 'We have no Ladies who have the Face, tho some of 'em may have the Impudence, to expect a Lampoon,' wrote Alexander Pope, who held the receipt of lampoons to be the prerogative of suitably attractive women. Later in that autumn of 1714, he lamented that there were 'no lampoons dispersed' as there was 'not a face that promises any'.[50] At Tunbridge in 1745 two women allegedly solicited a poet to lampoon them, and were rebuffed, appropriately enough, in a lampoon.[51]

It is important to notice that the sexual immorality exposed in lampoons, especially the winking references to women cured of infertility, nearly always involved offenders *who were already married.* Elite adultery was an acceptable target of satire at the same time that fornication was taboo. Consequently, single young women might be accused of hauteur, or coquettishness, or marital ambition, but nothing more serious. 'What Children delight in, and Men us'd to build Houses, Is the Name of two Girls that much do want Spouses,' ran one rebus circulated at Bath in 1740. They might also be taken to task for what they wore, like the 'two Young Ladies' who appeared in Elizabethan dress in November 1750:

In good Queen BESS'S Days, 'tis true,
They wore such Robes as these;
But 'tis a great Mistake in You,
To think they now can please.[52]

These were the worst things circulated about single women in a local print culture that could be savage to their elders, such as the targets of another rebus in 1740:

What makes a Fire, and washes our Clothes,
Is the Name of a Lady that hazards her Nose:
And the best of a Calf, and what carries Men to Jail,
Is the Name of the Man that is ty'd to her Tail.[53]

'Scandal' at the expense of married women persisted because of the belief that Bath provided wives ample opportunity to forfeit their reputation. The therapeutic rationale of resorts allowed married women to travel independently, and the simple presence of women unencumbered with husbands was enough to brand the resorts as hotbeds of adultery. Commentators noted that women were under less restraint in Bath than elsewhere, even the metropolis. 'Bath is the place of all England in which the fair sex at present take the most delight,' the Abbé Le Blanc asserted, 'and, consequently, where the greatest endeavours are used to please them.' Bath, for Le Blanc, was a completely feminine city, as dominated by upper-crust women as Oxford and Cambridge were by scholars:

If a foreigner would learn the language of the country, or get acquainted with the ladies of England, he ought to spend some time here. The women of quality are not easily seen in London; not because the husbands are jealous, but because the wives are reserved and inaccessible; whereas, on the contrary, here they are all ease and sprightliness in their behaviour. They make the most of the liberty of the country, and the familiarity which the waters afford them.

Le Blanc claimed (and his translator indignantly denied) that women, who in London would abstain from strong drink out of concern for reputation, drank spirits openly in Bath, where they were 'part of the tea-table equipage'. 'Bath tea', in fact, was a compound of 'arrack, lemons, and sugar', and could elevate 'the most gloomy dispositions'. Thus, while '[i]n London, a circle of ladies drinking tea is usually but melancholy company, … [a]t Bath, on the contrary, the tea-tables are extremely gay'. Women at Bath were 'quite another sort of creatures … than in London, and the constrained uniformity of their common life makes the difference the more remarkable'. For this reason, they went to great lengths to go there. A stay in Bath was 'perhaps, the fruit of six months meditation and intrigue: she must feign sickness, gain over the servants, corrupt the physician, importune an aunt, deceive a husband, and in short, have recourse to every artifice in order to succeed.'[54] Swift wrote of the young spouse of a senior clergyman whose 'doctor with a double fee / Was bribed to make the Dean agree' to take her to Bath.[55]

One particularly slanderous lampoon circulated in Bath around 1740 provides insight into the role that similar literary ephemera played in the life of the resort. These verses alleged that an elderly husband, the letters of his name elided to be unintelligible (except to the Company, of course), had promised £1,000 to the man who could impregnate his 'youthful airy Wife' and provide him an heir. According to the poet, she took advantage of the situation:

> *She who had always most obedient prov'd,*
> *Denied him not that Instant, how she lov'd!*
> *With all obliging haste, to Bath she flew,*
> *There tasted Joys, before she never knew.*
> *Resolv'd her Husband's Wishes to compleat;*
> *The Tall, the Short, she try'd, the Small and Great;*
> *And wond'rous things, she thought might Numbers do,*
> *Which never yet could be attain'd by Few.*[56]

Verses like these make us wish that lists of the Company survived from as far back as 1740 – the *Bath Journal*, with its list, began publication only in 1744 – until we discover that they are nearly exact copies of verses circulated in 1725.[57] Lampoons, then, should not be read as indices of sexual behaviour at resorts, but we might still ask why these satires, especially scurrilous verses like those just quoted, were recycled. Salacious lampoons created a climate of prurient speculation in which, as Sutherland asserted, 'every moment presents suspicion of gallantry', even when no visitors actually present were targeted. As Voltaire remarked on the execution of Admiral Byng, lampoons served 'to encourage the others'. Sutherland may not have realised that the ubiquity of 'scandal' was precisely the reason there was 'so little sin' in Bath.

Nash claimed as his purview exactly those aspects of social interaction that were the most likely flash points, especially dancing, gambling and gossip. He understood that in the hothouse atmosphere of a Bath season, malicious rumours could be prompted by nothing more than the awkward silence of those unused to being the focus of so much persistent male attention, and who may not yet have mastered the multifaceted etiquette that governed personal interaction in the polite world. Bath under his ascendancy became a safe place to learn the rules. Nash understood the importance of Bath's culture of gossip well enough to attempt to manage it, and his efforts did not go unrecognised. Nash's reputation for protecting reputations was assiduously cultivated, as one of many sets of lines addressed to him attests:

When Satire strives to blast the Fair-ones Fame
Thy Generous Care, defeats the Writers Aim
But when the Muse to Beauty homage pays
With equall Ardor you proclaim that Praise.[58]

In his capacity as a one-man anti-defamation league, Nash gained, as Goldsmith said, 'the friendship of several ladies of distinction, who had smarted pretty severely under the lash of censure'.[59] These connections (the redoubtable Duchess of Marlborough was Goldsmith's prime example) provided exactly the sort of relational capital which Nash needed to sustain his position. This network was crucial, and was

25. Nash relied on the support of social powerhouses like Sarah, Duchess of Marlborough, to buttress his authority

put to good use, especially in the necessary and honourable business of matchmaking. Nash, touting himself as 'Master of the Ceremonies, Regulator of the Diversions and Moderator of Disputes at Play', might justifiably have added 'Overseer of the Marriage Market'. Whether or not Nash deserves the credit for making Bath the most desirable venue for upper-crust courtship in the British Isles, contemporaries, in assigning him the credit, were promoting a particular set of social norms now more necessary than ever given the terms in which a changing economy was obliging them to understand their society.

5

Moderator of Disputes at Play

Circulation of Cash – Circulation decay'd –
Is at once the Destruction and Ruin of Trade; –
Circulation – I say – Circulation it is,
Gives Life to Commercial Countries like this:
What Thanks to the City of *Bath* then are due
From all who this Patriot Maxim pursue;
For in no Place whatever that National Good
Is practis'd so well, and so well understood!
What infinite Merit and Praise does she claim in
Her Ways and her Means for promoting of *Gaming*;
And *Gaming*, no doubt, is of infinite use
That same Circulation of Cash to produce;
What true public-spirited People are here
Who for that very Purpose come every Year![1]

So Christopher Anstey has his feckless anti-hero Tom Blunderhead, in daydreaming of his maiden speech in the House of Commons, encapsulate one of the central paradoxes of the new economy of the eighteenth century. In the heady days of the commercial revolution, the distinction between investment, speculation and outright gambling was notoriously blurred. Underwriters in Lloyd's Coffeehouse were as likely to accept wagers on the sex of royal infants *in utero* as they were to insure ship's cargoes, and the same government that sought to restrict gambling through legislation continued to sponsor lotteries throughout the century.[2] The position in which Georgian cultural critics found themselves is one that we share. We are torn between clinical concern over social pathologies and anthropological reverence for time-honoured cultural practices. In human cultures, gambling shares with imbibing a dubious dual distinction. As potentially addictive and therefore destructive behaviour, it, like drinking, is a social problem. Both, however, are also global and cross-cultural phenomena and have been so since ancient times. Gambling, for one sociologist, is 'a microcosm in which more general issues about the role of uncertainty and chance in human life are played out in concentrated form'.[3] Our historically rooted ambivalence towards gambling was recently encapsulated in the United States when William Bennet, a prominent American moralist, cultural critic, champion of 'Western culture' and author of a non-fiction bestseller ponderously entitled *The Book of Virtues*, admitted to losing an estimated 8 million dollars while gambling in Las Vegas over a period of ten years, a figure which included half a million dollars apparently lost in a single weekend.[4] Whether played in Catherine Lindsey's assembly rooms in Georgian Bath, or in a rural parish hall in twentieth-century Nebraska, or – once again in the form of government-sponsored lotteries – in corner shops all over the world, games of chance have an irresistible attraction which has not only defied all efforts at prohibition, but has actually seduced civil authorities into cooptation and sponsorship instead. Ironically, the commercialised form of gambling that William Bennet has now sworn off is one of the peculiar legacies of the Western civilisation that he has so tirelessly and uncritically defended. Perhaps no period is more illustrative of the partnership of gambling and civilisation than the European eighteenth century, and no place more so than Bath.

Gambling in Bath, according to the first Duke of Chandos, was '[t]he great business of the Place',[5] to such a degree that for most of the first half of the century one was nearly synonymous with the other. Its Master of Ceremonies was largely responsible for this association, so much so that the name of Nash was as closely associated with gaming as it was with Bath. Handkerchiefs were sold there emblazoned with Nash's portrait against a background of playing cards.[6] After Nash's death, his executor thought that Goldsmith's biography would 'be an Excellent Minitor [*sic*] to Youth against the destructive Vice of Gaming'.[7] In proclaiming himself 'Moderator of Disputes at Play', Nash recognised Bath's gaming culture as a critical, and possibly the most crucial, foundation of his sociable mandate there.

It was clearly the major source of his income. Nash once made the mistake of complaining to the Earl of Chesterfield of losing 500 guineas to 'that damned bitch fortune'. 'I don't wonder at your losing money, Nash,' Chesterfield replied, coolly, since boasting of gambling losses was properly the prerogative of grandees like himself, 'but all the world is surprized where you get it to lose.'[8] Not even Goldsmith was able to explain completely how Nash supported himself in high style for a period of about thirty years. His house in Bath was one of the largest and grandest there, and he was said to have an equally splendid house in London. He travelled in a coach and six with a full complement of liveried drivers, outriders and postilions, the Georgian equivalent of a stretch limousine. Chesterfield remarked that the suit Nash wore for the King's birthday in 1734 was so heavily laced with gold thread that 'he was taken by many at a distance for a gilt garland.'[9] His gambling losses, moreover, could run well into four figures – £1,400 at Bath very early in the autumn season of 1723, to give only one example – in the days when pounds were made of gold.[10] He would either have needed a steady stream of considerable income from one or two stable sources, or would have been constantly negotiating shorter-term arrangements. Either of these would have been difficult without anyone finding out – unless those who provided the income also had an interest in keeping their participation quiet.

There were certainly rumours about Nash's finances. Some accounts simply related that he had enjoyed extraordinary success as a professional gambler early in his career. Such success was possible if a gambler was in a position to stand as banker in games like basset or faro.

26. A game of basset. Which ever of the seated figures is keeping the bank enjoys a ludicrous advantage in this popular game of chance

Francis Fleming repeated a story that Nash had won £1,000 in seven weeks during his very first season at Bath.[11] Thomas Wilson heard that Nash 'won a vast estate of Lord Howard and the Duke of Bedford and generously gave it up again upon condition that he should have a Rent Charge out of these estates [of] £1300 pr. ann. [i.e. annually] for life'.[12] Other theories of the provenance of Nash's income had him serving as an aversion therapist to aristocratic compulsive gamblers through the accepted practice of 'tying up'. Nash, according to Goldsmith, entered into just such an arrangement with '[t]he late Duke of *B.*', who, if the same duke mentioned in a *Gentleman's Magazine* notice, was almost certainly the third Duke of Bedford, who died in 1732 with extensive debts. Nash advanced the Duke 'an hundred guineas to forfeit ten thousand, whenever he lost a sum to the same amount at play, in one sitting'. The stratagem was unsuccessful. Bedford, unable to stay away from the hazard table, was obliged to pay up after heavy losses at Newmarket in October 1731. Nash was very understanding, settling for £5,000 up front, with £400 a year for life thereafter. A notice announcing this agreement between Nash and '[a] certain Duke' appeared in the *Gentleman's Magazine* in 1732,[13] and Wilson's informant may have seen it. The arrangement may have been publicised when Nash tried to press this claim on Bedford's estate (of which there is no record in the Bedford archives at Woburn). He certainly needed the money, as he had recently suffered very heavy gaming losses himself, including £4,000 in one night at Tunbridge in 1730, after which he reportedly pledged never to play for more than £100.[14] According to Goldsmith, Nash successfully pressed a claim on the estate of Henry O'Brien, the seventh Earl of Thomond, for £5,000, which Thomond had promised him after Nash won his estate and then returned it.[15]

These stories would certainly account for Nash's ability to bankroll his ostentatious style of living, but both Wilson and Goldsmith in this instance have Nash behaving like a common sharper, no different from dozens of others, gulling less experienced players to the gaming tables. Nash might have made a tidy sum off fool's wagers like these, as Thomas Goulding suggested. '[Y]ou are such a hot-brain'd Man at Play,' Goulding's Rover tells Sir Humphry Harebrain, 'that I was assured of winning my large Bet when I made it, the first Time you ever came where there was deep Play.'[16] Might Nash not have descended on compulsive gamblers, and especially inexperienced ones, with this end in view? The suggestion that he was trying to help those he had fleeced is audacious enough to have originated with Nash himself. A scurrilous tract, purporting to be the memoirs of his mistress Fanny Murray, appeared towards the end of his life and claimed that Nash 'was originally a man of tolerable fortune' who, having depleted his finances through high living, had three sources of income: gaming, gifts from members of the Company and 'the pension which was allowed him', presumably as Master of Ceremonies. These gave him the 'means to keep up that appearance which he had long supported'.[17] Gambling had also provided him the opportunity to rise to prominence in Bath, one scene in which a quiet revolution in the culture of chance was played out.

~

The development of the public sphere in the eighteenth century has a compelling analogue in the emergence of the Internet in our own time, not least in that gambling (along with access to pornography) was among the first opportunities afforded by both. Much has been written about the second with reference to seventeenth- and eighteenth-century print culture,[18] and scholars are now beginning to look seriously at the first.[19] A large part of the period's anxiety over gaming stemmed from innovations in its organisation which effectively introduced high-stakes gambling into the public sphere. For most of the seventeenth century, this species of gambling was restricted largely to courtly culture. It has been conventionally argued that gambling presented a means for old-regime courtiers, members of the nobility who had lost their military function and much of their political power in the absolutist states of the Continent, to assert their status and buttress their continuing cultural authority. In encouraging high-stakes gaming at Versailles, to the extent of lending courtiers large sums for the purpose, Louis XIV reduced his formerly fractious nobility to dependence, which he further reinforced by reportedly restricting the privileged position of *tallière* – the banker in the most lucrative games of chance – to members of the highest-ranking noble families.[20] Courtly gambling, then, demoted money to the status of a plaything, as sums circulated among the neutered *noblesse d'epée* as inconsequentially as a shuttlecock in badminton. At the seventeenth-century court, the cash nexus was purely recreational.

It was in this same period, however, that mathematicians under courtly patronage undertook the mathematical analysis of gambling and introduced the study of probability. Among other findings, they determined that the odds in 'banking' games (in which one player in a group – the banker – took on the rest – the punters – paying off winning bets and collecting losing ones) worked in favour of the player who kept the bank. By the eighteenth century, once the potential for profit was clear to entrepreneurs, gambling was commercialised, with the proprietors of the 'house' initially taking a share of the proceeds from the individual 'banks,' and ultimately absorbing them. The interposition of the house diminished some of the appeal of gambling to aristocratic notions of honour, as these games were no longer confrontations between individuals but of the punters collectively versus the house.[21] Elites could still demonstrate their (putative) disdain for the money-based commercial economy. Sir Carolus Codshead, a character in Thomas D'Urfey's play *The Bath,* discounts his gambling losses as

> *a trifle ... not worth my mentioning. I never think on't, when 'tis over. Never count losses, nor gains at Play; not I, by my Ancestors. 'Twas the generous way of old; 'twas so in Harry the Eighth's Days.*[22]

Sir Carolus and others indulged their nostalgia to the delight of gaming entrepreneurs, willing pioneers in the brave new world of money, who laughed all the way from the metaphorical bank to the literal one.

With commercialisation, courtly conventions of gaming were gradually abandoned. Henry VIII's contemporary Baldassare Castiglione had stipulated in *The Book of the Courtier* that gambling was not a vice unless the courtier neglected other business to gamble, or played to win, or lost his composure on losing.[23] While there were those, such as Lord James Cavendish, who came to Bath with £2,000, nonchalantly determined 'either to double it or loose it back again',[24] the continuing value attached to this heroic detachment at the eighteenth-century gaming table is mostly evident from contemporary comment on its absence. Nash, who according to Goldsmith lacked the *sangfroid* necessary to be a successful gamester, set a very bad example. After losing £50 at Harrison's in 1721, he 'broke all the windows according to custom'; in 1734 he ended his evenings, as Chesterfield reported, 'with basset and blasphemy'. Of three surviving autograph letters, one is probably an apology for just such an outburst in the presence of Lady Jerningham.[25] Such lapses in decorum, together with the participation of women and the lower classes in gambling, were what most often aroused the comment of observers, and all were consequences of a courtly pastime becoming publicly accessible in the same way and at the same time that cultural production – literature, visual arts, theatre – became available outside of the charmed circle of the court. Instructively, it was coffeehouses, assembly rooms, the green rooms of theatres, and the spas – precisely the venues in which the public sphere emerged – that were the first sites of commercialised gaming.

In Britain the legality of gaming establishments outside the court was always murky. Courtly gaming in England, traditionally confined to the twelve days of Christmas, fell under the supervision of the Groom Porter to the Royal Household. The holder of this ultimately quite lucrative sinecure was responsible for procuring cards and dice, and for adjudicating any disagreements arising during the course of play. The Restoration saw the Groom Porter permitted to keep tables in his 'grace and favour' apartments in Whitehall Palace, and the 'Groom Porter's Lodge' became synonymous with gambling. By Queen Anne's reign, the purview of the Groom Porter had expanded to the licensing of gaming establishments outside the court. Such venues existed in London by 1705, and may have spread to the spas, where private gaming was already well established. It is possible that Nash arrived in Bath just as commercialised gambling was gaining a foothold there. At Bath 'banking' games seemed initially to float from place to place. The Duke of Kent was informed in May 1706 that because the basset bank, kept by a Mr Henley, was inadequate to the demands placed on it, 'Lady Basset ... will no longer appear in public at Mr Harrison's, but she holds court often enough at Lady Chanon's'.[26] The Mr Harrison referred to may or may not be Thomas Harrison, whose Assembly Rooms did not open for another two years. Wood related that until Harrison built his 'handsome Assembly-House ... at the Instigation of the new King of Bath', visitors 'were driven to the Necessity of meeting in a Booth to drink their Tea and Chocolate, and to divert themselves at Cards'.[27] By the 1720s visitors who chose to gamble had a range of houses to chose from. '[W]ee have a good dell of company in town,' one Bath resident wrote in late November 1722, 'and thay met every night ither at hayis rooms linsees or cornishes;' Harrison had

27. Georgian 'court' cards. Cardsharps were known to have decks made in which these higher ranking cards were slightly wider

already closed for the season, 'not thinking it worth his while'.[28] In 1725 Eliza Haywood wrote of her character Lady Playwell, who, although she swept 'all the Money' at Bath, 'was one of those who exclaim'd so violently against Gaming Houses', simply because 'there was nothing so great an Enemy to private Play, as the Encouragement it met with in publick'.[29]

While Nash's social ascendancy was probably not accorded by consensus of either Corporation or Company, it was certainly connected with Thomas Harrison. A visitor of September 1725 identified Nash not by any of his ascribed titles but as 'the greatest promoter of the diversions at Harrison's, and one of the greatest Gamesters'. Nash was so inseparable from the assembly rooms' proprietor in visitors' minds that it was 'thought that he shares with Harrison in the good profitts arising from these rooms'.[30] Nash and Harrison were ruthlessly pilloried as 'Sancho and Peepo' in a satire that appeared from the hand of Thomas Goulding in 1728. Here their relationship was made clear,

28. The Assembly Rooms as Nash knew them. Harrison's is the large building on the right; Lindsey's occupied the range of buildings across the street

as was the role of their silent partnership in Nash's social primacy at Bath. Goulding asserted that Nash won the confidence of male visitors by procuring for them, so successfully 'that at Gaming when he had lost his Money, they would very often lend him some, and set him up again'. According to Goulding, it was Nash's idea to collect subscriptions for building assembly rooms 'big enough for the Reception of the Company'. Because Nash was such a fixture at the gaming tables, he could not appear to be involved in this undertaking, '[f]or if the Nets are not discreetly placed, you'll catch no Game if the Birds are shy'. Once the new assembly rooms opened, Nash's role 'was to look out sharp, and bring Persons down to the Place, and [Harrison] welcomed them in ... And all the Money that the Gentry brought to Town, was spent in that Place.' Goulding related that a single roulette wheel in Harrison's netted £1,700 in one season.[31]

Like other forms of entertainment, gaming entailed a significant outlay on both equipment and personnel. Commercialisation resulted when entrepreneurs made the investments in plant, equipment and personnel which were beyond the capacity or inclination of most private individuals. By the eighteenth century both play and gaming had evolved highly specialised vocabulary and accoutrements. The apparatus necessary to gaming included tables with green baize tops and recessed bowls to hold counters, or with betting cloths specific to particular games such as faro or hazard. Hazard tables, for example, were generally oval, with indentations cut for the caster at one end and the croupier at the other. Skilled and specialised human resources such as dealers and croupiers were required in addition to the usual complement of footmen and other servants. As with balls, delegating the sponsorship of gambling to commercial entrepreneurs was a way of ensuring that those who wished to gamble would have regular opportunities to do so.

The increasingly central place of gaming at Bath and other resorts was a key element of their success, but was also more and more of a liability over time as gaming came to be viewed as the social pathology of affluent society that gin was for the lower class. Bath's close identification with gaming was enough of a liability to necessitate a fundamental redirection in the development of the resort. Like the Hindu deity Shiva, gaming was creator and destroyer, the engine of cataclysmic change felt beyond the circle of the resorts. The spas, especially Bath, became the forcing grounds of crucial social reconfigurations.

~

Georgian ambivalence towards gambling was reflected in a curious blind spot in attitudes towards play for stakes. Just as the wholesome (and domestically produced) beer that plebeians consumed was not equated with dangerously addictive (and foreign) gin, within polite culture playing games for money did not necessarily constitute gambling. In the name of sociability, games like ombre, quadrille and whist were regarded as innocent amusements, even when 'played for gold', with the equivalent of several hundred pounds changing hands. Thus later in the century, while Countess Spencer warned her daughter (Georgiana, later the famous Duchess of Devonshire, who did not heed the advice) to avoid high-stakes games like faro, basset, quinze (a prototype of blackjack) and lanterloo (a faster-paced, higher-stakes trick-taking game), she had no objection to sociable games such as whist and commerce, even when these were played for money.[32] Although critics might deride hombre and quadrille as trivial and superficial pastimes, they reserved genuine opprobrium for hazard, basset, faro and other such games played against a 'bank' (the terminology cannot have been accidental), games which powerfully symbolised the most pernicious aspects of commercial culture. Where sociable games among companions helped to weave the fabric of polite social relations, increasingly commercialised high-stakes gaming played out tensions that threatened the social fabric.

The salient differences between 'play' and 'gaming' were the level of stakes played for and the degree to which the outcome of play was determined by chance rather than skill. Parisian authorities, for example, distinguished between entirely permissible *jeux de commerce* and more circumscribed *jeux de hasard*.[33] Hazard, the most complicated specimen of gaming commonly practised in London or the spas, was relatively easy to master compared to ombre or quadrille, with their intricate rococo rules and conventions. Basset and faro, in common with dicing games like passage or the forerunner of roulette, 'roly-poly', were often idiotically simple to play and thus more accessible, which was important from the perspective of gaming establishments, as the odds in these 'banking' games were even more heavily stacked in favour of the house than modern casino games. For these reasons, and certainly because of the skill that they required, hombre, its variant quadrille and quadrille's derivative whist (together the ancestors of modern bridge) were at the apex of the gaming hierarchy. There was a sharp distinction between these and games such as basset and faro that writers on cards derided as mere games of chance. Distinctions between 'play' and 'gaming' became firmer once gaming acts increasingly subjected games of chance played against a 'bank' to the same restrictions as lotteries. In addition, 'play' was primarily sociable, while 'gaming' was primarily competitive, although the competition frequently took peculiar forms. As in the cockfights on Bali that the anthropologist Clifford Geertz memorably described, as much status was to be gained in the making of wagers as in the winning of them. Furthermore, those who 'won' benefited through (usually temporary) financial gain, but those who 'lost' with equanimity also 'won' through the same sort of conspicuous display that another anthropologist, Ferdinand Boas, classically observed in the Kwatiutl *potlach* ceremony.

Finally and most importantly, 'play' was less remunerative (for winners anyway) than 'gaming', as the amounts which changed hands at hombre and quadrille were inconsequential in comparison to those won and lost at the basset, faro and hazard tables. The structure of these games makes their disparity with sociable games clear. In basset, punters placed their bets on any of the thirteen ranks of cards. The game required multiple decks, as a complete suit of cards was dealt to each player for the purpose. Cards would then be dealt into losing and winning piles. A player betting on a rank in the winning pile had the option of forgoing his or her winnings in the hope that the rank would win again, in which case the payout from the house would be seven to one. The stake could be allowed to 'ride' three additional times, with the odds increasing to fifteen, thirty and finally sixty to one. The player in these cases would signal his or her intention by crooking the corner of the card, by which means decks of cards quickly became dog-eared and ultimately unusable for any other game. The prospect of large payouts in basset lured punters into braving increasingly steep odds, despite contemporary warnings that 'the dimmest eye may easily see, without a pair of spectacles' the magnitude of the house advantage.[34] Faro was a refinement of basset in that a betting cloth decorated with representations of cards replaced the layout dealt to each player, and an abacus-like device was introduced for keeping track of the deal. Punters could now bet on losing as well as winning cards, on combinations of two to four cards, and on the order in which cards would appear. Unlike basset, faro remained popular through the nineteenth century, and on both sides of the Atlantic.

Hazard was an exception among high-stakes games in that the 'bank' rotated from player to player, and thus could not be subsumed into the 'house', but rested with the 'caster' who handled the dice at any given point. The house may have claimed something like the payments expected of winners of 'box hands' – three winning tosses in a row – at hazard in gaming houses in the 1830s.[35] ('Craps' as played in modern casinos is essentially hazard adapted to allow the house to keep the bank.) The caster would name a number from five to nine as the 'main,' and then roll the dice. If the main was seven, for example and seven was then cast, the cast was then a 'nick', and the caster swept the stakes off the board. If the cast was a number from four to ten other than the main, that number was the caster's 'chance' (or the 'point' in modern craps). The caster then rolled the dice until either the chance or the main was cast. If the former, he or she again won all the stakes on the table; if the latter, the caster paid all bets, relinquished the dice to another player, and either sensibly left the table or (more probably) took his or her place in the ring of punters around it. A caster who rolled two ('ames-ace', or 'snake-eyes' as today) or three was said to be 'crabbed' (from whence 'craps') and immediately lost. Eleven and twelve were winning or losing numbers depending on which number was 'mains'. The game of hazard was aptly named, one writer pointed out, 'for it speedily makes a man or undoes him', and gaming novices were well advised to avoid it.[36] For this and other reasons, a seat at the 'gold table' in hazard was not for the faint of heart. As it was not directly supervised by the house (which had an interest in at least appearing to be on the up and up), the hazard table was especially attractive to cheats. All the proprietors could do was require that its dice be used, although loaded dice could certainly be smuggled in.

Gaming was made more hazardous by the presence of professional gamblers or 'sharpers' who, by fair means and foul, preyed on younger, less experienced and less streetwise players. A motif often found in the cautionary and satirical literature generated in Bath was of the naïve young visitor seduced into playing lansquenet. This game for two players, one of them very gullible, was deceptively simple. The player who was banker (invariably the cardsharp, teaching the novice) dealt two cards face up. He would then turn cards face up in the space between the first two cards until turning a card of the same suit as one of the first pair. If the card on the right matched the centre, the punter won. If the left matched the banker won. But the banker also won if the initial two cards dealt were of the same suit, tipping the odds ludicrously in his favour. Young Squire Blunderhead, the anti-hero of Christopher Anstey's *New Bath Guide* of 1766, is caught in this trap:

> *A Sum, my dear Mother, far heavier yet,*
> *Captain CORMORANT won, when I learn'd Lansquenet;*
> *Two Hundred I paid him, and Five am in Debt.*
> *For the Five, I had nothing to do but to write,*
> *For the Captain was very well bred, and polite,*
> *And took, as he saw my Expences were great,*
> *My Bond, to be paid on the Clodpole Estate;*
> *And asks nothing more while the Money is lent,*
> *Than interest paid him at Twenty per Cent.*[37]

One did not need to be as gullible as the Blunderheads to fall prey to sharpers, for it was in their interest to mix well with the Company. No less a figure than the Earl of Chesterfield could be seen in the assembly rooms paying with a coterie of notorious cardsharps.[38] (Chesterfield, however, had his reasons for his choice in companions. '"[I]f I play with sharpers and win,"' he remarked, '"I am sure to be paid, but if I win of gentlemen, they frequently behave so genteelly that I get nothing but words and polite apologies for my money."'[39]) John Macky, who was in Tunbridge Wells in 1714, possibly to spy on Jacobites, did not find as many ideological suspects as he found sharpers,

> *whose Trade is to go Genteel, and with a fine Address, mix themselves in all the Diversions here ... These People are easily discovered, by their more than ordinary Assiduity to Strangers. They are the first that bid you beware of Sharpers when they design themselves to pick*

> *your Pockets. All Shop-keepers are in Fee with these Fellows, and it is they who furnish the Dice for them.*[40]

The most naïve players could be very easily cheated by such transparent manoeuvres as being seated in front of a mirror so that their cards were visible. Sharpers also devised means of signalling to their partners and were known to conceal cards up their voluminous sleeves, in their elaborately ruffled shirts or even in their hats. There were various ways of marking cards – decks could be trimmed so that aces and court cards were slightly broader, and Charles Eaton, a cardsharp of the late seventeenth century, was known to insert very fine needles into the edges of cards so that the head barely protruded. Cheating at dice could be accomplished with loaded dice, or 'fullums'. A sharper would drill the 'pips', fill the cavity with mercury, and then reseal the hole with pitch. Alternatively the corners of dice could be filed. Other methods which did not involve tampering with the dice themselves required a great deal of manual dexterity and practice. 'Palming' dice involved taking both dice off the table but placing only one die in the cup, while concealing the second in the palm of the hand. The sharper had to note the position of the die in the cup, manipulate the die in his palm accordingly and then drop both simultaneously without rolling them. 'Topping' was a variation of palming, except that one die was held between two fingers rather than in the palm. One notorious gamester, Major Clancy, was very adept at 'slurring', or throwing dice across a table without their turning. By methods like these, Clancy was supposed to have won £6,500 in two years.

The sharper depended for his livelihood on a continual supply of such inexperienced and gullible marks – 'cullies' or 'bubbles', as they were known – and snaring victims often required the complicity of dealers, croupiers and other personnel in the gaming venues.[41] In the metropolis, even the cooperation of managers and croupiers did not suffice over time, as sharpers became less effective as they became more recognisable. 'Sometimes your Sharpers are so formidably remarkable, that few have the Courage to engage them,' remarked one observer;

'[t]hus they are disabled by their Skill, and their Eminency breaks their Business.'[42] Sharpers at spas, however, were abetted by the transient nature of the Company. Those who wondered why such shady characters 'could possibly have any acquaintance among the company at Bath' might be reminded that 'the company of Bath are constantly in motion. The company of one month are not the company of another',[43] and as a result there was no collective memory, apart from those such as Nash who by occupation or vocation spent the entire season there.

Nash drew a clear line between taking advantage of inexperienced players and playing fraudulently, either with doctored cards or dice, or sleight of hand such as 'cupping', 'palming', or the proverbial ace-up-the-sleeve. His scruples were good policy, as the law drew this distinction as well. Nash was credited (after his death) with pointing out notorious sharpers to their potential victims. One wonders if he ever did the opposite, and contemporaries wondered as well. Goldsmith certainly found that '[i]t was odd enough to see a gamester thus employed, in detecting the frauds of gamesters.'[44] A major selling point of the assembly rooms as gaming venues was the presence of Nash as a deterrent to cheating. '"I do not mind your playing in the rooms for guineas,"' Nash was supposed to have warned one young man about his new gaming partners, '"but they are dangerous acquaintance, and if you once meet them at a tavern you are sure to be undone."'[45] Members of the Company, having bought into Nash's self-promotion as Bath's benevolent autocrat, occasionally wondered why sharpers were tolerated at all. The King of Bath, argued one facetiously, needed courtiers with high-sounding offices, such as a Marshal of the Black Ace, to recognise the services of 'him who has done nothing but game all his life, and has reduced the most families to ruin and beggary'. Nash ought also to have at least one order of chivalry, and why not create Knights of the Four Knaves from among 'those who are every day making proselytes to the tables'?[46] Nash, for whatever reason, chose not to test his authority by attempting to bar sharpers from the assembly rooms, but the threat must have been present, and it would seem that a cardsharp with an eye to his career would take pains to court Nash's favour.

What concerned observers most was neither the presence of sharpers or cheats, nor the enormous stakes that were played for, but the gender profile of the gaming culture. If the presence of sharpers at the baize-covered tables alarmed them, the presence of women, and elite women at that, horrified them. '[O]ur hazard table is dubly Graced, by ye Dutches of Dorset, Lady Bristol, & more Ladys,' wrote one visitor from Tunbridge in 1730. 'Ye lat[t]er is very pitious often.'[47] The Countess of Bristol played polite games of quadrille, of course, but only to sit and rest her arm between bouts of hazard, the ancestor of craps, which she played energetically and for high stakes. As the autumn season of 1721 was getting under way, she lamented that play at hazard was 'very low, for most of the lady's play silver'. Lady Bristol looked forward to the arrival of 'several gamesters' who Nash assured her would arrive within the week, but three weeks later she was complaining about winning only £50 after throwing fifteen 'mains', an extraordinary run of luck.[48] Women may not have been more numerous in the gaming rooms, but they were certainly more noticeable, and drew comment more often than male gamesters did. 'Lady Betty [Southwell] & her sett play only at Quadrille,' Mary Chamber wrote from Tunbridge in 1730, 'but the Dutchess of Marlborough takes to losing her money at Roly-Poly.'[49] Richard Steele, horrified at the enthusiasm that the Duchess of Marlborough, Lady Bristol and other women of their class showed for gaming, attempted to draw their attention to this behaviour by having one of his foils, Nestor Ironside, describe 'Ladies' who 'share in these Diversions'.

> *I must own, that I receive great Pleasure in seeing my pretty Country-women engaged in an Amusement, which puts them upon producing so many Virtues. Hereby they acquire such Boldness, as raises them nearer that Lordly Creature, Man. Here they are taught such Contempt of Wealth, as may dilate their Minds ... I find my Soul exalted, when I see a Lady sacrifice the Fortune of her Children with as little Concern as a* Spartan *or* Roman *Dame. In such a Place as the* Bath *I might urge, that the Casting of a*

> *Die is indeed the properest Exercise for a fair Creature to assist the Waters; not to mention the Opportunity it gives to display the well-turned Arm, and to scatter to Advantage the Rays of the Diamond. But I am satisfied, that the Gamester Ladies have surmounted the little Vanities of showing their Beauty, which they so far neglect, as to throw their Features into violent Distortions, and wear away their Lillies and Roses in tedious Watching, and restless Elucubrations. I should rather observe, that their chief Passion is an Emulation of Manhood, which I am the more inclined to believe, because, in spite of all Slanders, their Confidence in their Virtue keeps them up all Night, with the most dangerous Creatures of our Sex. It is to me an undoubted Argument of their Ease of Conscience, that they go directly from Church to the Gaming Table: and so highly reverence Play, as to make it a great part of their Exercise on* Sundays.[50]

That throwing dice did not seem particularly ladylike to Steele did not stop other women from following Lady Bristol's example and 'playing deep' at hazard, passage, basset, faro, roulette or EO (a version of roulette devised to circumvent the gaming acts). Critics of gaming cited its inexplicable attraction to women as one of its most pernicious effects. For one moralist, the sight of women 'losing hundreds of Guineas at a Sitting' prompted men to 'go farther in Danger, and appear more brave in the Methods of Ruin'.[51] Lady Ambs-Ace, the scheming villainess of the 1725 comedy *The Bath Unmask'd*, was the archetypal 'female gamester'. '[M]y Seat at the Gold Table,' she declares, 'I would not exchange for a Throne, unless the Rules of Gaming were to be my Laws, and Sharpers my Privy-Counsellors.' Dice are her 'Deities,'

> *though I have no Sacrifice to offer them. Fame and Fortune ye have had already; my hourly Prayers ye have, tho' ye requite me ill. Yet such is the Power of your Charms that rather than want Offerings for you, I'll keep a set of Bravo's in pay, who shall cut Throats and rob Altars to adorn your Shrine.*[52]

For elite males, the green cloth which covered the gaming table had neatly displaced the field of honour. Honour, however, was a gendered concept defined differently for women than for men. The involvement of women in gaming attracted heightened attention because of concern, memorably depicted in Hogarth's painting of *The Lady's Last Stake*, that women gamesters risked their virtue as well as their financial resources (or more pointedly those of their husbands, who were in turn doubly endangered). There was also a largely unarticulated concern that women sought through gaming a measure of independence and escape from the strictures of a still patriarchal society. The gaming table, the green baize field of honour, was the only arena in which polite women could compete on equal terms with men.[53]

The resorts, with their gaming tables open to both sexes, were the centres of this social pathology, and Bath, appropriately enough, was the scene of the most celebrated admonitory text to appear in the Georgian period on the dangers of gaming. Its pathetic subject was Frances Braddock, one of two daughters of Lieutenant General Edward Braddock the Elder, and sister of the equally ill-fated Edward Braddock the Younger. Braddock Senior had retired to Bath in 1715 after distinguishing himself in the War of the Spanish Succession, and died there in 1725. Fanny's sister Henrietta followed him four years later, leaving the surviving sister with a total inheritance estimated at £6,000. Unfortunately, what would have appeared to a banker as the foundation of a comfortable annual income seemed to Fanny, with little understanding of the mysterious ways of finance, a fund of inexhaustible wealth. Accounts vary, but it appears that what she did not give away was gambled away, and in short order. In September 1731, having lost her inheritance, Fanny Braddock hanged herself in the house in Queen Square where, according to printed accounts, she had been reduced to working as a governess. Her death caused a sensation, as she was well known in Bath and elsewhere. Notices appeared in newspapers within a week, and the suicide was a notable topic of conversation at court.[54]

No one expects anyone they know and respect to kill themselves, and everyone reasonably close to the deceased feels somehow responsible, and therein lies the emotional impact of suicide. Although her friends and acquaintances seem to have known she had fallen on hard times, her death, and the manner of it, shocked them. Frances Braddock's death had to be explained, to have larger meaning ascribed to it, and to have responsibility assigned for it. Although she had gambled her fortune away, she did not fit the stereotype of the compulsive gambler. Fanny Braddock was no Lady Ambs-Ace, her acquaintances insisted. All of the accounts of her death, even the earliest, vigorously defended her character. 'She is generally lamented by all who knew her,' the *Gentleman's Magazine* reported, 'and was greatly esteemed for her genteel and courteous Behaviour, and good Sense.' John Wood, in whose house she lived for the last year of her life, averred that 'Her Behaviour was such as manifested nothing but Virtue, Regularity and good Nature in the preceding Part of Her Life.'[55] Moreover, she was closely associated with fixtures on the Bath scene, quite obviously with John Wood, but also with Nash and with Dame Lindsey, the keeper of one of the assembly rooms. The tragedy of Fanny Braddock upset them, but it also threatened them.

These associations may explain the 'Sylvia' narratives that appear as lengthy digressions in Wood and Goldsmith. Whatever else he said, Wood conveniently established that he was not in Bath when the death occurred, that he only heard about it on his return and that his relationship to her was that of landlord to tenant – she died owing him rent, after all. His contradictory account reveals little about how Fanny Braddock, under the posthumous pseudonym of 'Sylvia', ran through her fortune, except for laying the blame on Dame Lindsey, who was no longer alive to defend herself. Miss Braddock, Wood claimed, was completely beholden to Dame Lindsey by the time of his arrival in Bath in 1727, and would present herself at Lindsey's 'whenever a Person was wanting to make up a Party for Play'. Although her close association with a woman of dubious reputation saddled her with 'the Odium of her being a W[hor]e', Wood insisted that over three years of 'the strictest Observations', he could never 'perceive Sylvia to be tainted with any other Vice than that of suffering herself to be Decoy'd to the Gaming Table, and, at her own Hazard, Playing for the Amusement and Advantage of others'. Had he suspected otherwise, he implied, he would never have agreed to take her as a tenant in 1730.

Wood's defensive tone may cause us to question whether she was his tenant at all. Owing arrears of rent was one thing, but by Wood's own account 'Sylvia' owed nearly fifty guineas for only thirteen months in Queen Square, an amount which would have secured very comfortable lodgings in London for the same period of time. Did she *ever* pay rent? Was she even expected to pay? Was she in fact Wood's mistress? Whether or not Wood was keeping her, many contemporaries familiar with the arrangement must have suspected as much. His shock and anger at her death, at least, rings sincere. 'I have heard Hundreds in High Life Lament their not suspecting' Fanny Braddock's intentions, Wood fumed,

> *that they might have endeavour'd to prevent it, tho' it should have been at half the Expence of their Estates; and yet many of those People, when common Fame every where Sounded* Sylvia's *running out of her Fortune, would endeavour to draw her into Play to win her Money; and accept of whatever was offered them from her generous Hand!*[56]

Righteous anger like this was apparently more than her own brother could muster. According to Horace Walpole, when Lieutenant Braddock was informed of his sister's death, 'he only said, "Poor Fanny! I always thought she would play until she would be forced to *tuck herself up*."'[57] In Lydia Grainger's version of the story, published in 1733, it is her fear of her brother's discovering the extent of her losses, and of the prospect of being economically dependent on him, that drives 'Sylvia' to suicide.[58] By the time that Goldsmith's rendition of the story appeared, Braddock had risen to the rank of Major General, only to be deserted by his panicking troops and killed at Fort Duquesne.

Goldsmith based his account partly on Wood and partly on Lydia

Grainger. In Goldsmith's rendition, 'Sylvia' became attached to a 'constitutionally virtuous' but extravagant man with large debts, which she paid off over a number of years until her fortune was exhausted. Nash appears in this story as an adviser, first unsuccessfully urging 'Sylvia' to end her relationship, then inviting her to return to Bath with a promise of introductions 'to the best company'. Her social connections were impressive, whether or not she owed them to Nash, and whether or not we can believe John Wood that 'Her Levy ... looked more like that of a first Minister of State, than of a private young Lady.'[59] Lord Hervey, Vice-Chamberlain to the Royal Household and favourite target of Augustan satirists, knew her well, and women of his family, avid gamblers all, might have as well.

Was it Nash who introduced her to Dame Lindsey? According to Goldsmith, Nash was among the punters at Lindsey's on at least some of the occasions when 'Sylvia' was 'decoyed', for 'he directed her when they played'. This last circumstance would not have been lucky for her, as Nash in the year before her death had suffered serious reverses at the gaming table himself. He had reportedly lost £4,000 in one night at Tunbridge, enough to make him pledge never to play for more than £100 ever again; whether he kept his resolution is anyone's guess.[60] Is it accidental that Nash does not figure in Wood's account, or was he as guilty of taking advantage as Dame Lindsey was – or as Wood may have been? One reading of the sad tale of 'Sylvia' illustrated that women who were otherwise paragons of moral virtue could be reduced to abject misery in the grip of a destructive addiction. A closer and more critical reading reveals exactly how vulnerable women were once they slipped into the socio-economic margin. In a culture in which many observers, women as well as men, saw women as more morally susceptible and less responsible for their actions, the example of Fanny Braddock was a rallying point for the reform of manners. One journalist suggested that as

> *a Memento of the fatal Issue of Gaming, and a preposterous Fondness to keep, what is very improperly called the best*

> Company, *there may be represented in full View, by a masterly Hand, instead of Mr N–h, the Catastrophe of an unfortunate Lady, (who destroy'd herself in this Place) with the Circumstances of the Girdle, Closet-Door, and Noose, in the Attitudes and Agonies of that wretched Death.*[61]

Fanny's Braddock's suicide became such a lightning rod that those who, through commission or omission, were potentially culpable in her downfall felt compelled to defend themselves. By the time their defences appeared, however, the forces of reform had scored significant victories in Bath, triumphs which would change the shape of the city.

6

A Duke, an Architect and a Landlady

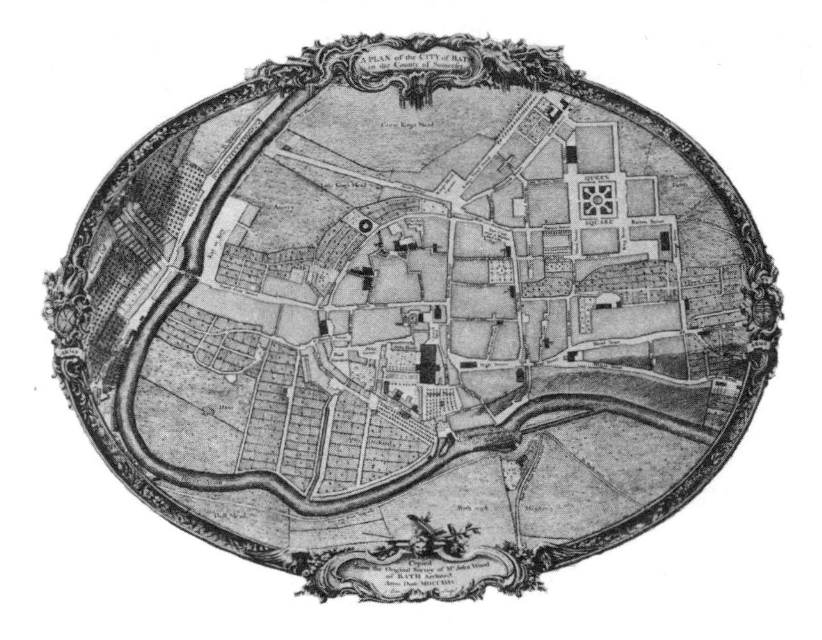

29. The Wood-Pine map of 1736

There can be no more pregnant epigraph for this chapter than the map based on John Wood's 1735 survey of Bath, engraved by John Pine and published in 1736. It stands in stark contrast to Joseph Gilmore's 1694 map. Like that, the Wood–Pine map is oriented with the north–south axis laid horizontally, but there all similarity ends. Peter Borsay, in comparing Wood's map with Gilmore's, notes that the borough wall, while still present on the former, is represented by a thin and barely detectable line.[1] The street plan is scrupulously rendered, while the architecture fades into oblivion. Landmarks like the Abbey and Guildhall are highlighted only as reference points. Only Wood's newly built Queen Square, larger than life, looks as if it might be a truly remarkable civic space; otherwise, the city looks empty of architecture – but full of possibility. The cartouche framing the map encompasses large tracts of suggestively undeveloped land, including the Abbey Orchards on the future site of the Parades, as if Wood meant to point out the potential for further development. If Gilmore's map represents a static pride of place, as embodied in solid citizens who like things very much the way they are, thank you, Wood's map is a real-estate development prospectus that presents a dynamic, and possibly controversial, vision for the future.

Wood's *Essay Toward a Description of Bath* famously began with a scathing indictment of accommodation in Bath before he began working there, an account quoted (usually uncritically) in nearly every history of Georgian Bath:

> *About the Year 1727, the Boards of the Dining Rooms and most other Floors were made of a Brown Colour with Soot and small Beer to hide the Dirt, as well as their own Imperfections; and if the Walls of any of the Rooms were covered with Wainscot, it was with such as was mean and never Painted: The Chimney-Pieces, Hearths and Slabbs were all of Free Stone, and these were daily cleaned with a particular White-wash, which, by paying Tribute to every thing that touched it, soon rendred the brown Floors like the Starry Firmament: The Doors were slight and thin, and the best Locks had only iron Coverings Varnished: With Cane or Rush bottomed Chairs the principal Rooms were Furnished, and each Chair seldom exceeded three half Crowns in Value; nor were the Tables, or Chests of Drawers, better in their Kind, the Chief having been made of Oak: The Looking Glasses were small, mean, and few in Number; and the Chimney Furniture consisted of a slight*

> *Iron Fender, with Tongs, Poker and Shovel all of no more than three or four Shillings Value.*[2]

Wood's assessment was corroborated, seemingly, by his early patron, the first Duke of Chandos, who found his rooms during his 1726 visit to Bath 'very miserably bad', with 'miserable furniture' that did not include 'so much as a Card Table', and 'lamentable' windows, 'which cou'd not keep out the least Puff of Wind'; in short, it was completely in keeping with the 'old rotten Lodgings' available in the rest of the city.[3] Joseph Gilmore's map, it would appear from Wood and his patron, papered over a great deal of disarray and decrepitude.

As it happened, neither Wood nor Chandos was an objective witness to the state of the hospitality industry in the early Georgian city, as both accounts were heavily inflected with self-interest. The architect, of course, sought to claim credit for the monumental changes which, to be fair, certainly were effected. Chandos, less extravagantly, was trying to bolster his position with a hard-bargaining tenant (the redoubtable Anne Phillips, of whom more later) who wanted adjustments made to her rent. '[I]f the situation in the late seventeenth century was as bad as sometimes said,' the social historian Sylvia McIntyre has written of Bath, 'it is surprising that visitors should have come at all.'[4] Celia Fiennes was favourably impressed with the building she saw in the late-seventeenth-century city, much of which was new and well furnished, and there were decided advantages to even older lodgings of the kind depicted in Thomas Johnson's 1672 drawing of the King's and Queen's Baths. The lodging houses shown rising on three sides of these baths often boasted their own entrances to the baths, which eliminated the need for Bath's notoriously surly and demanding chairmen. Even Wood acknowledged that new construction did occur, and under the auspices of prominent townsmen. By 1708, he admitted, improvements in Bath's physical plant had been going on for twenty years. Around 1720, Henry Bettenson began a group of houses at the south end of the city, while Thomas Greenaway began the houses of St John's Court. These buildings included what 'became the Palace of the King of *Bath*', which, appropriately enough, 'was the richest Sample of Building, till then executed, in the City.'[5]

In fact, for much of the time that it was a resort serving the Georgian power elite, Bath was a building site where finely dressed visitors in brocaded coats, hoop petticoats and sack-back dresses shared the narrow streets with sweaty labourers in leather aprons, and silk stockings in shoes with jewelled buckles stepped gingerly around piles of masonry. Wealthy visitors in the best rooms of the newest lodging houses might still be awakened at five in the morning by roofers 'covering in' a still-newer house across the courtyard. It flies in the face of our stereotype of the European eighteenth century to know that, far from being repelled by this aspect of their stay in Bath, members of the Company were fascinated by the city-in-progress, down to the raw materials of bricks, mortar and quarried stone. To our eyes and in our minds, Georgian classicism, with its insistence on proportion, harmony, unity and restraint, evokes the static politics, latitudinarian religion and confident complacency that we still associate with the period. We forget that this architecture, as it rose and displaced its Elizabethan and Jacobean antecedents, was to Bath's visitors the architecture of a brilliant and exciting future. We can sense this excitement from the accounts of fashionable visitors to Ralph Allen's quarries on Combe Down, or from the fanciful, quasi-utopian vision of Wood, who fetishised classicism with the enthusiasm of a Micronesian cargo cultist, as if he honestly believed that a resurrected ancient golden age would return if only he could reproduce its built environment.[6] The architecture that captured Wood's fevered imagination also appealed to visitors drawn to the newest and most favourably located accommodation.

Wood, of course, would have us believe that new buildings unnerved local residents as they rose both within and (more ominously) outside the borough walls. 'Citizens,' he reported, 'were so uneasy at the Sight of every new House that was begun, that, in utmost Despair, they cry'd out, "O Lord! Bath is undone; 'tis undone; 'tis undone."' He claimed that one of his key patrons, Robert Gay, distanced himself from the projected Queen Square development so that the Bath Corporation would not be deterred from electing him as one of the city's Members of Parliament.[7] Between the lines of Wood's acutely self-interested narrative, however, is a picture of a municipality using every means at its disposal to foster its growing resort economy. From 1708, for example, the Corporation secured a series of acts of Parliament allowing for the improvement of roads leading to the city, and for the cleaning, lighting and repair of its streets. It is important to remember that, until the 1720s, the infrastructure of Bath's resort trade – the facilities for bathing, accommodation and entertainment – were almost exclusively under the direct or indirect control of the Corporation. The inns and lodging houses crowded into the city centre were often the property of city aldermen or their family, and concessions (such as chairmen's licences) were often dispensed to poor relations. Local authorities were therefore ambivalent towards development, especially when undertaken by outsiders and in areas beyond their immediate jurisdiction, the medieval walled city and its 'liberties'. Mayor and aldermen were no less protective of their civic privileges than local governments everywhere else in early modern Europe. A city ordinance of February 1726 forbade those not 'free' of the city to keep shops in the city or liberties of Bath on pain of a £5 fine, and cited a number of retailers catering to the resort trade.[8] It is a telling point that the effort in 1720 to regulate the fares for chair hire effectively discouraged development further than 500 feet from the baths, Pump Room and assembly rooms.[9] Self-interest on the part of local authorities did not, however, extend to wholesale resistance to real-estate development, in spite of John Wood's efforts to impose such a narrative of conflict. If the Corporation did not take an active role in the expansion of the resort until after the middle of the century, its initial reluctance stemmed from lack of capital resources, and once private investors like the Duke of Chandos, Ralph Allen, Humphrey Thayer and Robert Gay took over development by supplying this capital, it was difficult for the Corporation to get its hand in.

The early eighteenth century in Bath witnessed the increasing prominence of private entrepreneurs in the business of housing and entertaining visitors. Real-estate developers such as the Duke of Chandos and entertainment projectors such as Thomas Harrison, interlopers in the eyes of a wary Corporation, were able to capitalise on the reality that Bath was outgrowing its medieval boundaries, which were still visible in the form of walls and gates. It was no accident that the emergence of private development coincided with Nash's rise to social ascendancy at the resort. Until the spa's amusement culture was solidly established, the idea of large-scale speculative building in the service of the unwell made many potential investors queasy. It was the medical community that had driven the redirection of Bath's economy in the seventeenth century, and development had been driven by changes in medical thinking. The new fashion for drinking the water, well established by the Restoration, made accommodation adjacent to the baths less imperative and removed a barrier to development outside the city centre.[10] 'From this area,' Alexander Sutherland declared, 'the inhabitants began to turn their heads from the *Loom* to that of entertaining strangers.'[11] The spa's medical *raison d'être* continued to govern its development for the first decades of the new century. Significantly, two of the key figures in Bath's development in the first quarter of the eighteenth century were health-care providers based in the metropolis. Robert Gay was a surgeon in Hatton Garden, just outside London's corporation limits, and the proprietor of Barton Farm, a large tract of land in the parish of Walcot, some few hundred feet north-west of the borough wall of Bath, and where much of the resort's subsequent residential development was located. Humphrey Thayer, an apothecary, was also Commissioner of the Excise, a lucrative government office, and possessed the capital to invest in Bath real estate, in this case a wedge of property nestled between the borough wall and the River Avon, an area which became the centre of Bath's amusement culture. He, like Gay, was well placed to gauge demand for mineral-water resorts, and to create it. Their involvement in promoting and developing the resort reinforced the notion that Bath existed so that the sick might recover their health. Consequently, no one in the Corporation or outside it could have imagined in the first quarter of the century that a convalescent centre would expand the way Bath did from 1728 onward. Aldermen, councillors, entrepreneurs and developers were still thinking on the scale of Tunbridge Wells or Epsom. Even the Duke of Chandos, who considered himself the first of Bath's developers to endeavour to build facilities to a higher standard than had been available before, was hemmed in by his own assumptions about the resort and its possibilities.

~

Over the course of the first half of the 'long eighteenth century' between the Restoration and the Regency, the city's hospitality industry adapted to the needs of an increasingly affluent clientele. At the same time, the growth of the resort in accordance with the needs of its polite clientele pushed local popular culture to the margins. Wood was able to boast later of displacement of popular entertainments by the development of the old Abbey Orchard, where in 1730 Catherine Lindsey's new assembly rooms opened on the former site of 'Smock Racing and Pig Racing, playing at Foot-Ball and running with the Feet in Bags, ... four of the Bath Diversions of those Days'.[12] The evidence for the changing social and cultural tone in Bath is not merely anecdotal. Ronald Neale found that while the capacity of the city's stables grew between 1686 and 1756, as we might expect given the rise in numbers of visitors, the number of beds belonging to inns decreased.[13] Visitors increasingly preferred lodging houses to inns, given that a standard course of bathing, drinking or pumping lasted five to six weeks. Inns provided short-stay accommodation, where all the needs of travellers – for example, food, drink and housekeeping – were provided by the management. Inns also could function as taverns and eating houses, and were often centres of local entertainment. Claver Morris, a country doctor who lived within a day's journey of Bath, entertained four friends there in September 1718 with dinner 'in the great new Dining-Room' at the Three Tuns, where they also heard a 'Consort of Musick'.[14] Lodging houses provided longer-term accommodation that afforded more privacy and where lodgers expected to see to themselves. Generally, they would be accompanied by their own servants, although the chatelaine and her staff were prepared to provide cooking and housekeeping for visitors who required it. John Penrose's Bath landlady, Mrs Grant, was exasperated when his family arrived on her doorstep in the Abbey Green without any servants. She condescendingly informed him that while servants at a boarding house might serve meals or run errands, servants in a *lodging* house would not, although they would clean rooms, make beds, light fires and cook. Alternatively, lodgers could hire servants locally for the duration of their stay, as the Penroses were able to do. Maids could be had for half a crown a week; the Penroses found a fifteen-year-old willing to work for two shillings a week plus meals, and two women who also lodged with Mrs Grant, no doubt appalled at their landlady's behaviour, offered the services of their maid for errands.[15] Lodging houses were more socially exclusive in other ways as well. While innkeepers were prepared to house travellers who turned up unannounced, lodging houses were usually engaged well in advance. Even after the building booms in the first half of the century, sets of rooms in Bath's houses were let mostly by word of mouth, and were really only available to visitors with the requisite social networks. 'If your Ladyship has any method of getting Lodgings at Bath,' Elizabeth Anson wrote to Lady Grey in August 1749, 'be so good to pursue it', as she had heard it was necessary to procure them at least three weeks ahead of arrival. Were Lady Grey not able to oblige, Lady Anson had other social connections to draw on: 'Miss Heathcote, Sir William's Daughter, who is going there, has promised to execute any Commission for me.'[16] By the early eighteenth century, even the wealthiest and best-connected visitors were having difficulty securing rooms for themselves, their families and their servants. 'The place can't be fuller than it has been for this last month,' William Brydges had written to his cousin James from Bath in 1711, adding that there were 'few lodgings now empty.'[17] A few years later, James Brydges and his wife, now the Earl and Countess of Carnarvon, planned a stay in Bath, but, as she wrote to her sister, Bath had 'been so full yt we could not get Lodgings'.[18] As wealthy spa-goers with capital to invest found it harder and harder to find suitable accommodation, investors from outside Bath soon recog-

30. James Brydges, first Duke of Chandos. His commercial ventures and business acumen made him an unconventional grandee

nised opportunities in the development of the spa. James Brydges, as first Duke of Chandos, was one of the earliest.

Chandos embodied all of the contradictions of the putative 'Age of Aristocracy'. He *was* an aristocrat, of course – his father held a barony, bestowed in 1554, and his family had sufficient influence to get him elected to the House of Commons as a Knight of the Shire for Herefordshire. For all of their lordly credentials, however, the Brydges were shrewd businesspeople, and their increasing fortune was tied up less and less in agricultural land and more and more in commercial ventures, including the Royal Africa and East India companies, joint stock enterprises which were then relatively new outposts in an already global economy. Young James's inherited aptitude and acquired skills led him into the mother of all venal offices as Paymaster General of Her Majesty's Armed Forces at the particularly opportune juncture of the War of the Spanish Succession. The payroll of the army and navy – from field marshals and admirals of the fleet down to private soldiers and jack tars fresh from the clutches of the press gang – passed through his hands, and as long as pay was disbursed at the expected quarterly intervals (and often when it was not), Brydges was free to invest the balances and pocket the proceeds. After eight years in office, he had accumulated a fortune of £600,000. His loyal support of the Whig interest won him the Earldom of Carnarvon upon the Hanoverian succession, and his support of Robert Walpole secured him the meteoric promotion to a dukedom in 1719. Chandos (as he was now styled) was one of the fortunate few South Sea Company investors who cashed in before its collapse in 1720, netting a rumoured £50,000, adding to a fortune thought by then to exceed £1 million.

As plutocratically wealthy as he still was, the South Sea Bubble was too close a call for Chandos to ignore, and he realised that his rent roll of only £10,000 left his portfolio heavily vested in paper securities and therefore dangerously undiversified. From the 1720s onward he turned his attention to real estate. He may at this point have remembered the odd correspondent over the years remarking how full the resorts were during their respective seasons, and how difficult it became to get lodgings, in Bath in particular. Chandos and his duchess generally preferred Tunbridge Wells, which was more convenient for London and for Cannons, his Edgware estate, although the Duke had bottled Bath water delivered in weekly consignments. It was not until Duchess Cassandra fell seriously ill in April 1726 that he ventured to Bath at all. After a week, once his terrible anxiety for his wife was past, he had time to observe the Bath scene, which he did not care for. The atmosphere was 'so different from my taste and manner of living, that I am already prodigiously sick of it[.] I fear I shall contract such a habite of laziness and indolence that I shall never be able to recover my self out of it.'[19] As if compelled to use the time that lay so uncomfortably on his hands, Chandos cast a calculating eye on the resort and its infrastructure. It occurred to him that, without too much expense, lodging houses could be built and fitted out that were at least more comfortable and convenient than anything otherwise available. Through the offices of Richard Marchant, a Quaker timber merchant, he began buying up houses in the block strategically located on the west side of the Cross Bath. Although the Duke took pains not to be identified as the purchaser, by August 1726 his uncle Francis Brydges averred that it was common knowledge among Bath residents that Chandos, using Marchant as his agent, had paid a rumoured £2,500 for the jumble of nondescript buildings around and upon the site of the Hospital of St John the Baptist, for the purpose of building a house, or a square, or 'God knows what'.[20] Of the hospital, an almshouse founded in the twelfth century, only the ground floor accomodated a few elderly poor residents; the floors above it had been 'privatised', and now contained a lodging house operated by one Anne Phillips. It was here that the Duke and Duchess of Chandos had stayed, and it became the nucleus of a complex of houses that he proposed to build around a central courtyard. The Cross Bath was only steps away by staircases from the first floor, while the parlours and dining rooms looked over the courtyard to the pastoral prospect of Kingsmead beyond.

Chandos was an experienced real-estate developer by this point, and well knew the legal hurdles that lay in the path of 'improvers', especially when dealing with urban corporations. Buying rental properties meant taking over pre-existing leases, and one of Chandos's new properties had been leased by the Bath Corporation, a situation which required delicate manoeuvring and negotiation, as did matters like water, sewerage, easements and paving. Fortunately for Chandos, the governor of St John's Hospital, one of the prime beneficiaries of his purchase, was, after October 1727, the brother of Bath's mayor. The Corporation, which gave John Wood fits in his efforts to run a sewer line and build lightboxes for basement kitchens, became much more tractable over time, and gifts like the fifty bottles of Madeira and claret that Chandos presented to Mayor Chapman certainly helped to grease the wheels.

Chandos made enquiries through Marchant about wages of craftsmen and the price of stone. He had asked Marchant to find a mason to do the work 'on the great' – that is, on a piecework basis. As for architects, Marchant recommended a number who were locally known, such as William Killigrew, who had rebuilt the hospital's chapel in 1723, and Benjamin Holloway who had worked in the Trim Street development. But it was an unknown 22-year-old John Wood who was selected in January 1727 as Chandos's architect.[21] Wood was a native Bathonian whose father and brother were involved in the local construction trades as well. Before signing on with Chandos, his major patron had been Robert Benson, Lord Bingley, a dispossessed Queen Anne Tory who had been Chancellor of the Exchequer. Bingley was Chandos's London neighbour in Cavendish Square, and they seem to have got along in spite of partisan differences (of course Bingley defected to the Walpolian Whigs in 1730). It was perhaps through Bingley that Wood first came to the Duke's attention. Wood also worked at Bramham, Bingley's estate in Yorkshire, and it was there that he drew up his first designs for Bath. That fact, and his bringing workers down with him to Bath, sustained a belief long held among Bath historians that Wood was a Yorkshire native. The first recorded contact with Chandos was on Wood's initiative, as the architect hoped that he would finance a building project proposed for Barton Farm, Robert Gay's parcel of undeveloped land north and west of the borough wall, and he sent the Duke a copy of the design. Chandos demurred, pleading that he was overextended with building projects, but only three months later settled with Wood for rebuilding Anne Phillips's house over St John's Hospital.

Wood's youth and inexperience must have been a deciding factor in Chandos's decision, and Chandos admitted as much. 'I was willing to incourage a young Man just coming into the World,' he told his banker, 'and imploy him in a Place where if he perform'd well he cou'd not fail of getting a great deal of Business of a like kind.'[22] Essentially, from Chandos's point of view, Wood was young and relatively untried, and therefore cheap, and besides, Chandos was doing him a favour. He did not know, as he later discovered, that Wood already had agreements for other projects in Bath when he settled with Chandos. His bid for rebuilding Anne Phillips's house was unrealistically low and of course there were cost overruns. Chandos initially agreed to pay Wood £1,600 in February 1727 but by August had already paid £2,000. The final tally for building the house was £3,139 2s. 9d., including items like half a guinea paid to a worker injured in laying the sewer.[23] Wood, under such budgetary pressure, could not resist the temptation to cut corners. Chandos chided him for using low-quality mortar, and was quite understandably furious at discovering that the 'pipes' from the water closets were not lead (as expected) but merely 'Boards nailed together'.[24] Wood had labour troubles as well, and Chandos resented being asked to intervene. 'I can by no means suffer that any One by Vertue of a Protection from me should screen himself from doing Justice to those they have Dealings with,' he wrote, but when a dispute with a mason over payment resulted in Wood's arrest, Chandos was angry enough to charge the offending magistrate with a breach of parliamentary privilege.[25] The architect's youth and inexperience contributed to his difficulties with workmen, and with Chandos's tenants; he was only in his early to middle twenties when he started building in Bath. Wood enjoyed getting his way, and that combined with youth and testosterone was a vitriolic concoction. Chandos certainly did not make Wood's job any easier, accusing him of bad faith within days of settling with him, and second-guessing him on the construction of cellars only a week after that. Within one month of work beginning, his new patron not only let Wood know that he was not trusted but also let everyone connected with the project know as well. '[C]ou'd I have imagined that I had been used in so vile & shameful a manner by you,' he wrote after Wood had been working for a year and a half, 'you shou'd never have been imployed by me again.'[26] Wood retaliated in passive-aggressive fashion by assigning bottom priority to the Chandos houses, where he was hamstrung in any case by a manipulative and controlling client.

This particular client's interference, of course, was his way of showing that he would not easily have advantage taken of him. It ought to be said that Chandos's knowledge of the most quotidian details of construction was impressive. He at one point delivered Wood a lecture on the proper hanging of shutters worthy of a home improvement programme.[27] If his familiarity with carpentry was unusual for a peer of the realm, his knowledge of indoor plumbing was astonishing. 'If the Water Closets prove a Nuisance to the House,' he scolded Mrs Phillips, 'it must be from the Ignorance of those who manage them; for if ye Plug is kept close & ye Bason always half full of water, no Smell can come from the Common Sewer.'[28] To be perfectly fair, Wood had given grounds for his scruples to be suspected, and he bore watching, especially as Chandos could not often inspect the progress of building personally. For his part, Chandos demonstrated after a time a grudging respect for those such as Wood and Anne Phillips who, in one way or another, stood up to his hectoring. He was not deterred from employing Wood to build two more lodging houses, and spoke well of him to his cousin William Brydges. In 1734, after all construction was complete, Chandos agreed to stand as godfather to Wood's daughter.[29] Most extraordinary of all was Chandos's admission to John Harris, Bishop of Llandaff, that he had been overly stringent in keeping Wood to his terms. Wood's shortcomings, Chandos wrote in recommending Wood to rebuild Llandaff Cathedral, were not due

> *to either his want of capacity, or understanding his business, or to his want of honesty, but purely to a want of due care in making his agreement, for as they were the first works of such a bulk which he undertook, he was, I believe, mistaken in his computations, and when he found this, to make himself whole as well as he cou'd, he got the cheapest matirials he coud buy, and, that he might save as much as was possible, finished them in so unworkmanlike a manner.*[30]

For all of the aggravation that the young architect suffered through his years of building for Chandos, the experience was invaluable. When Wood initially signed on, Ronald Neale points out, he 'was still an architectural novice without capital'. His dealings with Chandos, and the Duke's agents, were his 'introduction into the world of money and credit without which, for all his plans and building enterprise, he could never have laid one stone upon another'.[31]

~

Then as now, building was a complex undertaking, involving negotiations, logistics and all of the drama of the creative process. There is just as much to hold our attention once we move from the province of the architect to the more quotidian realm of the Bath chatelaine. Each unit of the ranges of building devoted to the accommodation of visitors was a distinct organism in itself. Fortunately the archives afford us a detailed glimpse into the day-to-day workings of two fairly typical lodging houses. John Wood paid his professional dues by enduring the ruthless browbeating of the Duke of Chandos, whose scathing letters to the architect, preserved in the Huntington Library, are often cited. Less well known, but interspersed with the Wood epistles in the Chandos Letterbooks, are equally splenetic letters to the Phillips sisters, Anne and Joanna, and Jane Degge, three of the tenants of the houses Wood built for Chandos in Bath. Anne Phillips was alone among them in being an established Bath lodging-house keeper, which gave her an advantage in dealing with Chandos, as she was familiar with the rental arrangements customary in Bath. If she was excited at the prospect of having her lodging house completely remodelled, she knew better than to make Chandos aware of it. As Wood began work, she and Chandos were negotiating her new rent. Chandos proposed that Mrs Phillips pay rent on a room-by-room basis, which was apparently not an uncommon arrangement in Bath. He initially asked for £300 a year for each set of rooms in the house that would let for £20 per week according to established rates for accommodation in Bath, and stipulated that the house would contain six garrets (for servants), two kitchens and two 'vaults' (basement rooms for pantries and storage).[32] Essentially, she would hand over the proceeds of fifteen weeks (on the assumption that her house was full to capacity). According to Chandos's calculations, this arrangement left her with the proceeds of the remaining five to ten weeks of the autumn and spring seasons taken together, in addition to what she would take from off-season lodgers. Chandos estimated that even after paying tradesmen, the parish tithe, poor rate and window tax, Mrs Phillips would clear some £400 annually, a very comfortable income in the early eighteenth century.

Anne Phillips was not about to succumb so easily and marshalled her years of Bath landladyship to counter these offers. She argued that her own rooms in the house, and those for her maids, should not be counted in the rental assessment, since she obviously did not let these to lodgers. Furthermore, she claimed that kitchens and garrets were never assessed in the computation of rent, perhaps because they were never engaged as separate lodgings (Chandos, in insisting that they be included, seems to have been aware of this).[33] Ultimately, Chandos recognised the futility of dickering over the assessment of rent room by room in a house that had yet to be built. By March he was proposing a lump-sum rent for the entire house. In April he was agreeing to let the house to her furnished, initially on a short lease of one to two years, given her uneasiness about the success of the venture. The completed house, he believed, would consist of seven kitchens and pantries, seven rooms on the first floor, sixteen on the second, seventeen in the attic and seventeen garrets. Relying upon a time-honoured negotiator's stratagem, he asked her to name the rent she would be willing to pay, stating his willingness to come to any reasonable agreement with her, on the understanding he would not have 'the World ... think I was either wholly ignorant or negligent of the Value of these Buildings'. He did not fail to mention, or at least to claim, that another potential tenant was interested in taking the house.[34] Two weeks passed and Anne Phillips had not only not taken the bait, but had the temerity to turn the tables and ask Chandos to name *his* rent. Giving in yet again, Chandos stipulated £350 per year, and her payment of all taxes but the Land Tax, as the least he would accept for the entire house. Finally, at the beginning of May, he capitulated, proposing £300 per annum 'clear of all Taxes', not drawing her attention, however, to his new expectation that she would now pay the Land Tax as well.[35] His omission and her inattention led to another round of wrangling, nor was that the end. Mrs Phillips, like the almshouse residents and any lodgers she might have had, was obliged to vacate the premises while the house was being rebuilt. Wood had underestimated the time necessary to finish the house as well as the cost, and she shrewdly exploited this reality to gain further concessions. The final arrangement was that she paid Chandos £300 a year in rent, payable in advance in quarterly instalments due on 25 March (or 'Lady Day', as the Feast of the Annunciation was known, the official beginning of the year under the 'old style' calendar), 24 June (Midsummer Day, coincidentally the Feast of St John the Baptist), 29 September (the Feast of St Michael and All Angels, or Michaelmas) and finally Christmas Day.

Once the roofing of Mrs Phillips's house was complete, it was time to assemble the furniture, so that it would be ready to move into the house as soon as the panelling was up and the paint dry. Against his better judgement, and with his sense of being imposed upon yet again very clearly articulated, Chandos acquiesced in furnishing the house. He naturally insisted (and for this we are grateful) that meticulous accounts should be kept and a thorough inventory taken of all goods with particulars of their distribution within the house. He was equally adamant about keeping the cost down. 'You know People at the Bath do not buy the finest of Goods to furnish their Lodging houses,' he advised her, and agreed with her in evident relief 'that the best sort of Furniture to put in ye house will be such as is plain but strong & good of the sort'.[36] After another two weeks, however, the gauntlet was thrown down once again:

> *As to what you say of the manner of furnishing the House I will deal very frankly with you & own my inclinations are to have it as well furnished as is just necessary to induce Lodgers to come to it, and that in the doing of this, my intentions are to save as much mony as I possibly can.*[37]

Chairs, tables and chests of drawers for the house came to £340 and change, while beds (including frames, mattresses, bedsteads and coverings) came to over £460, meaning that just over £800 was spent on furniture, and almost all, of course, on rooms for visitors. Servants, crammed into garrets, had also to be content with the cheapest and most minimal furniture. All twenty-four of the chairs for the garrets cost a total of £1 9s., or fourteen and a half pence apiece.[38] The total cost to Chandos of fitting out and furnishing Anne Phillips's house in the four years that she occupied it was £2,315.[39] The records of the furnishing of Jane Degge's house, owing to Chandos's entirely justifiable lack of confidence in her ability, are even more detailed. We know, for example, that thirty place settings of cutlery were purchased for a total of £1 7s. 6d., or eleven pence apiece, while twenty-six mirrors (including sixteen for garrets at a shilling each) cost £7.[40]

These accounts raise important questions about a critical stage in Bath's development as a resort economy. In the late 1720s local residents were deeply ambivalent and a bit sceptical about the putative benefits that their community drew from the spa. Like many residents of resort communities today, they suspected, often rightly, that the most conspicuous aspects of the seasonal economy were parasitic. Bath by this point had still not developed a manufacturing sector extensive enough to supply the needs of its growing accommodation, as the dramatic expansion of residential construction there had only begun. Many of the furnishings ordered for Anne Phillips and Jane Degge were produced locally, but the bulk were brought in from outside, usually from Bristol and occasionally from London. Somewhat less than £15 worth of goods were purchased for Mrs Degge from Mr Axford, a Bath brazier, as opposed to nearly £50 paid to a Mr Randall, his counterpart in Bristol. By the middle of the century, when even the Corporation was willing to trust in the continuing expansion of the resort, relevant segments of the manufacturing sector had grown in tandem with the construction trades in Bath. Where only three apprentice braziers and two apprentice cabinet-makers were entered in the entire second quarter of the century, in a single decade, the 1750s, seven young men were apprenticed as braziers and fourteen as cabinet-makers.[41]

We have only Chandos's side of his exchanges with Anne Phillips, and his letters are masterpieces of psychological gamesmanship. 'I am sorry to find you not altogether so steddy in your Resolutions as

I expected,' he scolded her at one point; 'it wou'd be exceedingly for my Advantage cou'd I find every one I deal with as punctual as myself.'[42] All that she could say to this invective was that micro-managing a lodging house was surely beneath his dignity, which was high flattery, given that Chandos had already displayed to her an encyclopedic knowledge of the mechanics, maintenance and cleaning of indoor toilets. Fortunately, she did not have to rest content with words. She had the advantage of interior lines of communication. Chandos, several days' journey away, was only able to be in Bath two or three times, for as many weeks, in all the years that he was building there. He depended for the success of his Bath ventures on intermediaries like James Farquharson, John and Walter Ferguson, Richard Lund – and Anne Phillips. Mrs Phillips's local contacts and her long experience in hostelry made her a valuable tenant, but also a difficult one. Her constant disputes with Chandos over rent, repairs, furniture, plumbing, the state of construction and other issues were critical manoeuvres in the high-stakes game of urban real estate. For all of their disagreements, and perhaps because of them, Chandos both understood Anne Phillips and needed her, much more than she ultimately needed him. Chandos's experience with Jane Degge bore this dependence out. She was the kinswoman of one of his land agents, and Chandos had long kept her in mind as a possible tenant for one of the Bath houses. In retrospect, it is highly amusing that she was the interested party behind his veiled threats to Anne Phillips. Mrs Degge was completely new to the business of hostelry, as it turned out, and Chandos was finally forced to tip his hand in asking Mrs Phillips to train her, in effect, in the essentials of letting accommodation. On one level, Jane Degge was the ideal tenant for an overbearing landlord such as Chandos, for she was precisely the opposite of Anne Phillips. She was manipulated into unfavourable terms of tenancy and was easily bullied into other concessions. She agreed, for example, instead of paying £300 a year or more in rent, to accept a lump sum once a year out of the proceeds of the house, essentially as remuneration for her management, while turning the profits over to

Chandos. The first year she was in the house Chandos offered £200 payable at Michaelmas; her second year she was offered only £150.[43] Her tractability, however, was a function of her inexperience and ultimately her incompetence. She did not know better, for example, than to allow lodgers to appropriate furniture belonging to other sets of rooms during their stay, which left some rooms underfurnished and therefore less desirable. While the lodgings around her were packed to capacity, her house was seldom if ever full. Mrs Degge became such a liability to Chandos that he elected not to renew her lease. 'I very much fear you will never succeed in this sort of business,' he wrote to her in January 1731. He had heard reports of her mismanagement at first hand (it helped her case not a bit that both complainants were titled), and given that three families had decamped from her house for more agreeable accommodation, it was not really surprising that her receipts for the previous month came to only £23. Five weeks later, he turned her out.[44]

The tone of his letters to Anne Phillips became much more amicable and conciliatory after the experience of Mrs Degge. She knew her business, she knew how to turn a profit and she was a useful agent for procuring furnishings, and Chandos probably appreciated by this point that if Anne Phillips could hold her own with him, she was more than a match for tradesmen, artificers, merchants or anyone else who might to overcharge or otherwise deceive her. His new, complaisant attitude emerged too late, however, and she cheerfully gave up her lease, disappearing from the Chandos Letterbooks into new accommodation, although, given her aversion to John Wood, not in any of his developments; perhaps she went into one of John Strahan's newly built houses in Kingsmead Square. Her sister Joanna supplied the place of the inadequate Jane Degge, and Chandos found her no less difficult to manage. She even had the effrontery to marry his estate agent, John Ferguson, so that Chandos found himself negotiating with at least one of those he had counted on to twist the arms of tenants in the past.[45]

Chandos discovered too late that his Bath houses were misbegotten investments and after seven years he was trying to sell them, with only mixed success. He managed to sell Anne Phillips's house for £3,400, realising a modest profit over what he paid to have it built, but the last of these houses was still on his hands at his death. The common wisdom in place by Jane Austen's day was that the closer a lodging was to the city centre, the *less* desirable it was. Chandos's houses, instructively, were directly athwart Westgate Buildings, so memorably disparaged by Sir Walter Elliot in *Persuasion.* Of course, by the Regency period Queen Square was also downmarket: 'We must be in a good situation,' Austen had the Musgrove sisters insist to their father; 'none of your Queen-squares for us!'[46] The Victorians might fetishise the antiquated (as opposed to the antique), but for the Georgians, newest was best.

The story of the Chandos houses is a minor episode in the history of the development of Bath and it assumes a disproportionate significance for Bath historians because it is so exhaustively documented. It does raise some important points, however. First, it illustrates what a radical departure the dramatic and expansive development of the resort outside the borough walls really was. As late as 1728 or even after, Bath projectors like Chandos were still thinking small. They assumed that Bath would be expanded and rebuilt only to the extent that was possible within the Corporation limits. Chandos's initial speculation was fuelled by a particular set of assumptions about the foundations and structure of Bath's resort economy. Bath, for Chandos, was a spa which primarily served the needs of invalids, and according to this reasoning it would make sense, for example, that proximity to the baths was the primary attribute for visitors seeking accommodation. He also believed that visitors in Bath for their health would not have standards higher than cleanliness, comfort and convenience. In these respects, Chandos was operating from assumptions no different from those that grounded the seventeenth-century Bath hospitality industry. Relentlessly business-like workaholic that he was, he could not imagine that large numbers of visitors would fritter away the time and money necessary to stay a season in Bath solely for the sake of amusement, and the idea of a local economy based completely on leisure escaped him. Long-term stability could not prevail in a pleasure resort; the needs of convalescents were much more dependable, and accordingly every detail of Chandos's houses, down to the chairs that he ordered, were planned for valetudinarians. These preconceptions were still plausible in the later 1720s, and informed Thomas Goulding's bid for pre-eminence at the resort. Goulding and his vision were much more consonant with Chandos's inclinations than Nash would have been, although to be fair the Duke never mentioned either man. Chandos and Goulding, more to the point, began their initiatives at the same time and admitted defeat at approximately the same time as well. Goulding lost to Nash, who successfully reasserted his magisterium. In a very real sense, Chandos lost to Nash as well. Nash won because his constituency, those whom Chandos dismissed as so many sybaritic profligates, reached critical mass in the 1730s. The newer and more luxuriously appointed development that Wood was building in Queen Square was more in keeping with the centre of conspicuous consumption and display that Bath was becoming.

7

Stone, Bricks, Mortar and Wood

31. Richard Jones, Ralph Allen, Robert Gay, and John Wood, by Thomas Hoare

The building of eighteenth-century Bath was put into motion with none of the calm, serenity and harmony which its architecture is supposed to invoke. If anything – as we have already witnessed in the machinations among the Duke of Chandos, John Wood, Anne Phillips and others – the Georgian Bath that we have inherited was shaped by the conflict of monumental egos and superhuman wills. The most important developments undertaken by Bath's leading architect were compromises, recastings, downscalings and redirections of his initial projections, so that large sections of the resort were topographies of John Wood's thwarted ambition. Wood, so often praised today for the elegant simplicity of his façades, simplified those designs only reluctantly and often angrily. Bath as we know it was not the work of one man or even three men, but of large consortia of entrepreneurs, builders, investors and the odd architect. The reconstruction of Bath was also, to the extent that one can apply the term to any sector of Georgian society, a middle-class enterprise. The Duke of Chandos was certainly never at the leading edge of urban development in Bath, and when he belatedly discovered this fact, he did his best to cut his losses and run. Bath was built *for* grandees, not *by* them.

The latter point is clear from Thomas Hoare's inexpert, almost primitive group portrait of the men who actually *did* build Bath in the thirty years between the first cornerstone in Queen Square and the last door-knocker in the Circus. Ralph Allen and Robert Gay, who could afford to have their portraits from far more skilled and practised hands, are seated (however stiffly) in the centre as a matter of course. Allen looks nothing like his other extant portraits; even a 1764 caricature bears a closer resemblance to Thomas Hudson's and William Hoare's work than this piece. Consequently we cannot know if the figures standing awkwardly on the left and right bear any resemblance to John Wood or to Richard Jones, Allen's Clerk of Works. We have a better idea what William Hogarth's kitchenmaid looked like, but, as in her case, it was a fluke that Jones and Wood were recorded in portraits at all. Here they are, though, the surveyor who designed Bath's new residential developments and the stonemason who built – or helped to build – many of them, together with the proprietor of the 'ground' and the supplier of the stone laid upon it.

Nash, of course, is not in this picture, and we can scarcely imagine he would have been miffed not to be recorded by such an inexpert hand. He frequently appears in Wood's *Essay,* however, supporting and encouraging the architect's plans, and proposing, even urging, new projects. It was Nash, according to the architect, whom the Hospital Trustees chose in February 1738 to present Wood's design for the General Hospital to the King and royal family, and to have the plan engraved. Ten years later, Nash was 'pressing' Wood to build new assembly rooms abutting the Parades.[1] As a key promoter (and indeed a projector) of Bath's growing pleasure and entertainment industry, Nash could claim much of the credit for Bath's surviving and surpassing any other contemporary British spa, and to that extent, it is due to him that Georgian Bath is still there for us to see.

That said, Bath would not have grown in the way it did without Ralph Allen's entrepreneurial drive, business sense and – one hesitates to say, but not for long – ruthlessness. Historians of Bath have often identified Allen as one member of the 'triumvirate' that created Georgian Bath. He stands as a logical counterweight to his fellow triumvirs, the temperamental visionary John Wood and the flamboyant *mondain* Richard Nash. Allen was an extremely pragmatic entrepreneurial type with an aptitude for problem-solving, an obsessive grasp of detail and a nose for opportunity.[2] All of these were virtues that the Duke of Chandos might have appreciated but, in contrast to that nobleman, Allen appeared – at least to 'polite' observers – to possess a streak of humility and humanity that preserved him from Chandos's neurotic need for control. Tributes came from Henry Fielding, who famously modelled Squire Allworthy in *Tom Jones* on Allen, and from Alexander Pope, who called him 'the Most Noble Man of England', declaring, 'God made this Man rich, to shame the Great; and wise, to humble the learned.'[3]

Allen's ventures were remarkably diverse. While still in his twenties, he convinced the Postmaster General to grant him the contract for the cross-posts, and then essentially reorganised the English postal system, micro-managing inefficiency and fraud out of existence, and making his fortune in the process. His profits were soon deployed in new ventures. For Allen, the development of Bath was part of a particularly harmonic convergence of opportunities. Building begins with raw materials and the means to deliver them. Accordingly, Allen purchased one of the thirty-two shares of the Avon Navigation, which in May of 1724 began the long-delayed project of canalising the Avon between Bath and Bristol. Four members of his family also bought shares, giving Allen enough of a stake to be named an officer of the company. The canal was fully operational by December 1727, and the following May Princess Amelia officially opened it by floating from Bath to Bristol on an elaborately decorated barge. By this time Allen had bought the limestone quarries on Combe Down from their previous owner, Mary Wiltshire. The oolite limestone quarried there was easy to shape and carve when first cut, and hardened with age, making it ideal construction material, but Allen found that stone intended for Bath was often damaged in transit by cart. The solution was a tram which carried the cut stone downhill, assisted by gravity, to the stoneyard at Dolemead, on the banks of the Avon, where it was finished and then wafted to its destination on the newly constructed canal.

Wood had come to Allen's attention as one of the contractors for digging part of the Avon Navigation, and Allen became a much more important patron than the Duke of Chandos could ever be. Wood was already designing Allen's townhouse in Bath when Chandos initially engaged him, and when the Duke became interested in the Avon Navigation and the Combe Down quarries as investment opportunities, it was through Wood that he made enquiries. Allen's initial partnership with Wood was directed towards undercutting local stonemasons, on whom Allen might have been dependent for quarrying his stone, by importing workers Wood brought from Yorkshire; for having resolved these transportation issues, it was the cost of labour that Allen addressed next, using an ingenious 'carrot and stick' approach. The 'carrot' was an innovation far ahead of its time. The houses which he had John Wood build for his stonemasons were the first purpose-built worker's housing anywhere in Europe. This shrewd investment reduced the cost of living for his workforce and enabled Allen to persuade them to accept lower wages. He was also able to argue that the resulting reduction in the cost of stone would increase demand, which would create more and steadier work.[4] For those holdouts among local stone-

32. Prior Park was built to promote the Bath stone taken from Allen's quarries nearby. Note the tramway in the right foreground

masons who declined these terms, Wood provided Allen the 'stick' in the form of stoneworkers imported from Yorkshire. The introduction of 'scab' labour created considerable resentment, and may explain labour troubles and incidents of vandalism on Wood's building sites in Bath. Richard Jones hinted at the dislocation that Allen and Wood wrought in the local stoneworking industry in relating that stone-masonry at Bath was once 'a very good trade, and [masons] had good prices for their work'.[5]

Allen tackled the problems of supply, distribution and labour with a view to reducing the price of stone, and then took steps to promote its use all over the kingdom, but especially London, where he supplied finished stone for St Bartholomew's Hospital at a loss. In this last objective he was unsuccessful, as the finished stone was too fragile to make the trip, and the labour restrictions imposed by the Corporation of London prevented his stonemasons from working on site. Allen received a decisive setback when Bath stone was rejected in favour of Portland stone for the building of Greenwich Hospital; Wood claimed that the samples of stone were inadvertently or even deliberately switched. The market for Bath stone remained regional, supplying the expansion of Bristol and Liverpool in addition to Bath, but Allen never gave up the effort to market the stone nationally. To this end, he put Wood to work on Prior Park, the house he built on the hills south of Bath.

Wood, although the architect of record, was not happy with Prior Park, and in the self-promoting *Essay,* he described the house as he would have liked to have built it. Neither of the houses Wood built for Allen, Prior Park and an earlier, overly ornate townhouse in Lilliput Alley, was reflective of the simpler style that the architect developed for the reconstruction of Bath. Unlike Wood's later developments, these were exhibition pieces meant to be seen rather than inhabited. Prior Park was built to showcase the properties and possibilities of Bath stone, which was quarried nearby. The magnificent gardens of the north lawn were visible from the house but not accessible from it, as Allen omitted the staircases in Wood's original design (the present stairs were added in the nineteenth century).[6] Allen may have feared that allowing visitors on the lawn would distract their attention from the house, which they approached from the level south front via the road for the stone-wagons. It was no accident that guests came up by the service drive. The class segregation supposed to be characteristic of Georgian development was quite deliberately turned on its head, as is clear from Anthony Walker's 1752 engraving of Prior Park, in which as much space is devoted to the tram loaded with stone on its way down from the quarry as to the house and outbuildings themselves. We see very clearly how the entire arrangement was an ingenious sales tool. Parties of several elegantly dressed women and men pause on the two-mile walk from Bath to admire the mechanical marvels of the tramway as much as the house and grounds; they would without doubt have visited the quarries as well. The stoneworks certainly made the intended impression on Elizabeth Anson, who, in addition to 'the power of Mechanics in the Crane at the Stone Quarry', admired an

> *Engine ... for turning the Stone Vases, the largest & most magnificent of wch ... are but six pound the pair; so that I should*

> *think ... you might have* Kouli-Kan's *Monument made here, ... and even if it should not answer it would be an experiment of no great cost.*[7]

The infrastructure for processing Bath stone was promoted as a tourist attraction before Allen even began to build Prior Park. The map of Bath that Wood published in October 1736 featured the obligatory legend decribing landmarks of note, among which was

> *A Crane for Loading of Barges with Free Stone; the Motion of lowering the Stone is the most Expeditious of any thing of its Kind, and allowed by the Curious to be a Masterpiece of Mechanism, to which Crane ye Stone in large Blocks seldom less than 5 or 6 Tun at a time, descend from the Quarries, at least a Mile and a half, by Machines contrived at the great Charge & Expence of Mr Allen the Proprietor of it, on which Account the Stone is sold for a fourth part less than heretofore, to the great Advantage of the Publick & Gentlemen that use it.*[8]

Like Chandos, Allen had little time for the amusements of the resort, except to the extent that they created a market for his stone by increasing demand for accommodation. Alexander Pope, for one, particularly enjoyed staying with Allen in Prior Park as it provided an excuse not to participate in the otherwise obligatory social round.[9] Allen certainly had dealings with Nash, as both were governors of the Hospital and both were keen to ensure that occasions like royal birthdays and visits were observed in suitable style. Nash would conduct balls, of course, and from the autumn of 1746 he would fire cannon that he acquired, appropriately or suspiciously, in the immediate aftermath of (or perhaps during) the forty-five. Prior Park would often be illuminated as well, and was by all accounts a spectacular sight from the town. Allen raised troops to fight the Jacobite rebels in 1745, volunteers who were on hand to parade and fire volleys on national celebrations like the Peace of Aix-la-Chapelle.[10] Beyond their enthusiasm for these public festivities and for the Hospital, their spheres of action did not intersect. If Nash stood for the seasonal visitors embodied in the Company, Allen personified (as a contemporary cartoonist asserted) the interests of professionals and businesspeople represented in the Corporation. As much as their attitude towards the expansion of Bath varied, at length it was they who profited. Moreover, their ambivalence was as instrumental as John Wood's determination in shaping Bath's architectural contours.

~

The profession of architecture as we would define it was still in its infancy in the first half of the eighteenth century, and John Wood and others like him were transitional figures in its development. Consider, for example, Wood's nonchalant disregard of the architectural plans he drew up for Chandos or Allen or the directors of the General Hospital. Those engaged in construction trades in the earlier eighteenth century held radically different assumptions about the uses to which their plans would be put. Often, 'blueprints', now seen as essential in construction, were not drawn up until after the fact. Wood's Circus was begun without a plan, and instead the first house, once built, simply served as the prototype for the remainder. The technical details found in modern blueprints were largely absent from Georgian architectural renderings, which were marketing tools aimed at seducing clients and backers rather than references useful for builders. It is no accident that collectors today find eighteenth-century architectural drawings so eminently suitable for framing. They were often intended as presentation pieces, and engravings after them were often sold, as in the case of the Bath General Hospital, to raise funds for construction. In this last case, once the money was raised, Wood simplified the design with the full consent of the directors.[11]

Building was also a much less centralised process than it is today, seeming by our standards collaborative to the point of chaos. Wood was much more adept at building exteriors than interiors, and willingly delegated the latter to carpenters, joiners, plasterers and painters, especially after the débâcle of the Chandos houses. More to the point, Wood really specialised in façades, which meant that in spite of the scope of his work (not until Robert Adam would any Georgian architect rebuild a city) he would never rank among the truly great architects of his day. Then again, his biographers pose a fair question: 'Is a great architect one who designs great buildings at great expense, or one who makes fine architecture available to all?'[12] Today we would call Wood a developer rather than an architect, and as his career progressed, he was less and less involved in the actual process of construction. Men like Richard Jones, who worked for Allen as a surveyor, built the houses, while Wood took out the construction leases from landowners like Robert Gay and then sublet plots to surveyors, masons, and others in the construction trades, who would build to his designs. And for all his flashes of temperament, Wood became increasingly flexible with regard to the plan of individual houses within his developments. As long as the street fronts conformed to Wood's plan, builders were allowed to configure the interior space as they saw fit. Each house, outwardly comprising part of a harmonious whole, would still have its own individual personality, which can only have appealed to buyers. The results of this arrangement are still readily visible today when the uniform frontage of any of his developments is compared with the anarchic disposition of the rear.[13]

This adaptation seems to us to be a stroke of brilliance, but it was no more than Wood's reluctant accommodation of the political realities of building. Reading between the lines of his *Essay* we find the wistful, and often bitter, musings of an architect at the mercy of his clients, who did not often get his way, as no prophet without honour in his own country ever does. For Wood had a vision for Bath, which he envisioned as a hyper-classicised utopia populated by what the intellectual historian Peter Gay has called 'modern pagans', eighteenth-century contemporaries who aspired to be citizens of a restored classical civilisation.[14] The architect wanted not only to rebuild Bath but to reconfigure its civic culture on classical lines. Bathonians would use his Royal Forum much as Wood imagined the ancient Romans had used theirs, and he envisioned his Royal Circus as an arena for games, where genteel Georgians would sprint and wrestle in the open air. On one hand, then, Wood represented modern paganism taken to its ludicrous extreme. He was so uncomfortable with the pagan and Mediterranean origins of classicism, however, that he formulated and posited an alternative Judaeo-British provenance for it. His architectural history owed much to Freemasonry, as well as to the same British national myth that underlay Bath's legendary past. Classicism, for Wood, began with the architects of Solomon's Temple and was only later appropriated by the Greeks and Romans. Naturally, its British origins predated the Roman invasion, having been introduced by ancient British kings like Bladud, who, according to tradition, had studied in Athens. As his twentieth-century biographers have pointed out, the architect was by no means alone in advancing his wildly imaginative and speculative archaeological hypotheses.[15] Antiquarians like William Stukeley believed along with Wood that if Stonehenge, for example, seemed less architecturally impressive than, say, the Temple of Vesta, it was only because the refinements of ancient builders had suffered longer from the ravages of time. Wood wrote as if he were rebuilding Bath as it had existed twenty-five centuries earlier, and it is really no wonder that the Bath Corporation found his initial development scheme 'chimerical'.

His perspective can only have been reinforced by the gradual re-emergence of the city's Roman past, a fortuitous consequence of the extensive redevelopment of Bath that he and others undertook. Wood must have been gratified by tantalising finds such as a bust of Minerva in 1727 and a mosaic floor in 1738. These artefacts anticipated the discovery in 1755 of the Roman Baths known to visitors today. Wood the Elder, had he been alive, would have been as disappointed as other Georgian classicists at the 'mean' appearance of the simple stone cistern with its niches, and would not have protested any more than any other contemporary when the Duke of Kingston covered them over again to build his private baths. The ancient baths were not rediscovered until the 1880s,[16] when they were suitably dressed up with statuary befitting a monument to Roman grandeur. Wood would surely have approved, and would no doubt have argued that the Victorians were only re-creating

33. The orderly façades of Queen Square belied the haphazard progression of its development

what the baths had obviously looked like once. He was inclined to view his craft not so much as architecture as historical reconstruction.

Wood's mission was to make classicism accessible in two senses. First, by locating its origins in the Old Testament (through the medium of Masonic beliefs) and in British prehistory, he strove to free it from the exclusive 'ownership' of classically educated elites. Second, by controlling costs and keeping external ornamentation to a minimum, Wood pioneered a 'pared-down Palladianism' that was within the means of the moderately affluent. By aiming his real-estate developments at the broadest possible market, he ensured that while he was certainly not the only architect working in Bath, he would be by far the most successful. Significantly, as eccentric as Wood's vision seemed, it was grounded in an understanding of Bath as a settled residential community. As early as the 1720s, Wood was thinking of his native city as a place for families to live and not merely as a resort for the *beau monde* to visit.

The *Essay* makes Wood's career seem less rocky and more seamless than it often was. The construction of Queen Square is a case in point. It would be easy to assume, following the *Essay,* that Wood designed the square as an organic whole in 1728 and then went systematically about the process of securing subleases for each of the lots. In fact, as his biographers Tim Mowl and Brian Earnshaw convincingly argue, Queen Square came into being essentially by accident. The architect had been trying with mixed success to develop the section of Barton Farm, Robert Gay's estate, closest to the Corporation limits. One new street, Barton Street, would run south into Saw Close and north into a second thoroughfare, modestly named Wood Street. Prevented from building southward, where other developments were preferred, he turned his attention to his own eponymous street, but aside from a block of four houses begun in 1729 on the north side running east of Barton Street, Wood could not attract interested builders. Then, very possibly, he learned through one of his contacts in London of the proprietary chapel recently built to serve residents of the posh new developments on the Grosvenor Estate, where Wood had worked for Lord Bingley. Residents (many of whom had a vested interest in advertising their conformity to the Church of England) could attend services to their liking in the ecclesiastical equivalent of a private club, secure in the knowledge that, unlike a parish church, this establishment would not have to receive all comers. Wood recognised a sales tool when he saw one, and after announcing at the beginning of 1731 plans to build the Chapel of St Mary the Virgin near the western end of Wood Street, he soon had more proposals for subleases than he had lots available. At about the same time, Wood suffered a setback when his abortive plans to build a circular mineral water hospital (his 'imperial Gymnasium') occasioned a falling-out with Robert Gay. Once he was back in Gay's good graces, Wood may have felt the need to counteract the failure of the hospital design, and the antidote that occurred to him was to turn the south side of Wood Street into the bottom of a square which was to become the largest public space in Bath until the completion of the Circus two decades later.

At that point in his career, Wood's competition in Bath was numerous and formidable. There was John Harvey, the builder of the Pump Room (which Wood genuinely admired), Thomas Greenaway, who constructed Nash's ornate, Queen Anne Baroque townhouse in St John's Court, and William Killigrew, who designed Thomas Harrison's new ballroom, which opened in 1720. His major rival was the Bristol architect John Strahan, who, like Wood, preferred to build rows of townhouses rather than the heavily decorated and expensive individual residences which other Bath architects tended to favour in the first quarter of the century. Strahan, again in common with Wood, also enjoyed the support of a major Bath property holder in John Hobbs, a Bristol lumber merchant, who owned tracts south and west of the Corporation limits.

Wood was no different from any other professional then or now in that he had to prove himself before he could realise even a scaled-down version of his grandiose vision. 'Starting small' and 'paying one's dues' do not quite do justice to the season in purgatory that Wood endured under his first Bath patron. His experience with Chandos paid off, however, in the acquisition of valuable contacts, most notably Chandos's banker, James Theobald, whose offices allowed Wood, with no capital of his own, to undertake the exponentially more ambitious developments of Queen Square and the Parades.[17] Prior to building Queen Square, for example, Wood was able to take out a lease of the ground for ninety-nine years from the landowner, Robert Gay, and then sell leases on the completed houses for ninety-eight years.[18] Chandos's persistent complaints about the house built for Anne Phillips and now known in Bath as the John Wood House did not deter Bath property holders like Humphrey Thayer from enlisting Wood in projects that were to distract him from construction he was still undertaking for Chandos.

Increasingly, Wood's new developments were intended for visitors who would rent entire houses rather than be content with sets of rooms within houses. These members of the Company came to Bath with a view to entertaining as well as being entertained, and to answer the demand, Wood's houses grew grander as the decades advanced. Queen Square, built between 1731 and 1736, contained quite spaciously appointed houses, such as number twenty-five on the north side, the central house under the pediment, which boasted five bays, a decorative

34. Nash's house in John Court still stands, although partially obscured by later construction

central staircase and large reception rooms on both sides on the first two floors. Other houses in the block were typical and comparatively simple terrace houses, with two rooms only on each of the first two floors and a staircase flying discreetly up the back.[19] As Wood planned the square, from the south side to the east, then north and finally west, his designs became more ambitious and elaborate. The south side (destroyed in the 'Baedeker Raids' of the Second World War, rebuilt and now housing one of Bath's more upmarket hotels) was relatively simple, as is the east side. The north side, however, is a near-exact replica of Henry Aldrich's Peckwater Quad at Christ Church, Oxford. The Parades, built in the 1740s, and the Circus, which Wood began and his son finished in the 1750s, contained more houses built on the scale of the largest units in Queen Square.

Queen Square was a success in that Wood found purchasers for all of the houses (he himself settled in number nine). As ambitious as the development became, the social profile of the initial twenty-seven purchasers was relatively humble, numbering only one peer of the realm (Earl Tylney), a baronet and two men styled 'esquire' (a designation already meaningless in the earlier eighteenth century, given that Nash pinioned it to his own name without blushing). Samuel Emes, a mason, purchased three of the houses, including a particularly choice corner unit. Wood admitted that, by and large, the initial development of the square was 'begun by People of moderate circumstances', and given the limited success of Chandos in the St John's Hospital complex, a building project as far removed as Queen Square was from the baths, the Pump and especially the assembly rooms must have seemed a risky venture indeed. Once it was completed, however, wealthier and more socially eminent purchasers invested in houses in the square. The London banker James Theobald, who had distanced himself from the project despite his friendship with Wood, purchased seven houses at one blow in 1740 from one of the original Queen Square investors.[20] By the time the *Essay* was published, Wood could boast that the square was occupied by 'People of Distinction and Fortune'.[21]

Wood's major competitor, meanwhile, proved to be less of a threat than he must have seemed initially. John Strahan was building Kingsmead Square just to the west of the borough wall at the same time that the first houses went up in Wood Street and, after Queen Square was finished, began Beaufort Square just south of it. Because he was more cautious, or less confident, or more level-headed, or less imaginative, or had more business sense, or less vision, Strahan ended up building for an entirely different sector of the real-estate market. Where Wood's houses were assessed at the higher end of the parish rating scale, Strahan's two squares consisted of houses at the next to lowest rate. The gap between the two architects' developments only widened. In the 1760s, when Wood's Circus was the choicest address in Bath, Strahan's Avon Street housed the city's red-light district. Wood built for the top of the market, those who subscribed for the balls and were listed in the *Bath Journal*, while Strahan built for the bottom, for those for whom no bells pealed because they arrived on the coach with the mail from London, or even on the day-barge from Bristol, and whose lodgings the city music left undisturbed, preferring their gratuities in silver rather than copper. It is notable, however, that there were lower levels of the market for Strahan to build for.

The Parades, the last of Wood the Elder's developments that he lived to see completed, were to have been his triumph. From his point of view, they were only the first phase of his Royal Forum, an ambitious development even by his standards, which would take up the whole of the pasture known as the Ham. An early proposal featured an open plaza 1,000 feet in length and 600 in breadth, which would straddle the Avon, with bridges over embankments linking the two sections and a great octagonal basin in the centre. Terraces fifty feet wide would surround the whole, over which magnificent ranges of building would rise. One of these ranges, a much more elaborate version of what was eventually built as the South Parade, would open on to a new set of opulent assembly rooms, including a theatre, two billiard rooms, a drawing room, several large anterooms and a 1,300-square-foot double-cube ballroom. If his earlier plans for Barton and Wood streets were 'chimerical', the Royal Forum thus projected was utterly insane. By 1740 Wood had reluctantly scaled his plan down to a 'New Square' on one side of the river only, with the addition of a new proprietary chapel, in the hope of attracting investors as St Mary's had for Queen Square.[22] The Parades would close the north end of the square, and construction began in 1740.

By virtue of their location, the Parades provided accommodation sacred to the pursuit of pleasure. Occupying the site of the Abbey Orchard, land which had passed into the hands of the Duke of Kingston, they overlooked the walks and were a brief stroll from both the assembly rooms and Orange Grove. Given its strategic location, the building subleases for the North or 'Grand' Parade were quickly taken up, especially since Ralph Allen took the lead, buying up some eighty feet of the total of some 200 feet of street frontage. Building proceeded quickly, with roofing completed after only eight months. Unfortunately, Wood lost creative control early on when one of the builders, almost certainly Ralph Allen, cut corners on the North Parade by (among other things) eliminating Wood's elaborate Corinthian columns and

35. As magnificent as they were and still are, the Parades formed only a fraction of the grandiose development that Wood originally planned

pilasters. Wood (very grudgingly) admitted that, these changes notwithstanding, 'the *Grand Parade* still deserves its Name'; it had replaced the Orange Grove as 'the principal Place of publick Resort in the City', and its twelve houses 'reflect a Beauty to each other, which has the Power of charming and delighting the Eye of almost every Beholder!'[23] The breach of trust was unforgivable nevertheless, and Wood abandoned the Parades to the builders around the time the northern range was being built. Without Wood's salesmanship to move construction lots, the remainder of the Parades went up as slowly as the Grand Parade had been built quickly, with the last sites subleased nearly a decade after construction had begun.

~

How little is to be expected from [the Corporation of Bath], in this particular, might have been guessed by their conduct to Mr Wood, *the architect, to whose extraordinary genius they are indebted for a great part of the trade and beauty of the place; yet they have industriously opposed his best designs, which, had they been executed, would have rendered* Bath, *in point of elegant architecture, the admiration of the whole World.*[24]

Wood now set aside the practice of architecture to immerse himself in its history and theory. It was in this period that the two editions of the *Essay* appeared, as well as his strange musings on the architecture of the ancient Hebrews and the Druids. His hiatus was suggestively timed. It would have allowed the architect – and any potential investors in his projects – to gauge the effects of the crackdown on gaming in Bath. In spring 1748 he resisted Nash's efforts to persuade him to build new assembly rooms south of the Parade, a tract of undeveloped land that Wood preferred to leave vacant as a reproachful memorial of the Royal Forum that never was.[25] When he began to build again, it was with the assistance of his son and namesake, and in an entirely new direction, literally and figuratively. Wood redirected his developments – and all future developments, as it turned out – to the hills north of the city, rather than the pastoral, less challenging terrain of the Ham, which remained undeveloped. Consequently, new construction drew the residential centre of Bath away from the amusement centre, so that ultimately – beginning in 1769 – new assembly rooms were built convenient to the Circus and the new streets that served it.

It was also during Wood's retreat from building that Tobias Smollett, in his *Essay on the External Use of Water* of 1752, took the civic leaders of Bath to task for neglecting the resort's infrastructure and for failing to appreciate Wood's efforts. By this time, mayor and aldermen were willing to listen and act. In 1753, for example, they passed new regulations for the baths – setting, for the first time in centuries, separate days for men and women to bathe – along the lines of measures that Smollett recommended.[26] The Corporation also underwrote the construction of Bladud's Buildings, begun in 1755 by Thomas Jelly, who closely followed Wood's elevations and designs. Wood, in fact, set both the pattern and the direction of construction in Bath after the mid-century.[27] The King's Circus was the first of his developments to be built essentially as he planned it, but as fortune would have it, he did not live to see it. At the beginning of the spring season in 1754, the cornerstone of the first house on the Circus was laid; by the end of that season, John Wood the Elder was dead, just short of his fiftieth birthday. A year and a half later, four houses had been built, including one for William Pitt, the rising star of the patriot Whig opposition to the ministry of the Duke of Newcastle. Pitt, according to Lady Anson, had rather different notions about his Bath residence than many visitors in the past. '[W]e imagine this place will be one of those where Mr Pitt will set up his standard,' she wrote, '&, by means of the great resort of people make followers, & spread his Politics through the Land.' She was very impressed with the Circus as it then stood, in spite of her hearing that 'Mr Nash thinks the whole will never be compleated.'[28] Nash might have been pleased that the Circus was completed in 1757, but by then he had more than buildings to worry about. His own anxieties may have led him to interpret the construction of the Circus several hundred yards uphill from the assembly rooms, rather than a few hundred feet away on level ground, as an ominous sign. On the other hand, the location of the most desirable and fashionable lodgings uphill from the Pump Room and the centres of amusement would entail exactly the sort of exercise that the influential Bath physician George Cheyne (of whom more later) urged on his patients and readers, and might perhaps have consoled John Wood the Elder, had he lived to note that the gymnastic displays he anticipated did not take place. At least the new spa might become a place of amusement 'calculated ... so as to improve, but not to impair health', where '[h]abit, in time, turns necessity into virtue', and where the wicked were gradually 'weaned from their darling vices'.[29]

~

> *Nothing [is] so common as to hear people say,* Bath will be over-built, Bath must be undone. *Those who make this prognostic enter but superficially into the study of human nature; they are but little versant in the revolutions of States.*[30]

By the time that Alexander Sutherland, a physician who gravitated between Bath and Bristol, published these lines in 1763, remarkable changes had taken place in Nash's Republic of Pleasure, among which the doubling of greater Bath's built environment was only the most visible. New construction was the physical manifestation of more fundamental shifts in the character of the resort and its clientele. 'The principal functions of the city changed significantly over the course of the eighteenth century', Peter Briggs has written. '[I]n 1710 it was mostly a health spa; in the 1720s and 1730s a haven for the fast set, seekers after fashion and gambling and sexual intrigue; and in the 1750s and later ... , increasingly a family resort and retirement community.'[31] These transitions were indeed analogous to 'the revolutions of States', at least in the sense that Sutherland's contemporaries understood the term. Even at that portentous date, now conventionally denominated as the dawn of the 'Age of Revolutions', revolutions were understood to restore the status quo, not to alter it and certainly not to overturn it. Just as the revolution of 1688 had purportedly returned England to a form of government that contemporaries liked to imagine had existed formerly, the architectural transformation of Bath, in the mind of its native son John Wood, corresponded to an idealisation of its past. While Sutherland did not share Wood's phantasmagorical conception of Bath's history, the Bath he knew in 1763 was closer to the ideal he envisioned for his community in moral as well as architectural terms.

Closer, but perhaps not yet close enough. Even after decades of 'improvement' of all sorts, Sutherland could not quite make up his mind how to feel about what had happened to Bath. He believed that the success of the spa had 'changed the manners of the people' of the city and that their 'narrow conceptions' had been broadened. He realised, however, that these benefits to the local population had come at a cost to society at large. The material and cultural enrichment of the average Bathonian resulted from the kind of developments that in the past had been the unmaking of civilisations:

> *While Roman and Gallic liberty remained, Romans and Gauls preferred rural employments to unmanly amusements ... While rural exercises strung the nerves, mineral waters were rarely wanted. Baiae and Bath were mean country towns; the peasants*

their inhabitants rarely tasted their waters. As liberty decreased, Rome *and* Paris *increased. Baiae became the summer residence of Emperors, Patricians, and Plebeians.*

Sutherland put his finger on the paradox that lay at the heart of spa culture. He must have recognised on some level that the resort that provided his livelihood was predicated on the pursuit of the same pleasures that caused the infirmities its water was supposed to cure, and consequently his analysis of Bath was occasionally reminiscent of Bernard Mandeville, whose *Fable of the Bees* posited that the pursuit of luxury and the indulgence of vice were ultimately beneficial to the public. 'While national debt, extravagance, indolence, or ailments continue to increase, Bath never can be undone,' he declared, 'Bath will, in time, become one of the largest and most elegant cities in the world.'[32] The ever-present tension in Bath between the quest for health and the quest for diversion was the *primum mobile* of the resort economy. By the time Sutherland wrote, even the Bath Corporation had recognised this reality and had begun to invest in the infrastructure of the resort for the first time since the building of the Pump Room. These new perspectives on the resort changed the character of the thing being observed, often in ways that the observers had not expected.

8

Libertines and Methodists in Sickness and in Health

In Crowds the *Ladies'* throng, Where *Pleasure* calls,
To *Gaming-Rooms*, to *Concerts*, and to *Balls*,
BUT NONE TO CHURCH! – *What for?* No *Men* are there.
Must *Belles* on one another only stare?[1]

But *none to Church!* – 'Tis false! your pious Fools,
Polish'd *no higher* than by *Bible Rules*,
Lame, *Old*, and *Ugly*, thither run in Sholes;
THEY'VE nothing else to do but *Mind their Souls*.[2]

Bath yields a continual Round of Diversions, and People in all Ways of Thinking, even from the Libertine to the Methodist, have it in their Power to compleat the Day, the Week, the Month, nay almost the whole Year, to their own Satisfaction.[3]

Goldsmith may have cited 1738 as the high-water mark of Nash's ascendancy at Bath in the knowledge that the very next year witnessed ominous portents of things to come. As we have seen, had Wood's Parades been built as the architect intended, Nash would have had a palace worthy of his title, but by 1739 these ambitious plans had collapsed. In those same two years, a key source of Nash's authority and income was threatened when the first gaming acts in nearly thirty years classified a number of popular 'banking' games as illegal lotteries and put pressure on local government to enforce the legislation. Bath's reputation as a gambling mecca had troubled some prominent residents for a long time, but continuing adverse publicity, stemming in part from Fanny Braddock's suicide, convinced resort interests of the need for either reform or a public relations counter-offensive. Like Las Vegas in the 1990s, Bath sought to refashion its image, and its Master of Ceremonies saw the wisdom of cooperating with this effort, even appropriating it in an effort to reinforce his own public standing. Nash was persuaded, perhaps, by yet another confrontation on his own turf, not by a rival King of Bath but by self-anointed agents of the King of Kings.

Religious reformers were lured like flies to Bath by the odour of moral corruption, and among them was John Wesley, who visited and preached in the spring of 1739. Two sermons had already drawn crowds numbering in the thousands, which raised the possibility that Methodist zeal would infect the resort's service sector. To a traditionalist frame of mind, Wesley was usurping the duty of masters to oversee the religious lives of their servants, and any figure among resort interests who combined such a point of view with a sufficiently forceful personality was likely to confront the preacher at some stage. After the fact, of course, Wesley wrote of anticipating his confrontation with Beau Nash, his peer in self-promotion, with relish. 'All Bath ... was big with expectation of what a great man was to do to me there,' he related, 'and I was much entreated not to preach, "because no one knew what might happen."' Consequently, Wesley claimed, 'the rich and great of this world' smelled blood in the water and turned out in force, swelling Wesley's audience and raising its socio-economic profile. Wesley, as he meant his reader to understand, was now facing what a stand-up comic would call a difficult room, were he not preaching one of the open-air field sermons for which Methodists were famous – or notorious – and he certainly did not want his audience to laugh, at least not at *him*. Wesley's assertion that all were sinners, 'high and low, rich and poor, one with another', was too shocking to those belonging to the *beau*

monde, and too gratifying to those outside of it, to provoke laughter, and he interpreted the silence of his more affluent listeners as their 'sinking apace into seriousness'.

If he noticed a large white hat moving purposefully through the crowd to where he stood, Wesley did not remark on it, but only noted that Nash appeared as 'champion' of the pleasure-seekers of Bath, 'having forced his way through the people'. Nash, by Wesley's own account, saw himself as defender not of the sybaritic Company but, in this case, of Church and State by law established, and accordingly cited the Conventicle Act to the effect that Wesley had assembled an illegal gathering. When Nash asked under what authority Wesley was preaching in Bath, Wesley, high churchman that he was, cited apostolic succession and then pointedly turned the question around to Nash, asking, 'Pray, sir, are you a justice of the peace or the mayor of this city? ... by what authority do you ask me these things?' Nash, instructively, had no immediate answer. He admitted he only knew of Wesley 'by common report'. 'Is not your name Nash?,' Wesley then asked, and upon confirmation, replied, 'Why then, sir, I trust common report is no good evidence of truth.' With this the 'champion' was forced to quit the field.[4]

We have only Wesley's word for his encounter with Nash, of course, and it is worth noting that when his sometime patroness, the Countess of Huntingdon, read Wesley's account of the exchange, she tried to dissuade him from publishing it.[5] Goldsmith, however, found clerical poison pen letters among Nash's papers, including a priceless missive from the Presbyterian divine James Hervey, warning Nash that 'so long as you roll on in a continued circle of sensual delights, and vain entertainments, you are dead to all the purposes of piety and virtue: you are as odious to God as a corrupt carcase that lies putrefying in the churchyard'.[6] Nash's motivation for keeping letters like this one is unclear, although he was probably flattered to be such a conspicuous target for godly proselytisers. In his way, Nash understood, as John Wood did, that Bath was at the interface of religious life during a peculiar period in which establishment complacency and evangelical zeal alter-

36. Selina, Countess of Huntingdon, found Bath irresistible even after her conversion

nately confronted and accommodated each other. That Bath should become a centre of evangelical religious revival was less anomalous than it may seem to us. What evangelical reformer could resist Bath, with its unequalled opportunities for wagging of fingers, clucking of tongues and the odd exemplary conversion, not to mention shopping? Philip and Mercy Doddridge, eminent Dissenters surreptitiously fond of Bath, seem to have collected converts, the more spectacular the better, as it afforded opportunities to describe in salacious terms the depravity of former lives. Doddridge excitedly wrote to his wife about young Mr Godwin, a former pupil who had led a life 'of ye most profligate & abandon'd wickedness', including stealing from his father 'to support his Whores & other lewd Companions'. He was now 'a most eminent penitent & quite a New Creature'.[7]

Nash may even have played the part of a prospective convert, if only to gratify Selina, Countess of Huntingdon, the reformed Bath *mondaine* who reportedly prevailed on Nash to hear George Whitefield at her house. Lady Huntingdon was the epicentre of Bath's religious revival long before the construction of her chapel there in 1765. She has been an easy figure for writers to stereotype, and they have been aided by a backhanded nineteenth-century biographer, A. C. H. Seymour, who is responsible for one often-quoted vignette:

> *The frequent visits of Lady Huntingdon to Bath, during a period of twenty-five years prior to the opening of her chapel in that city, were attended with the happiest results. Wherever she went she invariably produced an extraordinary degree of attention to religious subjects ... Wherever she was, and in whatever company, her conversation was on religion, in which there was this peculiarity, that she spoke of the sins and errors of her former life, her conversion to God, the alteration in her heart and conduct; and she plainly said to all, it was absolutely necessary that the same change should take place in them, if they would have any hope in death.*

Likewise, we are told that her attempts to proselytise among her own class were met with amused indulgence, and with occasional reproofs, such as one from the Duchess of Buckingham, who found the teachings of Lady Huntingdon's clerical protégés

> *most repulsive, and strongly tinctured with impertinence and disrespect towards their superiors, in perpetually attempting to level all ranks, and do away with all distinctions. It is monstrous to be told that you have a heart as sinful as the common wretches that crawl on the earth. This is highly offensive and insulting; and I cannot but wonder that your Ladyship should relish any sentiments so much at variance with high rank and good breeding.*[8]

In contrast to what Aaron Seymour claimed, however, Lady Huntingdon was averse to confronting unregenerate Company, and discouraged others from trying. She advised John Wesley more than once against offending powerful individuals and institutions (she was more partial to George Whitefield anyway), and there is an apocryphal account of her escorting a particularly obstreperous Quaker preacher out of the Pump Room.[9] It was only in the 1760s, in fact, that the Countess became a major figure in the Methodist movement,[10] and available accounts of her life in Bath were written retrospectively with her role as 'Queen of the Methodists' (as Horace Walpole called her) in mind.

Moreover, Lady Huntingdon's letters indicate that even after her conversion in the summer of 1739, she continued to enjoy 'sensual delights' like wine, spirits and tea, and the 'vain entertainment' of gossip, especially gossip generated in Bath. She also continued to keep what she herself called 'worldly Company', and she relinquished any efforts to convert members of her own class after the 1750s.[11] For all of their moralising, religious reformers such as the Countess and prominent dissenting divines such as Philip Doddridge were comfortable in the 'sink of iniquity' that was Bath. 'Please to press my Compliments *to all my Bath Friends*,' Doddridge wrote in 1746, and when his wife, Mercy, was in Bath the 1742–3 season, there was no shortage of God-fearing company for her to associate with: 'Dr Stevenson Mrs Chandler Mrs Vanderplanck Mrs Axford Mrs Remington Miss Nesbit &c present their service.' She must have gone shopping with some of these, since she lived lavishly for the spouse of a nonconformist clergyman. 'I have been forced to buy several things here,' she admitted to her husband, '... as gloves, ribbons, and silk, not to mention Bath lace, which you know must follow of course.' Doddridge immediately promised her 'more Money when you want it. My Dear Mistress once more good Night.'[12] Further evidence that the Doddridges were not the wet blankets of contemporary stereotype is provided by his correspondence with Frances, Duchess of Somerset, and their friendship with Lady Isham, the wife of Sir Justinian Isham, a leading Tory. There is a danger in yielding too quickly to long-standing cultural stereotypes of what the eighteenth century called 'enthusiasm'. In Bath, religious reformers adapted to their surroundings and sought to fashion a species of politeness that encompassed evangelical piety, clean living and high moral standards.

At the other end of the spectrum, establishment Anglicanism inspired fierce loyalty among those who do not seem to us to be particularly religiously directed. Nash, for his part, was a creature of the establishment and faithfully attended services at the Abbey – at least no contemporary observers have suggested otherwise, and they have plenty to say about his other failings, and about the negligence in religious observance of other members of the Company. Although reputedly orthodox in his religious beliefs, his confessional history, like his political principles, was part of his carefully cultivated mystique. One rumour about his misspent youth had him converting to Catholicism and entering the French service.[13] Nash always showed a high regard for clergy of the established church, listening with good grace to sermons on the evils of gaming before circulating among the pews collecting for the General Hospital.[14]

Emile Durkheim's dictum that organised religion is the means through which society worships itself was possibly never truer than it was in the established church of Georgian England. In Nash's day, Anglicans were served by three parish churches – the Abbey (formally Sts Peter and Paul), St James's (south of the borough wall) and St Michael's (north of it and in disrepair). In these parishes as elsewhere, the fabric of the church was an architectural and spatial expression of social taxonomy. In older churches, the graves and memorial plaques of affluent parishioners were visible indices of the relative prominence of local families. Pews, often comfortably appointed with cushions and high wainscoting, and fitted with doors and locks, were more often than not private property. We can well imagine the appeal of services to those whom the verger would deferentially and ceremoniously conduct to a well-placed box pew on a typical Sunday. In a place like Bath, however, visitors would forfeit these privileges in the city's three parishes, where pride of place belonged to others. The Abbey, for example, was the parish church of the Bath Corporation, and mayor and aldermen had suitably prominent seating. A proprietary chapel, such as that of St

37. John Wood's Chapel of St Mary the Virgin admitted worshippers by paid subscription and was as exclusive in its way as the Assembly Rooms

Mary the Virgin, which John Wood built near Queen Square in 1732, resolved a number of social dilemmas. Consequently, when Wood announced his intention to built his chapel, subleases were taken up on seventeen additional lots in the square.[15]

For Anglicans, religious observance often seemed to be part of the amusement culture of Bath. Samuel Richardson's expansion of Defoe's *Tour* included church attendance as part of the obligatory round: ''Tis also the Fashion of the Place,' the emenders claimed, 'for the Company to go every Day pretty constantly to hear Divine Service at the great Church, where are Prayers twice a Day.'[16] Clergy were conspicuous in the lists of the Company available from 1744 onwards, and there is no reason to believe that this pattern did not hold for earlier seasons in the eighteenth century. Bath was no holiday for men of the cloth, as they were dragooned to preach in the Abbey and elsewhere, and were effectively forbidden from much of the prevailing entertainment. They could not join the dancers, or the voyeurs at the Cross Bath, or the card players, and certainly not the high-stakes gamblers, without raising eyebrows. Satirical verses allegedly delivered to a parson at the faro table warned clergy off behaviour that did not comport with their estate:

> *A* Levite *Gaming, makes the Saying true,*
> *The Harvest plenteous, but the Lab'rours few.*
> *Does Tables please you?* Moses's *does produce,*
> *Tables much fitter, for a* Levite's *Use.*[17]

Even Roman Catholic recusants, still subject to penal legislation, had a place of worship at the Bell-Tree Inn at the end of Bell-Tree Lane (now Beau Street). Once the rectory of St James's Parish, it was converted into a lodging house that to all external appearances was no different from any other accommodation in that part of the town. On its second floor, however, was a Roman Catholic chapel administered by Benedictines. This tiny devotional space was equipped with vestments, crucifix, tabernacle, pyx, reliquaries and even a tin thurible, which would have given neighbours olfactory notice of the activities there even if the celebrant intoned as quietly as he could manage. Mass was celebrated here, according to one recusant observer, with all the pomp and ceremony possible in such a small place.[18] The chapel's presence and location were an open secret among both locals and Company. When Alexander Pope's dear friend and fellow recusant Martha Blount had the indiscretion to take Ralph Allen's coach to the Bell-Tree one Sunday, Allen (a public office-holder) was seriously annoyed, occasioning a rift with the poet. Unlike Bath's future mayor, its Master of Ceremonies held no office he was in danger of losing, and Pope assured his friend that, as a favour to the poet, Nash would take her to Mass whenever she desired.[19] By 1753 the Bell-Tree Chapel was openly mentioned in guides for visitors, and by the next decade the *Bath Journal* was recording the congregation's donations to the General Hospital.[20] They were thus allowed to participate, for whatever reason, in a critical manifestation of the resort community's evolving self-concept.

So little giv'n at Chapel Door –
This People doubtless must be poor:
So much at Gaming thrown away –
No Nation, sure so rich as they.
Britons, *'twere greatly for your Glory,*
Should those, who shall transmit your Story,
Their Notions of your Grandeur frame,
Not as you give, but as you game.[21]

So Mary Barber chided spa-goers after a disappointing collection for the local charity children, and although the visitors taken to task were at Tunbridge Wells, the Company at Bath were equally vulnerable on account of their parsimony in the midst of self-indulgence. Wealthy visitors had long been admonished to contribute to the relief of the poor in Bath. Thomas Ken, the late-seventeenth-century Bishop of Bath and Wells, advised them to 'give [alms] in this place to those poor Christians, who come to the Bath for the Cure of the like Distempers as the Rich do, but have nothing to sustain them, or to defray the Charges of their Cure'.[22] Indeed, by Nash's day charitable donations were as obligatory as subscriptions to the balls, walks, assembly rooms and coffeehouses. In 1736 Thomas Goulding warned new arrivals to Bath that they would be importuned in turn 'for the Curates . . . , for the Charity-School . . . , for decay'd Gentlemen . . . , for the Poor Strangers . . . ' and finally 'for the Wretched Lepers'.[23]

Bath was geared to recovering and maintaining the health of the affluent, but illness and infirmity struck the poor as well, and they too came to Bath in droves. Cynicism on the part of local authorities contributed to the pressure on an already inadequate system of poor relief in Bath. As an act of Parliament passed late in Elizabeth's reign granted sick indigents the right to use the baths without charge, parishes found the temptation to use the pretext of illness to export their poor irresistible, so much so that Bath successfully pressed for the repeal of this act in 1714.[24] Its repeal might have thinned the numbers of the indigent in Bath somewhat, but the poor were with the Company always, and the fact that Bath's three parishes were no longer obliged to regard them as residents for the purposes of poor relief meant that even more were forced to beg for their sustenance from passers-by. The Company and others of the more affluent visitors to Bath were stricken with the crisis of conscience which daily confronts urban dwellers in our own time. Then as now, the impulse of the affluent was to keep the poor out of sight, an especially keen imperative in a place as devoted to high-end consumer culture as Bath was – and is still. Those who refused to give alms suffered persistent guilt over having left undone those things which they ought to have done, while those who did open their purses (often the same people on different days) laboured under a nagging suspicion that they had been hoodwinked. Cynics claimed that 'sturdy beggars' found the opportunities for mendicancy in Bath too good to resist. Ultimately, the solution was mediated public assistance administered through a corporate charity supported by public subscription.

In 1716, two years after legislation allowing the poor free use of the baths was repealed, the London banker Henry Hoare and Lady Elizabeth Hastings, Lady Huntingdon's sister-in-law, proposed building a general hospital in Bath for the poor. Seven years passed before a fundraising subscription was begun in autumn 1723, with Nash as one of six collectors. The prospectus published that October explained the hospital's objectives in revealing terms:

> *The principal End aim'd at by this Contribution, is to provide for poor Lepers, Cripples and other indigent Persons resorting to Bath for Cure, well recommended, and not otherwise provided for, and to discriminate real Objects of Charity from Vagrants and other Impostors, who crowd both the Church and Town, to the Annoyance of the Gentry resorting here; and who ought, by the Care of the Magistracy, to be Expell'd and Punish'd.*[25]

In one month a little over £270 was raised, and most of it entrusted to Humphrey Thayer to invest in South Sea Company bonds. Thayer, like his fellow hospital trustees Robert Gay and Ralph Allen, was already engaged in profitable real-estate development in Bath in the 1720s, and little was done other than to designate John Wood as the architect. By 1731 only £60 had been added to the sum in Thayer's hands. A decision in that year to admit those who donated at least £20 as governors of the hospital failed to attract donors, and in the next six years less than £50 was raised. The ten trustees, including Thayer, Gay, Allen, Nash and George Cheyne, publicized an estimate of £2,500 for building and furnishing the hospital according to Wood's design.

The problem was securing somewhere to build on. Robert Gay pledged a parcel of land near the Hot Bath, but when the planned hospital was enlarged without consulting him, he balked at donating a larger tract. Once opportunistic real-estate speculators muscled in, the deal was dead. When the hospital was finally built, it was on the site formerly occupied by the theatre, which closed in the wake of the Licensing Act of 1737. The site was unsuitable because of its small size and its location in a noisy street a considerable distance away – and uphill – from the springs.[26] Wood originally proposed to link a circular hospital with an improved bath complex, including renovated baths and an enlarged pump room, so that facilities for the affluent and the indigent would be under one roof in an 'Imperial Gymnasium'. Instead of being housed in facilities integrated with those for the Company, the charity patients were shunted into an inconspicuous corner of Bath under the borough walls. The location of a site was a spur to donations, however, as was the publication of Wood's modified design, and in less than a year funds for the General Hospital totalled £2,082, which approached the funding target closely enough for construction to begin in July 1738. It took nearly four years to build and opened in May 1742.

The General Hospital's charity patients were admitted through an exhaustive vetting process. Space was severely limited. For all of the publicity surrounding collections for and donations to the hospital,

38. William Oliver and Jeremiah Peirce examine prospective admissions to the General Hospital

it was chronically under-funded and consequently could not operate at full capacity. 'The Building is capacious enough to admit upwards of an hundred Patients,' John Penrose reported in 1766, 'but the Subscriptions and Benefactions will not maintain more than seventy; for which Reason the Governours do not think it adviseable at present to admit more than that number.' Prospective patients were required to have a medical diagnosis submitted to the medical staff of the hospital, who would then determine if the patient was a suitable candidate for admission. Soldiers and sailors could be admitted on the recommendation of their commanding officer. An approved patient was then placed on a waiting list and the ministers of her or his parish would be advised by letter once a vacancy arose. The patient would be expected to present this letter on arrival, along with £3, provided by the parish overseers of the poor, to cover the cost of return passage – or of burial. Anyone turning up at the hospital on spec without documentation and 'caution money' would be refused entry and turned over to the local authorities as a vagrant.

Once patients were admitted, their behaviour was carefully regulated. Male and female patients were kept rigorously separated, and foul or abusive language was forbidden, as was smoking or playing with cards or dice. The several dozen patients resident at any given time compensated for their lack of numbers by their visibility. '[E]ach of the Poor belonging to the Hospital,' Penrose related, 'wears on his or her Breast, in conspicuous manner, a circular Piece of brass, with the Words Bath Hospital, and a Number, on it.'[27] Donors watching from the Pump Room as the hospital residents were handed into the King's Bath could see their guineas at work, and should they fail to take the point, the patients were paraded to the Abbey at regular intervals for the charity sermons used to herald fundraising efforts.

The annual charity sermons for the hospital were cleverly calculated appeals which accomplished multiple publicity objectives. They established first of all that the hospital residents were uniformly deserving objects of charity, and second that the Company were morally obliged to contribute towards their maintenance and treatment. The Company assembled in the congregation were reminded that the poor who sought admittance to the hospital were the servants who had attended their affluence, the labourers who had helped to bring their wealth into being, and the soldiers and sailors who had protected it, and had often damaged their health in this line of duty. The dirty and dangerous labour of the poor residents was often contrasted with the idle and frivolous lives of their masters,[28] who were then expected to shift uncomfortably in their pews before disgorging suitably large sums. It was the publicity and intimacy of life among the Company at Bath that compelled its constituents to open their pocketbooks. When collection boxes for the General Hospital were installed at the Pump Room and the hospital itself, only very small sums were collected from them.[29] The publicity that by mid-century attended the annual collections from congregations, those of the establishment, dissenters and recusants alike, was an effective pressure tactic obliging partisans of church and chapel to match their outward show of piety with an equally conspicuous display of charity.

As treasurer to the hospital, Nash was its most conspicuous and energetic fundraiser. In the previous eight years, he had collected just over £250 during regular fund drives for the hospital, and donations through him constituted over half of the total collected. This amount was certainly considerable – at the upper end of five figures in modern British and American equivalents – but it seems modest considering that well over £8,000 was reportedly raised by the time that the hospital opened, and infinitesimal given Goldsmith's description of Nash's fund-raising tactics. The *Life* relates the story of the unidentified duchess who asked to be 'put down for a trifle', having no money on her, while Nash was soliciting donations at Wiltshire's. 'I will with pleasure, if your grace will tell me when to stop,' Nash offered, before blithely proceeding to transfer guineas from his own pocket into the crown of his white hat. The duchess grew progressively angrier as Nash dropped ten, twenty and then twenty-five guineas into his hat. (Guineas, incidentally, were gold coins and as such they were *heavy*, much more so than the ersatz sovereigns that load pocket change in Britain today. Walking around with a pocketful of twenty-five of them – at least – must have been a bit like carrying a brick.) Nash finally agreed to stop at thirty; later, in a better frame of mind, the duchess gave an additional ten, on condition that her donation be anonymous and the sum not mentioned.[30] Forty guineas at one blow from a single donor was no mean achievement, but it was an achievement Nash did not often repeat. In only two of some twenty collections recorded in the *Bath Journal* were his *total* solicitations in excess of forty guineas, and the mean was around fifteen. The anecdote of the duchess's forty guineas may have been intended to suggest that much more money was raised through Nash than was reported to the public. It certainly signalled his determination to be the most visible representative of the resort's new culture of charity as well as its established culture of amusement. In this objective, at least, he was successful. When Nash's statue was unveiled in the Pump Room in time for the autumn season in 1752, it surprised no one that he should be shown with a plan of the General Hospital, as if the whole enterprise had been his idea. The General Hospital, after all, contributed significantly to the comfort and convenience of the Company. It was a cosmetic charity which allowed well-heeled visitors to enjoy the spa's amusements and amenities unmolested by their consciences, secure in the belief that the legitimate medical needs of the deserving poor were being met. A relative handful of impoverished invalids were very well – and conspicuously – cared for, so that visitors now had an excuse to rebuff the remainder. More positively, however, the hospital fostered ties between the Company and the community at large that had not existed before, as it was a source of civic pride in which visitors, through their contributions to continuing fundraising efforts, could claim a share. In addition, it helped to remind an often dubious public of the medicinal character of the spa, an emphasis that critics like Thomas Goulding, Tobias Smollett and Alexander Sutherland continued to urge.

> *I should be glad to send you some news, but all the news of the place would be like the bills of Mortality, palsy four, gout six, fever one, and so on. We hear of nothing but 'Mr such-a-one is not abroad to-day.' 'Oh no,' says another poor gentleman, 'he dyed to-day.' Then another cries, 'My party was made for Quadrille to-night, but one of the gentlemen has had a second stroke of the palsy and cannot come; there is no depending on people, nobody minds engagments.' Indeed the only thing one can do one day one did not do the day before is to dye.*[31]

> *The Physicians here are very numerous, but very good-natur'd. To these charitable Gentlemen I owe, that I was cured, in a Week's time, of more Distempers than I ever had in my Life.*[32]

The Abbey ranked with the Pump and assembly rooms as one of the venues where the Company assembled *en masse* at regular intervals. It also forcefully reminded visitors of the resort's rationale – as it does still. A visit to the Abbey will disabuse twenty-first century visitors of the received wisdom that Georgian Bath was all about conspicuous consumption and conspicuous display, and that the supposed therapeutic value of the water was a transparent excuse for visits to its pleasure grounds. To register the point, they need not even pass within striking distance of the verger's desk, where, after an oppressively cheery 'Welcome to the Abbey!' they will be genially but firmly dunned for a donation. The objective is visible from just inside the west door: row upon row of memorial plaques on the north wall, over 600 in the Abbey in total, more than in any other church in the British Isles. To see them all, one must grease the verger's palm (yes, one must), pass into the nave and brave the sight of hideous contemporary altar frontals and pulpit hangings. Members of the Company bulk large among the recipients of memorials, among them Susannah Isham, who died at Bath in June 1726. Her father, the Tory politician Sir Justinian Isham, noted her passing in an uncharacteristically brief missive: 'I am in so great concern that I am able to write no more but that your Poor Sister Su died at the Bath upon Sunday last, where she is to be buried. I pray God I may live to see the death of no more of my Children.'[33]

Many families came to Bath with the objective of marrying their daughters there, but there were many others, such as the Ishams, who buried them there. As they lived in the days before refrigeration, formaldehyde or cremation, so people were buried where they died. The sheer density of the Abbey memorials testify that plenty of them did die, no great surprise, given that many of them were seriously ill when their arrival in Bath was heralded by the same Abbey bells that would ultimately announce their departure from this world. The therapeutic promise of the water, while the transparent excuse of some, was the last desperate hope of others, so that in Georgian Bath discomfort, disease, decrepitude and death were omnipresent spectres at the feast. Sir Justinian was not the only voluble Bath correspondent reduced to unaccustomed terseness when death intruded there to claim a relative or close friend.

Unless and until they resulted in death, however, infirmities, whether one's own or other people's, were prime fodder for correspondence and conversation. There was, for example, the hapless baronet and Member of Parliament (a patient of Dr Cheyne) who arrived in Bath suffering from 'an habitual *Diarrhoea,* attended with extreme *Flatulence* ... and *Indigestion*'.[34] In the spring season of 1749 the *Bath Journal* carried an alarming account of 'a Woman, in the Parish of Calne', about fifteen miles east of Bath, who 'voided a Stone, which was seven Inches long, and five broad'. Not the sort of item, one would have thought, to form matter for polite conversation at Pump, walks or assembly rooms, but it attracted enough notice and comment for the paper to run a clarification the very next week, soberly relating that 'The Stone (mention'd in our last ...) is seven Inches three Quarters in Circumference longways, and Five and a Half broadways, and weighs about three Ounces.'[35] Part of the attraction that Bath continued to exert on those with real and imagined illnesses was the ready availability of sympathetic interlocutors, and for this reason there were no doubt full complements of hypochondriac visitors who had no intention of getting better. There were also patients susceptible to the psychosomatic effect of the water, or the iatrogenic effect of a physician's attention. If they believed that the water would make them better, or if their physician told them that they were getting better, they felt better. Mineral water, as water, was certainly healthier than anything else a Bath convalescent might drink.

At the time of writing, it is not yet possible to bathe in the water, although the imminent opening of the new 'Thermae Spa', built with National Heritage funds, will allow visitors to bathe in a restored Cross Bath and Hot Bath, as well as the glass-enclosed 'New Royal Baths'. User fees are steep – £10 for a soak in the Cross Bath and more for the others – in consideration of the unlikelihood of awkward encounters with either charity hospital patients or lepers. One can still drink the water in the Pump Room for the more manageable sum of fifty pence. No one has described the taste more accurately than Celia Fiennes: 'its very hot and tastes like the water that boyles eggs'.[36] It is difficult to believe that this warm, cloudy, lightly sulphuric water – much milder than hot mineral spring water available elsewhere – made visitors like George Grenville 'giddy' and thus unable to write long letters.[37] Of course, Grenville, if he was typical of 'water drinkers' in Georgian Bath, drank at least a pint a day. William Oliver recommended a daily dosage anywhere from one to three pints, and in some cases as much as two quarts, taken in most cases half a pint at a time.[38]

39. The King's Bath in 1765. Compare this scene with Thomas Johnson's drawing. Hospital patients bathed here with humbler visitors. The Pump Room is at left

In spite of their professional differences, Bath's medical community energetically advertised the spa by touting 'the healthy qualities of the waters', and, as the literary scholar Simon Varey asserts, played as important a part in the development of Bath as Nash, John Wood or Ralph Allen.[39] Bath's medical providers knew better, or in Cheyne's case learned better, than to prescribe water other than that of Bath. Locals were so incensed at Cheyne for sending Lady Walpole (wife of the prime minister) to Spa in the Austrian Netherlands that he 'durst scarce walk the streets', and a rumour made the rounds that he was directing the Prince of Orange, due to pay a visit later that year, to Bristol instead of Bath. '[T]he lower people think it better to let people die here,' he protested, 'than send them elsewhere for their recovery.'[40] Moreover, Bath physicians' recommendations concerning the appropriate timing of their patients' treatment coincided to a suspicious degree with the autumn and spring social seasons. Smollett was puzzled that 'by the peculiar sagacity of the learned' in Bath, 'the bathing time is limited to the most severe season of the year'.[41] Doctors usually knew better than to recommend courses of therapy that would interfere with the amusements, perhaps suspecting that their patients, unless truly incapacitated, would not allow their doctors to impede them from entertaining themselves, as Sarah Scott's companion Mrs Coles did. '[C]ould an Old Woman cloathed in Gray,' Sarah's sister cattily remarked, 'have done a more serious thing than to have taken physick on a Ball night[?]'[42] Nash modelled an appropriately cavalier attitude towards medicine. When Cheyne asked if he had followed his prescription, Nash retorted (reportedly) that he would very likely have broken his neck had he 'followed' it, having flung it out of a second-storey window.[43] As ambivalent as visitors may have been towards any medical advice they received, the medical community of the resort were useful to them in other ways. For members of the Company to put themselves under the care of the right Bath physician was to secure an entrée of sorts. Bath's medical practitioners were very well placed, for example, to procure the most desirable accommodation (in fact, like many if not most Bath householders, retailers and professionals, they kept sets of lodgings in their houses). Dr George Cheyne kept his eye out for rooms for Lady Huntingdon. 'Let me know how long you shall stay here and what rooms you shall want,' he wrote to her in August of 1734, 'for the best are beginning to be secured already.'[44]

Many patients' health would genuinely improve, especially if they avoided being 'physicked', as Sarah Scott was in the winter of 1753. She put herself in the care of a Dr Hartley, who subjected her to blood-letting (which she thought had 'been of a little service to me') and gave her medicines twice a day. 'I find there is a small quantity of mercury in them,' she wrote to her sister, 'but of so innocent a sort as not to confine me, as a proof of which I am now going to the Play.' Three weeks later, she had to apologise for not having written:

> *My poor body has been entirely void of any [strength]. My head was excessively bad all last week. ... [O]n sunday ... about the time of dinner I was taken immoderately sick, fainted away, to which a convulsion fit succeeded, which lasted an hour & half, without the least return to my senses, my speech was some time*

> *longer returning, & I have ever since been so faint I have scarcely been able to speak much less to do any thing ...*

Her physician was concerned, of course, but not unduly alarmed by these developments. As she reassured her sister, he

> *saw no reason to apprehend any danger; my disorder seemd a weakness he coud by no means account for, nor comprehend, but there was no appearance of any thing dangerous; & he gives me hopes that when I have recover'd this shock I may perhaps find myself in an easier state of health than before.*

Sarah's sister, the redoubtable Elizabeth Montagu, reposed an equally unjustifiable degree of confidence in Dr Hartley and urged her sister to follow all of his directives.[45]

Hartley, by Bath standards, was a fairly conventional practitioner. George Cheyne, on the other hand, beloved as he was, struck many of his contemporaries as highly unconventional, even eccentric. As a pioneering advocate of preventive medicine, Cheyne was at least a century and a half ahead of his time. 'Most Men know when they are ill,' he told his readers, 'but very few when they are well. And yet it is most certain, that 'tis easier to *preserve* Health, than to *recover* it; and to *prevent* Diseases, than to *cure* them.'[46] He was an early exponent of now commonplace medical beliefs, arguing that mental well-being was linked to physical well-being, that vegetables were healthier food than red meat, that exercise was beneficial and that excessive drinking was unhealthy. His *Essay of Health and Long Life*, as his biographer notes, 'was quite unlike the multitude of books produced by his Bath colleagues ..., all of whom extolled Bath's virtues but gave little practical advice'. Cheyne, on the other hand, gave 'specific instructions the patient could follow'. As a result, the *Essay* was spectacularly successful and had six printings in 1725 alone.[47] By the middle of the century, it had gone into its tenth edition, and made Cheyne a wealthy man – because his advice worked.

Much of this advice, however, ran counter to everything the Bath of

Beau Nash stood for. In his 1733 treatise *The English Malady*, Cheyne took particular aim at the habits of the elite, which as a resident of Bath he had ample opportunity to observe. His topic was 'melancholia', which we would call depression, a condition that he linked to luxury. 'A debilitating, luxurious diet' in turn 'must necessarily beget an Ineptitude for Exercise', and too much leisure depressed the spirits. When, as in Bath, '*Assemblies, Musick Meetings, Plays, Cards* and *Dice* are the only Amusements', a lax habit of body necessarily followed. Elites had much to learn from their inferiors. '[T]he *Food* and *Physick* proper and peculiar to the middling Sort of each *Country* and *Climate*,' Cheyne argued, 'is the best of any possible for the Support of the Creatures ... placed there.'[48] He went even further in expostulating with a sceptical Samuel Richardson in December 1741:

> *If you enter upon a Vegetable Diet, will you not live higher than Nine Parts of Ten of most of the People of Great Britain? All below Farmers scarce taste Animal Food Six Times a Year and the Bacon most Persons who are Farmers eat almost no more than you will of Butter and Salt of the same Nature with their Pork. Cheese is generally the highest Food they get and yet one Tenant is generally supposed to out-live Three or Four Landlords at an Average.*[49]

Cheyne was often taxed with his advocacy of vegetarianism, which he viewed (correctly) as a particularly efficacious preventive measure against gout, which the medical historian Roy Porter has characterised as a 'patrician malady', as status-enhancing as it was excruciating.[50] According to Goldsmith, Cheyne urged the vegetable diet on Nash, who then 'would swear, that his design was to send half the world grazing like Nebuchadnezzar'. On another occasion, Nash was supposed to have told Cheyne, 'my neighbour's Cow ... is a better physician than you, and a superior judge of plants, notwithstanding you have written so learnedly on the vegetable diet'.[51] In fact, Cheyne was too well aware of the ingrained dietary habits of his patients to recommend that any of them abstain from meat, or alcohol for that matter, except under close supervision and as a last resort. Abstinence occasioned 'the worst kind of Hysterical and Hypocondriacal Disorders', which we might recognise as withdrawal symptoms, 'and all their black and dismal Consequences ... which is a Disease far worse than the *Gout* it self'.[52]

For a number of reasons, Cheyne's work was outstanding publicity for Bath in comparison to the writings of his medical colleagues, as many of his recommendations coincided serendipitously with patterns in the demography of its clientele and in its physical development. The water, to Cheyne, was 'an Antidote, to almost all the *Chronical* Distempers of an *English* Constitution and Climate', but it was an especially effective solvent of the 'urinous salts' that he believed, not incorrectly, to be the cause of gout (actually caused by a build-up of uric acid, which then forms crystallised deposits on bone tissue, especially around joints). By incorporating Bath water into a therapeutic regimen for gout in particular,[53] Cheyne was effectively promoting the spa to an elite clientele. He also held Bath's water to be the best medium in which to dissolve the more astringent, 'vitriolic' or 'fetid' medicines, especially at cold or temperate times of year (neatly coinciding, again, with Bath's own season).[54] He advised his readers that their dwellings should not be on top of hills, or near large bodies of water, mines or swampy and damp areas, 'but either in a *champaign* Country, or on the *Side* of a small Eminence, sheltered from the *North* and *East* Winds',[55] which describes, more or less, Queen Square and the Circus, John Wood's developments north and west of the borough wall. Cheyne's recommendations on exercise were also congruent with the direction of building as well as the daily round that Wood and Goldsmith later described. Walking was the 'most natural' exercise, followed by riding horseback, for which invalids could permissibly substitute riding in coaches. Walking up a gentle gradient (as a visitor lodged in the Circus or the streets surrounding it would ultimately have to do) was superb exercise for the lungs, although Cheyne also recommended (rather disconcertingly) talking in a loud voice. Badminton, played in the assembly rooms during the day, was good for promoting perspiration. Otherwise sedentary people should exercise two to three hours a day, one half before dinner, the main midday meal, and the other before bed.[56]

> Reading *must be light, entertaining, and diverting* ... Conversation *must be easy and agreeable, without Disputes or Contradiction. The* Diversion *innocent and inexpensive, else the Remorse and Reflexion afterwards will do infinitely more Prejudice than the present* Amusement *can recompense; and it must end at seasonable Hours.*[57]

Subtly and otherwise, Cheyne also pointed the way to the gradual reform of manners and a changing cultural tone in Bath.

~

As important as its baths and their promoters in the medical community were, Bath would not have grown in the way it did in the first half of the eighteenth century if it had not held any other attraction than the therapeutic properties of the water. It took nearly thirty years for a critical mass of investors and developers to accept what observers like Ned Ward had been saying from the previous century, that Bath was better known as a pleasure ground than a health spa, and it was the pursuit of amusement, polite and otherwise, that was driving the numbers of visitors to the resort. By the middle of the century, there were voices calling for a re-emphasis on the resort's therapeutic function, which had been long neglected. Tobias Smollett protested:

> *The corporation of* Bath *seems to have forgot that the ease and plenty they now enjoy, and to which their fathers were strangers, are owing to their Waters; and that an improvement upon their Baths, would, by bringing a greater concourse of company to their town, perpetuate these blessings to them and to their posterity.*

He tacitly reminded his readers that humbler folk than the Company visited Bath, and in fact they may have done so in greater numbers. The dilapidated condition of the baths was of particular concern, especially the King's Bath, long ignored as a plebeian venue. It was filthy, as anyone could see from the residue which adhered to the sides of the bath, and it was exposed not only to the elements but to the gaze 'to the eyes of all the company, in the Pump-room, as well as to those of the footmen and common people, whose curiosity leads them to look over the walls'. Surely women, even plebeians, would not care to 'mingle with male patients, to whose persons and complaints they are utter strangers', in a bath into which '[d]iseased persons of all ages, sexes, and conditions, are promiscuously admitted'.[58] Smollett recommended that the baths be redesigned to take account of what he viewed as advances in medical understanding, and that new regulations be imposed to segregate the sexes in the baths, standardise the fees paid to attendants and extend the hours of bathing. His writing was well timed, as the Corporation was willing to listen. In January 1753 they set alternate days for men and women to bathe at all four baths, adopting Smollett's regulations (on this point, at least) wholesale.

Other more gradual changes were already afoot. We have already seen how Elizabeth Montagu's younger sister, Sarah Scott, was in robustly poor health all her life, and under the supervision of her physician, Dr Hartley, was more than usually subjected to courses of drinking Bath water, in addition to mercury-laced ministrations that did little to improve her condition. So dependent did she become on the largely psychosomatic effects of Bath water that, in 1749, she took the once unthinkable step of staying there over the summer to continue her therapy in the off-season.[59] Finally, in 1756, she purchased a house that had once belonged to Dr William Oliver in Batheaston, three miles to the north-east. It was here that she settled, and when she periodically ventured into Bath itself, she had a convenient pied-à-terre in the house of her cousin Lady Barbara ('Bab') Montagu in Beaufort Square. It was in Batheaston that Elizabeth Montagu now stayed on her visits to Bath, rather than her customary lodgings near the Orange Grove.

There is less and less observation of the Bath scene in their letters. Sarah rarely went to the assembly rooms and took little interest in anything that happened there.

In its broad outlines, Sarah Scott's decision to settle in Bath was typical of a pattern that emerged in the resort after the middle of the century. Bath gradually acquired a larger and larger community of more or less permanent residents, such as Sarah Scott, Lady Bab Montagu, James Quin the actor and William Pitt. Nash's scepticism over the building of the Circus was portentous; he could not understand why Wood was building houses intended for long-term residents rather than short-term seasonal lodgers. Wood and, more importantly, Allen were from the late 1740s envisioning Bath as not just a pleasant place to visit, but as a pleasant place to *live.* Wood was not thinking of tourists when he wrote of the wide availability of provisions at relatively low prices in Bath. For elderly or infirm retirees, Bath's location in a valley relatively close to the shore protected it from extremes of temperature. And there were certainly plenty of doctors.

Appropriately enough, Cheyne, the most progressive of them, was an early promoter of Bath as a pleasant place to settle as well as to visit. In putting Bath forward as a residential community rather than merely a seasonal resort, he prefigured Wood's *Essay* by over twenty years. In 1720 he told his readers that Bath was

> *the fittest place in* Britain *to spend their Life-time with the greatest Ease and Pleasure; take all the Advantages of the Place together, ... the regular way of living; the Excellency of the Provisions; the Warmness, Cleanness and Neatness of the Housing; the Conveniency of the free, fresh and open Air of the neighbouring Downs for Exercise; the Easiness of the Amusements; and the Advantage of what Conversation one desires; I say, taking all these Advantages together, I can affirm, from near twenty Years Experience, without Suspicion of Flattery, or Fear of Contradiction, that* Bath *is the Place.*[60]

The Bath envisioned by Cheyne was the sort of place that the Hampshire gentleman John Ambrose could contemplate retiring to in 1768, with a real prospect of passing 'the Remainder of my days in quietness'.[61] The *New Bath Guide*, published annually from 1762, heralded the city's transition from seasonal spa to residential centre, indicating in its first edition that 'a great number of gentleman have taken houses and reside here all the year.' Ten years later, Ambrose numbered among the 'many ladies and gentlemen, who formerly only paid it a yearly visit,' but had become permanent residents.[62] John Ambrose was in good company, but it was not the Company of Nash's day. As crowded as the balls, walks and assembly rooms still were, the collective solidarity that had bound visitors of means was quickly unravelling.

9
Old Beaux Knash

Didst thou increase in virtue as in size;
Were lux'ry banish'd, with each baneful vice,
Th'infernal arts of scandal, cards, and dice;
The vagrant herds that every street infest,
And insolence, with vigorous care suppress'd;
Did no base miscreants, to themselves unjust,
By mean exactions liberal minds disgust;
From distant countries Thanes in crowds should fly,
Proud in thy domes to shun the winter sky.[1]

John Wood's Circus, once completed in spite of Nash's speculation, was a symbol of the new direction that Bath was taking, if these verses written on its completion in 1758 are any guide. Its evocation of classical virtue was a hopeful sign that Bath would indeed become the city that Alexander Sutherland described, where '[s]obriety, frugality, and simplicity reign', and where '[y]oung rakes who, in town, spend their time in taverns or stews, hardly find a moment for either'.[2] It seemed to many contemporaries that any prospect of a more wholesome atmosphere at Bath would be undermined by the Company's pet vices, and especially by gaming. Bath was already becoming the family resort of Jane Austen's novels, and gaming was not a family-friendly activity. In a satirical piece that appeared in 1750, a mother at Bath finds her nine-year-old son seated at the EO table, where he proudly announces that he has won a shilling. Her only remarks on 'seeing the pretty Infant so innocently engaged' are that 'you are better in a Room, you don't wear your Breeches out so fast, and you can't get so much Cold: you have better Luck than I; be sure you mind how you play, For I must go to my Party'.[3] By the 1740s Bath was the centre of high-stakes gaming, and gaming operatives there led the way in concocting stratagems to flout anti-gaming legislation. Consequently, Bath became the focus of efforts at suppression. As it happened, new directions in Bath's development as a resort community coincided with initiatives on the national level to effect the decline of the spa's gaming culture.

Under the Gaming Act of 1710, gaming losses in excess of £10 were not legally enforceable, and, if paid at the time of loss, were recoverable by civil suit if the action were filed within three months of the loss. Since privilege of Parliament was disallowed under the gaming acts, peers and members of the House of Commons would not be able to put off litigation, as they normally would while Parliament was in session. Additionally, winnings over £10 were punished by stiff fines of five times the amount won. This legislation resulted in periodic crackdowns in Bath. In 1713 magistrates there fined and jailed the operator of an illegal gaming house and fined a pair of sharpers caught with doctored dice. In 1731, possibly in the wake of the well-publicized, gaming-related suicide of Fanny Braddock, the local authorities made overtures towards suppressing faro.[4] In most cases, however, laws addressing gaming, like those against duelling, were more honoured in the breach than the observance. Moreover, legislative efforts to curb gaming had the unintended effect of giving gaming greater cachet. Since winners could not go to law to collect, paying one's losses became more a matter of honour than ever. A refusal to pay, or, worse yet, a legal action to recover losses, was tantamount to an accusation of cheating. Even opponents of gaming for stakes admitted that it was an established cultural practice sanctioned by the involvement of elites. No money saved or recovered through the provisions of any legislation could possibly compensate a punter for the loss of face inevitably involved in confronting those who had won his (or just as often, her) money. A cautionary anecdote, liberally fictionalised but illustrating conventional assumptions about the Bath scene, tells the tale of a young military officer who in a drunken stupor loses £2,000 to a notorious sharper. When his father, citing the gaming act, refuses to honour the promissory note in the sharper's hands, the young man finds himself fighting a duel in which he is 'dangerously wounded'.[5]

The reasons behind the ineffectiveness of the gaming acts were acknowledged even by their proponents, one writer noting after the very comprehensive act of 1745 that passing or even enforcing legislation would be to no purpose while the insincerity and hypocrisy of the ruling class was evident for all to see. The Thomas Harrisons and Catherine Lindseys of the world were privy to the secret vices of elites, and what magistrate would not balk at prosecuting keepers of gaming houses when he saw them 'caressed by his superiors'? Neither could it escape anyone's attention that every gaming act from 1710 on specifically exempted royal residences from its provisions. The language of the Patriot Whig opposition was even employed to depict gaming arising from the collusion of the ministerialist 'court' in the corruption of the young. 'Politicians,' it was said,

> *never discouraged Practices of this Kind [gaming], because they frequently tended to the Support of political Designs; young Gentlemen of great Parts having been drawn in thereby to ruin their Fortunes, and been forced to become Slaves to the ambitious Designs of these great Men, though never so detrimental to the Publick.*[6]

Opponents of gaming persisted nevertheless, and if official indifference was as determined as this rhetoric represented, the persistence, and persistent success, of efforts for ever newer and more-improved gaming acts were all the more remarkable.

It was already clear that indemnifying punters against excessive losses was not going to put a dent into deep play. An act of 1699 had forbidden lotteries on the grounds that the odds of winning or losing were not clear to those who bought tickets. Proceeding from that premise, the Gaming Act of 1739 classified three specific card games – ace of hearts, faro and basset – along with the dicing game of hazard as illegal lotteries under the terms of the earlier act. Gaming interests aggressively sought and exploited loopholes in the law, and successive gaming acts were passed to eliminate each of these. When the simpler game of passage was promoted as a replacement for the proscribed hazard, a new gaming act forbade all games involving dice with the exception of backgammon. Gaming establishments at Bath and elsewhere thus fell back on roulette (or 'roly-poly'), which was not played with cards or dice. A legislative response was delayed for five years while the dust from the fall of Robert Walpole settled, but the effort was comprehensive when it came. Roulette was classified as an illegal lottery, together with any game involving numbers or 'figures'. By this last term the pips on cards and dice were clearly understood, but gaming interests quickly noticed that the act did not mention letters of the alphabet. Thus was born EO, a modification of roulette devised specifically to evade the technicalities of the 1745 Gaming Act. Instead of numbers around the rim of the wheel, as in roulette, letters – E for 'even' and O for 'odd' – were represented. House and punters alike seized upon the expedient with enthusiasm, if we can believe Charles Burney's report of seeing 1,000 guineas in a heap at an EO table in Bath in the season of 1747–8.[7]

As it turned out, in developing the expedient of EO, gaming interests were whistling in the dark. Gaming opponents had perfected a formula for the effective suppression of games of chance, at least in public venues. A new feature of gaming acts from 1739 onward was a provision which fined local authorities £10 for every case in which they were guilty of failing to enforce the provisions of these acts. It was fruitless to threaten local officials in this way, however, without giving them the means to do what the law expected. The 1745 act finally empowered equity courts to order the repayment of gaming losses, a previously disputed point which had hamstrung the earlier legislation.

40. Dicing games such as that shown in Philip Mercier's The Gaming Table *were outlawed by successive Gaming Acts*

It also authorised magistrates to subpoena witnesses to violations, so 'that Servants, Waiters, Standers-by and Players themselves are liable to be summoned and obliged to appear, and give Evidence'. All that was needed now was a test case to demonstrate to local officials that gaming could be suppressed in the face of pressure from gaming interests. Where better than Bath?

> *In the City of Bath this pernicious Practice was grown to an enormous Height, the keepers of those Houses were caressed by People of great Rank and great Fortune, Persons who had great Influence over Tradesmen, and upon whom the Magistrates of that City had no small Dependance; this made these People think themselves secure, and thought they were not in Danger of being punished, or suppressed; but to the honour of the Magistrates, they soon found themselves mistaken; the Magistrates did their Duty,*

> *and that most abominable Scene of Gaming and Fraud was totally suppressed.*[8]

If gaming could be suppressed in Bath, surely it could be suppressed anywhere. Then again, if gaming were to be rooted out anywhere, it had to be eliminated in Bath first. EO signalled the determination of gaming interests in Bath to skirt the law and there was undoubtedly enormous pressure on Bath magistrates to at least appear vigilant. Once there was a legal consensus that EO was covered by the 1745 act, the local authorities in Bath staged a well-publicised crackdown. In January 1750 a private gaming room near Westgate was raided and at least a dozen punters arrested. The table was seized and burned in the street outside. During the next autumn season, a series of additional raids closed private tables that had since proliferated.[9] Magistrates at Tunbridge Wells took similar action the next year; 'The Justices of Peace have done great service to the imprudent part of our company by prohibiting Gaming,' Elizabeth Montagu reported to her husband that summer. She indicated, however, what she thought to be the real intent of the measure in praising the local authorities 'on acc[oun]t of the servants who have one temptation less to be idle & bad'.[10] These very conspicuous efforts on the part of local officials generated enough publicity to satisfy reformers of manners that magistrates in Bath and elsewhere were taking their duty seriously. The suppression of EO in Bath in particular was highlighted as a singular incidence of official vigilance. One raid was clearly timed to coincide with the King's birthday on 30 October, ordinarily observed with a ball and other public celebrations which were dutifully recounted in the newspapers. The *Bath Journal,* after describing the ringing of bells and firing of cannon, the Corporation dinner in an illuminated Guildhall, followed by entertainments for gentry and nobility at both assembly rooms, soberly related that 'the Sheriffs went (by Order of the Mayor) to the several Places in this City, where *EO* Tables were kept, and suppress'd the Playing at any of them'. The paper discounted a rumour 'that several Ladies cry'd, when they heard the News'.[11] In case any doubt remained that Bath meant business about its prohibition of gaming, visitors in the very next season were greeted with a pamphlet '[i]n which Notice is taken of the Suppressing of the favourite Game of EO'.[12]

Visitors who wished to gamble for high stakes would always find the means to do so, if they were sufficiently wealthy and well connected. One Bath resident identified Lord Chesterfield among the players in the autumn season of 1754 who 'shut themselves up from the World that no one may see their folly in losing the sums of money which they are so kind as to distribute daily among sharpers'.[13] An anti-gaming tract of 1757 (an epistolary adaptation of the Fanny Braddock story) implied that deep play went on unabated at Bath.[14] Although high-stakes banking games were not completely eliminated, they were banished from public venues such as the assembly rooms and coffeehouses, and therefore removed from Nash's sphere of influence.

For Nash, the writing was on the wall. Verses in the *Bath Journal* indignantly denied suggestions in '*some Lines handed about*' that Nash was complicit in the management of the EO syndicate:

> *... why the Invective 'gainst* generous *NASH?*
> *Who ne'er, but with HONOUR, augmented his* Cash.
> *His Soul is* too great, *and* too noble *his Mind,*
> *Than to* herd *with the Rooks, or to* prey *on Mankind.*
> *'Tis plain then, O BATH! that of Heaven thou'rt the Care,*
> *Since NASH still* directs *thee, and ATWOOD's* thy
> Mayor.[15]

Nash strove to link his name with the reforming magistrates, even sitting with them through sermons 'on the Michiefs of Immoderate Gaming'.[16] It helped that the last, and most effective, of the gaming acts stipulated that the portion of fines which did not go to informants would find its way to the coffers of the Bath General Hospital. His diminished income had already made him vulnerable to attacks on his integrity. In April 1748, he was compelled to defend himself from the charge of embezzling from the subscriptions to the assembly rooms:

> *I think it hard, after above Forty Years being a Fool, and Slave to the Publick, I should be accus'd of getting Money by the Publick SUBSCRIPTIONS; I now appeal in the Publick Rooms, who receive the Money; to the Musick, who are constantly paid by the Receivers, if ever they were defrauded of a Shilling; or, that I ever touch'd a Six-penny Piece of it. Indeed, when there was any small Surplus left, those that think I got any of it, may find it in the Hospital Charity-Book. ... It has cost me more Money annually, on the Publick Account, than any Ten that ever came to Bath; And if it was not for the Sake of the Bath, and Company, I would leave 'em to the Confusion I found them in.*[17]

Nash's protestations of innocence did nothing to abate these accusations. In December 1751 the *Bath Journal* reported a strict accounting of the 'Subscription for the Musick at the Pump and Balls, and Rooms', challenging 'Fools and Lyars' to 'find out what is sunk in this Account', adding that Nash had paid four guineas towards 'the Musick Books'.[18] Within a decade of Nash's death, it was not only assumed but openly advertised that the very subscriptions under contention in his day would provide the Master of Ceremonies with the bulk of his income.

Ultimately, Nash was forced to show his hand, confirming what many of his contemporaries had long suspected. If there was a signal that the gaming culture of Bath was seriously ailing if not dead, it was Nash's desperate attempt to recover – at law – what would have been ill-gotten gains had he been paid as he thought he deserved. Consequently, the introduction of EO is also the only innovation at Bath for which sufficient documentation exists to give Nash all the credit he is due. Nash died in a state of litigation against all of the proprietors of assembly rooms in Bath and Tunbridge Wells. His suits contended that, in the wake of the 1745 act, Nash, at the behest of the proprietors, consulted attorneys about the legality of EO and, receiving favourable reports, ordered EO tables for each of the assembly rooms in Bath and Tunbridge from William Fenton, a London cabinet-maker, at a cost of £25 per table. Nash alleged that in exchange for acting as intermediary, and for continuing to attract visitors to the rooms, each of the proprietors was to allow him a share of the proceeds from EO – 20 per cent at Wiltshire's and Simpson's. This arrangement, Nash disclosed, was largely identical to silent partnerships he had held with the operators of other gaming houses at Bath, citing in particular the examples of an EO table at Morgan's Coffeehouse and the 'Faro Bank' at Lindsey's (as Wiltshire's was called until 1737). In each of the first two years after EO was introduced, John Wiltshire paid Nash £170, but 'considerably less' in 1748, due to a decreased volume of visitors. Nash then claimed that Wiltshire and Simpson jointly offered him an annuity of £100 in lieu of his one-fifth share, which he refused.[19] Each of the defendants denied that Nash was ever to have any fixed percentage of the 'take' from EO, and would only admit that Nash received periodic gifts of cash in recognition of his services. More to the point, the defendants, in answering, stripped away all manner of vital fictions that had sustained Bath's amusement culture. At the same time that they confessed their belief that EO was indeed illegal under the terms of the gaming acts, they questioned what was supposed to be unquestionable, the institutionality of Nash's social authority.[20] This public abjuration of his sovereign status was an injury he could not long survive, either figuratively or, as it turned out, literally.

~

Trembling with Palsies, and decrepit age
Let N[as]h stand foremost in the crowded page.
That child of eighty! own'd without dispute,
Thro' all the Realms of Fiddling, absolute:
Alas! Old Dotard, is it fit for thee
To couple dancing Fools at eighty-three?
Go, get thee to thy Grave, we're tired all
To see thee still, still tottering round a Ball.[21]

In Nash's case, reversal of fortune was cruelly timed. Without the means to keep up appearances – and appearances were everything to Nash – he began to show wear and tear, and look his age. Nash's age had always been an important adjunct of his public persona. While it advanced, it did so imperceptibly, and he always seemed to be agreeably but indeterminately past his prime. Three undergraduates visiting Bath had called him a 'batter'd old beau' when he was only fifty – but in 1725 the late middle age in which he seemed to be suspended suited him very well. Once Nash's image dominated the Pump and assembly rooms, and decorated fans, handkerchiefs and snuffboxes, he was as ubiquitous and ageless as Chairman Mao in Beijing. Even once he began to age perceptibly, he did not lose his appeal. Nash, according to one observer in 1736, looked 'younger than he did about 20 years ago', and another commentator years later named him one of the finest-looking old men he had ever seen.[22] His inevitable decrepitude was the more striking as a result, and seemed to come on suddenly without warning or mercy. Once Nash entered his eighties, his age began to be a topic of conversation. Horace Walpole saw a wager in the betting book at White's on whether Nash or Colley Cibber, the octogenarian Poet Laureate, would be the first to die.[23]

For the last several years of his life, Nash had suffered 'fits' – seizures of one kind or another, possibly strokes or even cardiac arrests. The fact that the seizures we know about occurred in the rooms demonstrated his continuing dedication to his position, and signalled to the Company that the end (of what, precisely?) was near. A 'fit' at Tunbridge in August 1753 convinced Elizabeth Montagu that he would soon relinquish his 'empire over Mankind'.[24] Nash recovered by the following spring, only to get gout in both feet. He insisted on going to the assembly rooms anyway, although he struggled with the unfamiliar cane – 'he puts his Leg down first and rests his Weight on it,' George Scott reported, 'and then touches the Ground with his Stick'.[25] After this bout of illness, Nash was markedly less energetic in his collections for the General Hospital, which now averaged only four or five guineas, and there were occasions when he had no donations to report. In March 1760, he survived another seizure in Wiltshire's Rooms. 'I cannot but think unhappily for him,' Scott wrote, 'as he is at best hardly alive.'[26] By October he was unable to walk. '[H]e is now carried about in an elbow Chair with Poles between two Chair-men,' Scott reported, and Mary Delany saw Nash ('the poor wretch') 'wheeled into the Rooms' to settle a dispute at the ball.[27]

By that late date it was happy for Nash that his authority was invoked at all, for poverty and decrepitude had already sapped his influence even over the arrangements for the balls. In 1754 the Wiltshires and the Simpsons began to schedule the balls across three seasons, each with its own subscription, and introduced new charges of half a guinea a head for men and a crown for women. These rates were less than the 'household' subscription of two guineas, but were assessed on more visitors. No longer would men receive extra ball tickets to dispense as patronage to women of their acquaintance or whose acquaintance they wished to make; women would now have to pay, or be paid for, themselves. We, of course, would tend to see this development as more egalitarian; women could now join the amusements in their own right and not as guests of the men. Contemporaries were more likely to complain, along with Sarah Scott, of the 'insolence' with which Walter Wiltshire and Charles Simpson insisted on the new tariffs.[28] For others, it was an ominous sign of change. 'Mr Nash has lost his power,' John Archer wrote, 'as the gentlemen have carried on a subscription for the balls contrary to his inclinations.'[29]

Nash was ill equipped emotionally and dispositionally to deal with the physical (and increasingly mental) infirmity which now beset him. He was heard to utter dire prophecies of the chaos that would envelop Bath once he was gone. A rumour that James Quin, the celebrated actor who had recently retired to Bath, had been approached about taking on the mantle as Master of Ceremonies sent Nash over the edge. Relations between Quin and Nash were already strained, as the actor, in seeking to broker a settlement between Nash and Simpson and Wiltshire, had come to believe Nash was making unreasonable demands. Nash received a copy of a badly spelt and punctuated letter purportedly sent by Quin to Lord Chesterfield soliciting support for his bid to displace Nash. The letter is dated from Bath 3 October 1760, only ten days before Quin's deposition

41. James Quin in Hogarth's portrait from earlier in the actor's career. After his retirement to Bath, he repeatedly declined offers to succeed Nash as MC

in the case of *Nash* v. *Wiltshire*. 'Old beaux Knash has mead himselfe so disagreeable to all the companey that comes here to Bath,' it began, 'that ... the best companey declines to come to Bath on his acctt.' When Nash berated one young woman for refusing to dance, 'the companey was so much offended ... that not one Lady more, would dance a minueat that night'. The country dances were dominated by haberdashers, mechanics and innkeepers, in contrast to the squadrons of duchesses and countesses that had once appeared at the first ball of the season. Nash 'by his' pride and extravigancis has out lived his' reasein' and 'it would be happy for thiss' city that he was ded'.[30] Fateful words, these.

Perhaps the letter, which George Scott and Goldsmith were certain was a forgery, was the work of Simpson, or one of the Wiltshires, or their supporters; perhaps Nash held it in reserve to discredit Quin's testimony (Quin deponed that Nash had offered to settle with the Wiltshires for an annuity of £100, but had then killed the deal with an additional demand for £350 in legal fees[31]). Nash, according to Quin's biographer, was never satisfied that the actor had no designs on his position and nothing to do with the letter, and time for a reconciliation proved very short. Nash's last attack occurred just as the winter season of 1761 was getting under way. He was in the assembly rooms among the card players on 8 February – a Sunday, as Philip Doddridge and the Countess of Huntingdon might have noted with satisfaction – when he collapsed in his chair. Four days later he was dead.

~

View him in every various Station,
You'll find none like him in the Nation;
GARRICK himself wou'd scarce have ventur'd,
To play the Parts in him concenter'd:
The Beau, the Scholar, Courtier, Cit,
The Man of Honour, and the Wit,
Though not a Bully, bravely blunt,
Nor apt to give, nor take Affront!
The Moralist, the Man of Pleasure;
But not... a Hoarder up of Treasure.
There ne'er was such a Contradiction;
He seem'd both real, and a Fiction ... [32]

Easter was early that year, so that 17 February, a Tuesday, was in the middle of Lent – not really the most appropriate time to bury Nash, who might rather have chosen Shrove Tuesday, even if it meant shuffling off his mortal coil and joining the choir invisible a fortnight earlier. The eight bells of the Abbey, muffled for the occasion, pealed in solemn parody of their greeting of visitors who arrived in private coaches. The coffin, adorned with blue-violet pall and black plumes, was carried out of the little house in Saw Close where Nash had been reduced to taking rooms, and where his body had lain for the last four days. It was five in the afternoon, so even if the day had been sunny, the weather was negated by the impending winter darkness. The cortège may have wound into Westgate Street, and then possibly turned into Stall Street before passing into the Abbey churchyard, passing the Pump Room. Or perhaps a more circuitous route was chosen, north from Saw Close, past the Bluecoat School, an appropriate place for the children of the charity school to join the procession to sing an appropriately dreary hymn:

What's our comfort here below,
Empty bubble, transient shew;
Wrapt in the body's vile disguise,
None truly is until he dies.

Lest we imagine diffident wailing in cracking, off-key, West Country adolescent voices, children of the charity school, boys and girls alike, were taught to sing, and were by all accounts quite good.[33]

The cortège would then have followed the upper borough wall east to High Street. This route would taken them past the General Hospital, which might have been the first 'station' – perhaps the procession halted here, so that the beadles of the hospital could take their place behind the hearse, followed by those patients well enough to walk, limp, hobble on crutches or be wheeled in Bath chairs down the bumpy cobblestones. The 'poor ... , the lame, the emaciated, and the feeble', together with the rich, powerful and well fed, moved east and then south into High Street, coming to a second stop at the Guildhall. Perhaps it was here that the mayor and aldermen took their places. For years the Corporation of Bath had held themselves apart from the seasonal amusement culture, jealously holding their own observances of royal birthdays, so possibly it was only at their front door, once the procession was in sight of the Abbey, that they took their prominent places in it. The six longest serving aldermen of Bath walked alongside the hearse, preceded by three clergymen – perhaps the incumbents of Bath's three parishes – in white surplices and black stoles. Perhaps it was also at the Guildhall that the city waits, which had serenaded many a wealthy newcomer in expectation of a gratuity, moved into position to relieve the children of the Bluecoat School from torturing their vocal cords in the cold and damp. They were supplemented by 'Mr Nash's band', which had very likely attended Nash's coffin from the beginning of the route. Together they played the 'Dead March' from Handel's oratorio *Saul.*

From the Guildhall, everyone might have gone directly into the Abbey churchyard. The General Hospital patients would certainly have welcomed this result, and perhaps they were permitted to leave the procession at this point and take their seats. Might not the others have then taken a detour through a side street into and then around the Orange Grove, on to the Terrace Walk between the assembly rooms? It might have been here that Charles Simpson and Walter Wiltshire waited to follow as chief mourners the casket of a man who had still been litigating against them at his death. From this third station the procession could have headed east past the walks to circumnavigate the Parades. At some point the now quite substantial convoy would have to negotiate the narrower streets of the old city to reach the Abbey. It would have been difficult to avoid the construction site where the Duke of Kingston was building his new private baths, where six years earlier workmen had discovered the remains of Roman Baths. As the procession passed under the Abbey façade, where stone angels negotiated Jacob's Ladder as they had for a quarter of a millennium, and through the west door, the funeral sentences began. Perhaps the charity children sang them. The Corporation had, after all, voted fifty guineas towards the expense of a suitable funeral, just as one year earlier, they had out of pity voted Nash a monthly pension of ten pounds, under the cover of a subscription to his memoirs.

One of the beauties of a set liturgy is its capacity for confluences of all kinds, harmonic, dissonant and even ironic, at no time more apparent than at those junctures which confront the living with the dead. No one knew better than the assembled aldermen, for example, the truth of the words which now reverberated through the Abbey, as they applied to the monarch who lay in state:

We brought nothing into this world, and it is certain we can carry

> *nothing out. The Lord gave and the Lord hath taken away; blessed be the Name of the Lord.*

The previous June, Nash had led the ball for the twenty-second birthday of the Prince of Wales, but five months later, when local worthies processed to herald the accession of the same young man as King George III, Bath's own King had been notably absent. The three kingdoms were still (officially) in mourning for their late monarch when Bath lost its titular king.

The procession was now through; the catafalque in place, the participants had filed off into stalls, pews and ranges of stools. The psalms were announced, and sung competently if not confidently by the choir, and less so by the congregation. George Scott, already engaged in settling Nash's estate, might have nodded in appreciation in his pew on hearing that 'man walketh in a vain shadow, and disquieteth himself in vain: he heapeth up riches, and cannot tell who shall gather them'. Nash's executor (and his heir, had there been anything other than debts to inherit) was his nephew Charles Young, assisted by his attorney, William Yescombe. George Scott became their agent, which effectively meant finding means to discharge debts of something over £1,200. This amount (a sum respectably in six figures in modern equivalents) seems modest given the way that Nash had lived, but his magnificent house in John Court had been sold, as had his coach and coach horses. All that remained were one or two gold snuffboxes, an agate *étui* or instrument case, mounted with gold and diamonds, sixteen miniatures and several pastel portraits by William Hoare. The portraits, originally valued at eight guineas each, were advertised for sale at five apiece, but generally sold for half that sum or even less. Nash's last mistress, Mrs Hill, berated Scott over 'Mr Nash's Things being sold for Nothing', and Scott himself was incensed when five of the portraits were sold as a lot for a scant six guineas. When the miniatures were put up at auction, Scott bid three guineas for the lot, apprehending that they would sell for far less. Aside from these few effects and Nash's small (but, according to Scott, surprisingly well-selected) library, there was only a dubious debt of a few hundred pounds supposedly owed Nash from the estate of an anonymous peer. If Nash's estate had any percentage of the sales of Goldsmith's biography (the 1,500 copies of the first printing sold in four days), it was not enough to satisfy his heirs, who accused Scott of profiting disproportionately from the book's proceeds.

Goldsmith heard, and reported, that the crowd watching the procession was large enough to fill not only the streets, but the rooftops along the route, which gratified the shade of someone who lived to be the centre of attention – and who was now occupying it for the last time:

> *O spare me a little, that I may recover my strength, before I go hence, and be no more seen. … Glory be to the Father, and to the Son, and to the holy Ghost, as it was in the beginning, is now, and ever shall be, world without end, Amen.*

'From the first letter of Saint Paul to the Corinthians, the fifteenth chapter,' began the parish clerk from the lectern under the pulpit. 'Be not deceived;' the apostle warned, 'evil communications corrupt good manners.' At last, a positive reflection on Nash's promotion of civility and discouragement of malicious gossip, and from such an unexpected source.

> *So also is the resurrection of the dead; It is sown in dishonour; it is raised in glory: It is sown in corruption; it is raised in incorruption; It is sown in weakness; it is raised in power.*

'In the midst of life we are in death.' We are now at the graveside, wherever that was – for we do not know for certain where Nash was buried. The Corporation voted funds for his funeral, but not his burial; could Nash have found his way to a pauper's grave? The stone memorial in the Abbey is that only, and more to the point was only installed in 1770, nearly a decade after his death. It may have been a (mercifully) thin crowd that saw him deposited in the grave.

Forasmuch as it hath pleased Almighty God of his great mercy to take unto himself the soul of our brother Richard here departed, we therefore commit his body to the ground, earth to earth, ashes to ashes, dust to dust. . . . We give thee hearty thanks, for that it hath pleased thee to deliver this our brother Richard out of the miseries of this sinful world . . . .

(Farewell, Joan Sanderson, farewell, farewell)

Death, as those in the entertainment industry know, can be a good career move. As days passed and epitaphs accumulated, Nash was to be credited with quite substantial achievements. Nash, asserted one eulogy, had 'revived Architecture,' and all of Bath was 'a Monument of his Address.'[34] This was quite a compliment for someone who had never underwritten so much as a single building lease. Moreover, Nash's aura of irrefutable authority was never brighter than it was in the decade after he died, as selective memory worked its magic on his reputation. Those who remembered Nash, or claimed to, or thought they did, clucked their tongues at the slow but (to them) perceptible downward spiral of Bath's social institutions. 'We are in a sad way here, robb'd on all sides,' George Lucy wrote in April 1762, complaining that whatever money cardsharps allowed him to keep while he stayed in Bath he would lose to highwaymen on the roads just outside of it. The cause of this deteriorating social fabric was clear: 'I think one may draw a parallel between what Rome was before the time of Sixtus Quintus and what Bath is now, since the death of Nash.'[35] The decline of Bath after Nash's death became a convention of subsequent literature on the Georgian resort. It is a better memorial to Nash that very nearly the opposite was the case.

10

The King is Dead; Long Live the King

Impotent Posterity, In vain shall fumble to make his Fellow.[1]

Perhaps the most apposite memorial to Nash was that Masters of Ceremonies had been instituted at other resorts, so inextricably was Bath's success associated with him. Scarborough engaged Charles Jones for this purpose as early as 1740, and Bristol Hotwells had acquired an MC by the middle of the century. For the past several years, the Hotwells had been advancing itself as the logical summer retreat from the spa, in preference to Tunbridge Wells. Its Long Room may have been 'very hot & disagreeable' and its pump room 'a poor shabby place' with 'only one scurvy fiddle by way of musick', as Lady Caroline Brydges complained when she visited in August 1751, but the Hotwells did have a 'Master of the Ceremonys',

> *one Mercer formerly a Hautboy in my Grand fathers band of musick he scrap'd acquaintance wth me to my great astonishment & was more amazd when I found all the acquaintance he had wth me was by knowing my Grandfather before I was born.*[2]

The pattern that Nash set almost guaranteed Bristol's first incumbent an inauspicious debut. Mercer was clearly striving to imitate Nash, but unsuccessfully. It took nerve ('assurance'), combined with an instinctive knowledge of how far to press the familiarity one assumed, for socio-economic mongrels like Nash and Mercer to banter with a nob like Caroline Brydges. The Hotwells' promoters persisted, however, with some success. In June 1753 the *Bath Journal* began listing arrivals for the summer season there, as it had always done in the autumn and spring seasons at Bath. These lists indicate that the Hotwells was more the family resort that Bath was becoming; there were more couples with children listed, although there was still a fair number of unaccompanied men. As the arrivals for Bath thinned out and became socially more humble, the list for the Hotwells became more numerous and more august. In the middle of June, the Company at Bristol included the Countess of Albemarle and her son, the Earl of Jersey, Lord and Lady Sutton, Lords Fielding, Kettleby and Villers, Sir James and Lady Creed, Sir Harry Hamilton and thirty-five others, including five military couples.[3] By the end of the decade, Bristol Hotwells boasted two assembly rooms, and ten years after that, its own Master of Ceremonies was in a position to contend for the Bath post.

~

In Bath itself, it was soon clear that Nash had created a role too large for anyone else to fill. James Quin, who was certainly mentioned as a successor to Nash, was not interested, and the monarchy of Bath became 'an employ that almost went a begging'.[4] Nash was immediately succeeded as Master of Ceremonies by his deputy, an elderly French dancing master named Jacques Caulet (anglicised to James Collet). While Nash expected this outcome, he was not optimistic about Caulet's chances of success.[5] Graf von Kielmansegge, a Hanoverian nobleman in England for the coronation of George III, was nevertheless highly impressed with Caulet, who was 'still very active and diligent' although 'nearly seventy years old ... he dances like the youngest, and is civility itself to every one'. While Kielmansegge 'could not find praise enough' for Caulet, his remarks reveal problematic aspects of the new MC's demeanour. He was especially attentive to foreign visitors, which gratified Kielmansegge but may have irritated the xenophobic base of the Company. Furthermore, the agility which Kielmansegge and George Scott so admired bordered on hyperactivity. The way that Caulet 'rushed about with us for hours, showing us everything which was in the slightest degree worth noticing',[6] must have reminded even Kielmansegge of an overly affectionate retriever.

George Scott, Nash's executor, was also initially pleased with Caulet. Scott echoed Kielmansegge, repeating that, despite his age, Caulet was 'as lively as he need to be; if any Thing too much so, and like a true Frenchman will dance into his Grave'. Only three months after Nash's death, Caulet seemed to be well established as his successor, securing election as a governor of the General Hospital in May 1761.[7] Caulet, according to the Bath musician Francis Fleming, was 'ever studious to please' and 'commanded in a great measure the *esteem* of the company'. These backhanded compliments signalled the trouble that was to follow. Bath's new monarch was not sufficiently regal, and 'rather ... glided smoothly through than cut any great figure in his seat of sovereignty'.[8] A royal visit in his second season as Master of Ceremonies, that of the Duke of York, was Caulet's undoing. He had assisted Nash at Bath and Tunbridge for a number of years, but had never dealt directly with such an august visitor, and his inexperience, compounded with the pressure and anxiety that the highly strung Caulet certainly felt, was the making of disaster. '[P]oor old Nash is missed upon this Occasion,' Scott wrote in December, as Caulet was proving 'by no means an Adept in his Office'. By February Scott was calling him 'a weak, ill-bred Frenchman', particularly citing 'his Behaviour to the Duke of York, [which] was a Comedy of Errors'. Although the Duke of York had behaved 'with the utmost Politeness and Regularity' in the face of Caulet's blundering, the spa was embarrassed. One year later, Caulet was out of office and Samuel Derrick – through means uncertain and for reasons unclear – was chosen in his stead.[9]

Derrick, unlike either of his predecessors, was a modestly accom-

42. Samuel Derrick had vision and determination, but lacked the presence to succeed as MC. His tenure was correspondingly tumultuous

plished occasional writer, translator and critic. He knew Samuel Johnson and James Boswell, although both had mixed feelings about him. Boswell called him 'a little blackguard pimping dog', while Johnson (according to Boswell) believed that he had 'nothing to say for himself but that he is a writer. Had Derrick not been a writer, he must have been sweeping the crosses in the streets and asking halfpence from everybody that passed.'[10] Johnson spoke kindly of Derrick after the latter's death, however, and Boswell was gracious enough to record it.[11] Derrick may at least have been acquainted with Goldsmith, his fellow Irishman. He had worked (unsuccessfully) as an actor and in 1752 published *The Dramatic Censor,* his critical gloss on Thomas Otway's *Venice Preserved*, the most popular non-Shakespearian tragedy on the Georgian stage. This tract was intended as the first instalment in an ambitious series encompassing all of the leading pieces in the London theatrical repertory, but, like so much else in its author's life, failed to rise to outsized expectations.

James Quin's biographer, who wrote while Derrick was still alive and in possession of his 'throne', related that Derrick's candidacy had been advanced immediately after Nash's death by a peer whom he had complimented in a poem. This proposal, made 'half in jest and half in earnest', was taken up by women of the Company

> *who had been obliquely praised in the same piece, and they imagined it would be no small feather in their cap if they could say they had the Master of the Ceremonies for their panegyrist. Accordingly, Mr D[errick] was, by these ladies' interest, without opposition elected.*[12]

Derrrick's papers, preserved in the Victoria and Albert Museum, tell a slightly different story. Nash anticipated that Caulet, as his deputy, would succeed him, and other members of the Company may have expected this outcome as well. Consequently, Derrick showed no immediate signs of aspiring to the white hat. In August 1761 he was preparing for a trip to Ireland, which, if undertaken, would have precluded his opening the autumn season at Bath. The following February and March, a close friend was writing to ask Derrick 'where you live, how you live, and whether you live or no'.[13] Derrick was only pitched upon after Caulet's unsuitability became apparent over the course of his four seasons in office. Caulet was probably dismissed through the efforts of influential cliques among the Company, and Derrick chosen in time to open the first season in 1763.

By the time that Derrick was seriously mentioned for the post (as seriously as the post was ever discussed, that is), Goldsmith's *Life* had appeared, with its (admittedly guarded) appreciation of Nash's knack for doggerel verse. Goldsmith recognised and alerted his readers to the fact that literary ephemera – verses, lampoons and the like – whether printed or privately circulated, were important means of social control at Bath and other resorts. Derrick now seemed as apposite a choice for MC as an established writer, critic and editor as he was an odd choice on account of his stature and demeanour. Smollett's Tabitha Bramble, to cite a fictional example, 'knew it was convenient to be well with the Master of the Ceremonies, while she continued to frequent the Rooms; and, having heard he was a poet, began to be afraid of making her appearance in a ballad or lampoon'.[14] Although he agreed that Derrick was a 'wretched' writer, Samuel Johnson believed that '"it was his being a literary man that got him made King of Bath".'[15] Derrick's experience in the theatrical and literary worlds made him familiar with the need for promotion and the means to effect it. He also had a grand vision for Bath at what must have appeared to be a time of fundamental transition. The early 1760s saw an effort to cast Bath in an international light and attract more visitors from the Continent. Derrick had already turned his pen to promoting the spa as a *European* resort before his appointment was formalised. Bath, he wrote in 1762, was 'undoubtedly one of the most elegant, pleasant, and convenient spots in Europe'; there was 'no place in the world, where a person may introduce himself, on such easy terms, to the first people in Europe'; no place in Europe could provide 'a more delightful retreat for the young and old, healthy and infirm, than this little city'.[16] It is possible that he worked in conjunction (rather than competition) with Caulet, whose nationality and solicitation of continental visitors were remarked upon.

Furthermore, Derrick's theatrical background was a bona fide qualification for the highly performative post of governing Bath's amusements. After all, James Quin had been suggested as a replacement for the ageing Nash, and Nash considered him a credible threat. Quin had turned down any such overtures, having through long stage experience better sense than to take over a role so closely associated with another performer. Derrick, on the other hand, innocently stepped into the unenviable position shared in our own time by the not-quite-famous television actor who takes the lead in the second or third cast of a popular Broadway or West End production. He compounded the mistake through 'strict conformity … to his predecessor's conduct', assuming that 'foppery and extravagance were … necessary appendages' to his new office, down to the detail of the white hat. Nash had always joked that he wore the oversized white tricorne from the knowledge that it would never be stolen or taken by mistake. Derrick's white hats, on the other hand, were constantly being purloined. '[H]e has actually lost two,' an observer reported, 'and is now consulting three hatters upon the proper cock of the third.'[17] Younger men of the Company, knowing intuitively that Derrick's grace and favour were nearly worthless, probably regarded the new MC's white hat as a prize souvenir, a trophy to be displayed to their friends. 'Instead of assuming an authority which was placed in his hands,' Derrick, according to Francis Fleming (whom he had dismissed), 'submitted to the caprice, insults, or controul of those who should have been his subjects'.[18] He had only been Master of Ceremonies for one season when Scott pronounced him 'by no means to be of Consequence enough to conduct Matters at Bath'.[19] A substantial contingent among the Company apparently agreed. In September 1763, instead of preparing to open his second season at Bath, he was writing letters to his old supporters begging their aid in securing his reinstatement. In March the following year, Derrick was receiving his mail at the Smyrna Coffee House in London, where he was once again scrabbling a living as a writer. His replacement in Bath was the 'artfull french man' Caulet, who, according to Derrick and his supporters, engaged in 'under hand dealling' to regain the post. It was another year before friends could congratulate Derrick 'upon being thoroughly established at Bath', or at least as established as ever he would be.[20] Quin's biographer casts the retired actor as the 'kingmaker' in this episode, advising representatives of the Company how best to remove Derrick and then coming around to support Derrick after being bribed with a shipment of fish.[21]

Derrick, short and slightly built, had none of Nash's physical presence, and the necessity of making himself conspicuous exposed him to ridicule. One writer – who came out in Derrick's defence – responded to suggestions that Derrick's 'deficiency of stature' prevented him 'from discharging the high duties of his office' by suggesting that he be permitted to use stilts in the assembly rooms.[22] In *Humphry Clinker*, Smollett has Lydia Melford describe Derrick as 'a pretty little gentleman, so sweet, so fine, so civil, and polite, that in our country he might pass for the Prince of Wales' – the heir apparent being all of four years old when the novel was set. In the novel, Derrick attempts to eject Tabitha Bramble's dog, Chowder, from the rooms, but the dog 'seemed to despise his authority, and displaying a formidable case of long, white, sharp teeth, kept the puny monarch at bay'. Derrick is reduced to 'bawling to the waiter' and 'making remonstrances upon the rules and regulations of the place'. Mrs Bramble is incensed, and 'when the Master of the Ceremonies offered to hand her into the chair, she rapped him over the knuckles with her fan'.[23] In all fairness, it ought to be said that Derrick and Smollett were friends – Derrick had stayed in the writer's house in Chelsea – and that *Humphry Clinker* was not published until 1771, two years after Derrick's death. It is still clear, though, that even those who were friendly with and even close to Derrick – Johnson, Boswell and Smollett among them – often held him in humorous contempt.

If the posthumous *Derrick's Jests* is any guide, Derrick's conduct towards visitors did not help his cause. When reproached at the Abbey for not helping several older women into their pews, he retorted that he was only paid to attend the Company 'in the Long-room'. The Derrick of the *Jests* also has a sharp tongue which he wields without mercy, circumspection or subtlety. Derrick 'could never bear to hear an absent person traduced and ridiculed'. But he was perfectly willing, if the *Jests* are any guide, to ridicule both men and women of the Company to their faces. If some of the remarks recounted there were actually made in the circumstances described, Derrick would have been repeatedly thrashed. Remarks credited to him charged women with promiscuity and saddled men with cuckoldry, quite serious imputations in the eighteenth century. Where Nash, as evidenced in his own *Jests*, had the reputation of protecting visitors, especially women, from slander by tongue or pen, Derrick never let propriety stand in the way of opportunities to be thought a wit. 'Though Mr Derrick's behaviour to the ladies was in general polite,' the compiler of the *Jests* allowed,

> *he would sometimes make complaisance give way when he had an opportunity of saying a good thing. A very ordinary lady one day*

> *asking him his opinion of* patching. '*Oh! Madam,' said he,* 'patch *by all means, but wear only one, and let that be a* mask.'[24]

For all of the obstacles he faced (and put in his own way), Derrick took his duties seriously and performed them as conscientiously as his constituency would allow. He attempted to suppress the ringing of bells for new arrivals and the playing of music outside their lodgings, with a view to relieving residents of noise and newcomers of importunate musicians. He dropped hints to the Corporation that the Pump Room was in need of further expansion (it had been enlarged once in 1751).[25] His greatest challenge was regulating the balls, particularly standards of dress, which the vicissitudes of fashion had made impossible. Derrick, unlike Nash, was not a creature of fashion himself and did not possess the sense of style that would have allowed him to be flexible. If women had worn hoop petticoats and lappet tops to dance minuets for Nash, then they would do so for Derrick, even if it was a nuisance to remove the hoop in the (*much* more crowded) ballrooms in order to stand up for the country dances. The continuing insistence on old-fashioned court dress opened the possibility of the kind of pratfall that Smollett has John Melford describe:

> *I was extremely diverted, last ball-night, to see the Master of the Ceremonies leading, with great solemnity, to the upper end of the room, an antiquated Abigail, dressed in her lady's cast-clothes; whom he (I suppose) mistook for some countess just arrived at the Bath.*[26]

What was worse, where Nash had recognised that social rank was best observed tacitly, Derrick gave place, and required others to do so, at the top of his lungs. The very first of a set of regulations promulgated in October 1765 stipulated that 'No Chair or Bench can be called on Ball Nights for any person, who does not rank as a Peer or Peeress of Great Britain or Ireland.'[27] The endearing epigrammatic dogmatism of Nash's regulations was entirely absent from Derrick's exasperated inventory of prohibitions, which were reminiscent of the irritating but ineffectual barking of an irate Pomeranian.

~

The failure of Nash's successors stemmed from the single aspect of his position that they were determined *not* to copy – the irregular compensation of uncertain provenance. James Quin, according to his biographer, refused the post from a belief that 'he could never expect to gain in quality of Master of Ceremonies' the annual income of £1,200 to £1,400 he had given up at his retirement from the stage.[28] Caulet received 'emoluments', possibly from the proprietors of the rooms, prompting Francis Fleming to remark that Caulet might have held on to his post, the Duke of York notwithstanding, 'had he promoted the diversion of the four aces as much as he did shuttlecock'.[29] Derrick's compensation became a matter of public discussion. He indiscreetly published his correspondence in 1767, in which one correspondent, congratulating him on his appointment, wished

> *to know if you have any fixed salary annexed to your diadem. Are your revenues sufficient to maintain a sovereign prince in a state of independence? Though I have no doubt of your reigning in the hearts of your people, yet I would rather you owed your support to settled revenues than voluntary contribution.*[30]

Derrick, in addition to drawing a modest annual salary of £50 drawn out of the subscriptions, staged benefit nights for himself. Nash had used benefit nights to compensate musicians and as an *ad hoc* fundraising tool in cases of charitable contingencies, but had stopped well short of benefiting directly and with public knowledge. While benefit nights were effective means of compensating particular performers, whose admirers would then make a point of turning up, it reinforced Derrick's dependence on the Company and exposed him to their contempt. Derrick was said to have cleared £150 from one benefit ball in April 1767. 'Oh Shame! Shame! Shame!' exclaimed John Penrose, 'that such an insignificant Puppy should receive so rich a subscription.'[31] No one knew where Nash's money came from (until it was gone), which meant (as the Earl of Chesterfield sagely observed) that everyone 'wondered' in every sense of that word. Their curiosity and amazement contributed materially to the Nash mystique.

The received wisdom, reiterated by Quin, Scott and Fleming, that no subsequent Master of Ceremonies would ever rise to the pre-eminence Nash was able to achieve did not, incredibly enough, deter aspirants to the position, and it is testimony to the success of the Nash myth that there were any aspirants at all. There is a note of pride in the way that Quin and Scott adverted that they had been approached to take the 'throne'. 'Under the Rose,' Scott informed one correspondent,

> *You are to know, that I was principally concerned in the Management of the Bath Affairs for the last five or six years we were there; and I have the Pleasure to think I was of some little Use in that City, where I spared for no Pains to serve the City in general, and prevent the Company resorting thither, from falling into the Snares of Sharpers ... they began to press me to conduct the Business of the Place, if any Thing that passes there deserves that Name.*[32]

How Scott was supposed to have served as *de facto* MC when (as he insisted more than once) he did not go to the rooms belies his professed disdain for Bath's amusement culture and everything connected with it.

When it was clear that Derrick was on his deathbed in the spring season of 1769, no fewer than three candidates advanced their claim to the white beaver hat, and the bitterly contested elections in the weeks that followed resulted in physical confrontations, requiring the intervention of the local authorities. One reason for such keen interest in the position in 1769 was clear: no one now pretended that the post was not highly remunerative. In 1748, Nash had dispatched an open letter to the *Bath*

Journal indignantly denying that *any* of the subscriptions to the assembly rooms went into his pocket, but now the assumption was that much if not most of the proceeds from subscriptions would revert to the Master of Ceremonies. Once he had paid the musicians and the other expenses of the assembly rooms, he was entitled to the balance, a figure which would only increase once John Wood the Younger finished building the new Upper Assembly Rooms, then under construction and in the centre of the vast new residential developments now projected in every direction from the Circus. What the sovereignty of Bath had undoubtedly lost in authority it now gained in lucrative potential. Control of the subscriptions, which already amounted to at least £2,000 per year, was the spoils of victory. '[']is a Prize well worth Contention,' one set of verses ran, 'Attended with so good a Pension.'[33]

The newly apparent desirability of the Bath 'governorship', and the resulting competition for the post, meant that for the first time a 'job description' was written for it, in order to explain why the Company should be interested in the outcome, and why such a post should even continue to exist. The Master of Ceremonies, according to a partisan of one of the candidates, was 'to be the Guardian of the young People of both Sexes, [and] to keep them out of the Hands of Gamblers and Fortune-Hunters'. A supporter of his opponent agreed, praising his own candidate as 'an Enemy to every Kind of Vice', adding that his election would assure 'all Parents and Guardians' that 'Young Persons of Rank and Fortune can now pass the Season at *Bath* as safely as the beauteous *Godiva* passed through *Coventry*.'[34]

On 16 March 1769, when Derrick was ill but not yet dead, Charles Jones – possibly the same man engaged as MC at Scarborough in 1740 – circulated a paper announcing his candidacy for the post. He must have been a familiar figure at the gaming tables, for in promoting his bid for office he solemnly pledged to 'bid adieu to Play'. It was perhaps for this reason that Jones was not an impressive candidate, and his circular was the first and last notice of his candidacy.[35] The remaining two contestants were Major William Brereton, Derrick's second-in-command and, like him, an Irishman, and a Mr Plomer, whose forename is not recorded. Plomer was already Master of Ceremonies at Bristol Hotwells, which had been actively promoting itself as an alternative to Tunbridge Wells as the obvious off-season respite from Bath. Scott, and doubtless others, felt that it was through the support of Irish members of the Company that the otherwise ineffectual Derrick had held on to the post for as long as six years, and this issue of nationality was a point of tension in Bath that erupted over the question of Derrick's successor. Due to their relative proximity, Irish gentry were always numerous among the Company at Bath, and were stereotyped as fortune hunters and social climbers. Plomer's partisans played to these prejudices, asking rhetorically whether Bath was to 'be absolutely governed by the transient Visitors from another Nation'.[36] Brereton's supporters retaliated in kind, capitalising on the humbler social profile of the Hotwells, which persisted in spite of the newer and smaller spa's efforts to publicise the presence of high-ranking visitors. In one mock advertisement, a number of 'Citizens of Bristol' proposed 'to travel to *Bath* in the One-Day Barge', subscribe to the balls and vote in the election, thus tipping the balance in Plomer's favour. To reinforce the point, the 'signatories' were identified with such trades as rope-maker, bottle-maker, sugar-baker, 'Grocer and Quaker' and 'Currier, left off Business'.[37]

Derrick expired early on the morning of Tuesday 28 March. '[P]oor fellow,' an observer commented at the news, 'I hear he is gone in a miserable manner, I hear his privities were cut off and his belly left quite bare!'[38] Whether or not any such literal violence was actually visited on this King of Bath's mortal body, the refusal of Jones, Brereton and Plomer to wait until he was actually dead was a figurative assault on Derrick's official body. The War of the Bathonian Succession was afoot before the reversion of the throne was even effected.

John Wood had written that the post was in the gift of the Bath Corporation, patronage that the city fathers declined after Nash's death, leading Goldsmith to posit that the Master of Ceremonies was chosen by the Company, although the procedure was nebulous. Three 'Kings' had been chosen by the spontaneous consensual acclamation

– or at least acquiescence – of the Company. The years since Derrick's accession had witnessed agitation for political reform nationwide, with particular attention being given to questions of the franchise, representation and the legitimacy of elections. No matter where one stood on specific issues (for example, whether or not the radical journalist and indicted pornographer John Wilkes ought to be seated as Knight of the Shire for Middlesex), serious consideration was now paid to electoral processes in the political nation as a whole. When it appeared that the titular throne of Bath was soon to be vacant in 1769, all of the candidates and their constituents agreed that Derrick's successor would be chosen by election. While everyone in Bath – or at least the contestants and their respective cliques – had now a clearer sense of the proper consequence of the Master of Ceremonies, there were no precedents for the management of a contested election for the post (and very little precedent, for that matter, for an *uncontested* election). It was not known when and where the poll should be held, or who would possess the franchise, or, to complicate matters, who had the authority to decide these questions. The erstwhile candidate Charles Jones hilariously issued a public appeal to the Lord Chamberlain to assert his jurisdiction in the matter.[39] Both sides understood that the Master of Ceremonies was elected by subscribers to the balls, but disagreed over questions such as voting *in absentia*. A pro-Brereton writer complained that Plomer's supporters were trying to fix the election through a flood of absentee subscriptions. The Breretonians and the Plomerites effectively held their own elections and waged a pamphlet war denying the legitimacy of the other candidate's poll. Brereton's election occurred before Derrick's corpse was cold – it was a ball night, after all, and someone would have to lead the minuets, although it does not seem to have occurred to anyone (on Brereton's side, at least) that perhaps a brief period of 'court mourning' was in order. The poll, held in the afternoon at Gyde's Rooms (as Lindsey's/Wiltshire's had become by that point) numbered 262 votes for Brereton. Plomer's party, evincing a concern for decorum, declared that no election could decently take place until at least three days had elapsed after Derrick's death, and announced an election to be held Friday 31 March at Simpson's, in which 267 ballots were cast for Plomer.[40]

By the beginning of April there was 'most violent work' between the two contenders.[41] A letter was circulated from one Joseph Fell, charging Brereton with extortion and cheating at cards. David Garrick took Brereton's side, publishing verses disparaging the 'Bristol smugglers'.[42] Hand-wringing over the 'Virulence and Acrimony' that had violated 'the Decencies of private Conversation' was joined with bemusement that the contention over such a trivial office had become as aggravated as the continuing agitation over John Wilkes, the opposition polemicist whose election to Parliament by the county of Middlesex had been repeatedly invalidated:

> *Whilst neighbouring Kingdoms disagree,*
> *And talk of Wilkes and Liberty,*
> *Pensions, Prerogatives, and Pow'r,*
> *... A lowlier Theme I humbly sing,*
> *Of whom hereafter may be King*
> *Of* Bladud*'s realm, where Mirth should reign,*
> *But Discord now the Waters stain;*
> *That Place, where* Venus *should preside,*
> *The fiery* Mars *does seem to guide.*[43]

Matters came to a head on the evening of 11 April, when both Plomer and Brereton appeared at Simpson's to take up the post to which each believed himself duly elected. The result was 'a most violent quarrel' which rapidly progressed 'from words ... to Blows'. According to one Bath resident, 'the Magistrates were sent for [and] the riot act read three times'. The fracas ended 'after an hour and a half's dreadful confusion', and the next day 'eight writs were issued out against several of the bruisers'. The *Bath Chronicle* corroborated this account, adding that '[n]ever was such a Scene of anarchy and confusion remembered in this city'. The situation was so grave that the local magistrates forbade public or private balls until further notice.[44] Public reaction ranged

43. Chaos descends, post-Nash. A 1769 cartoon illustrates the riot at Simpson's over the election of Derrick's successor

from shock and horror to merriment. Although surviving accounts suggest that it was the two male principals who began the fisticuffs, a cartoon illustrating the confrontation (entitled 'Female Intrepidity, or the Battle of the Belles') foregrounded the presence of women among the combatants, as did sets of verses written to commemorate the fracas that erupted in Simpson's ballroom:

> *Pins and Pomatums strew the Room,*
> *Emitting many a sweet Perfume;*
> *Each Tender Form is strangely batter'd,*
> *And odd Things here and there are scatter'd;*
> *In Heaps confus'd the Heroines lie,*
> *With horrid Shrieks they pierce the Sky;*
> *Their Charms are lost in Scratches, Scars,*
> *Sad Emblems of domestic Wars!*[45]

44. A former military officer, William Wade was better suited for the post of MC, but Bath's amusement culture had grown too large to be managed by one person

It must have seemed to the amused and appalled alike that Nash's dire prophecy of the chaos that would descend in his absence had been realised. The day before the riot, the *Bath Journal* had portentously suggested that the ball surplus be spent on a memorial plaque for Nash, in recognition of his having kept amusements in order, and implicitly in reproach to those who would succeed him.[46]

~

The 'Bath Contest' of 1769 was resolved much like the Great Schism of the papacy had been three and a half centuries earlier: the rival claimants stood aside after receiving suitable concessions, and a compromise candidate was chosen by consensus. This was Captain William Wade, elected on 13 April. Wade was described as the nephew of Field Marshal Wade, Bath's long-time MP; he was probably a great nephew, but was not, as was long rumoured, an illegitimate son. It was Captain Wade's privilege to open the new Upper Rooms in 1771, in the Card Room of which hung his own equally new portrait by Gainsborough. His suit suggested the officer's scarlet he (unlike Nash) was indisputably entitled to wear, while his hat – a small, discreet black tricorne – was too clear a negation of Nash's style not to be deliberate. In its place were a badge of office – a gold medal, enamelled blue, worn on an indigo ribbon – and a corsage of what appear to be roses, thistles and shamrocks.

Subscriptions increased, of course, but Wade soon found that the crowds made his post unmanageable. It was no longer in the interest of the proprietors of different assembly rooms to cooperate with each other, and it was several years before Wade could establish a ball schedule that gave the rooms an equal share of custom. In fact, there were now enough visitors to support both sets of rooms. Consequently, Wade was the last Master of Ceremonies to preside at the Upper *and* Lower Rooms. When he resigned in 1777 (after being named correspondent in a divorce suit), it made more sense for each of the rooms to choose its own 'master', paid for by the management out of the subscriptions. The minuet, that communal sacrament witnessed as compliantly as the elevation of the host on the other side of the confessional divide, also fell victim to crowds and to fashion. The traditional dance was abandoned for the 'long minuet', in which several couples danced at the same time, meaning that more members of the Company could participate, and also that the ordeal would be over sooner. The dress code was also relaxed considerably. The dancers shown in Henry Bunbury's engraving wear the fashionable dress of the 1780s. Ultimately, even the long minuet disappeared, although John King, Master of Ceremonies in the Upper Rooms in Jane Austen's day, tried unsuccessfully to revive it. Even more gradually, the Assembly Rooms themselves fell out of fashion, as 'at homes' became the preferred forum for social interaction in a locale where more and more of the Company were in fact 'at home' rather than merely visiting in season. Jane Austen had Catherine Morland wade through an uncomfortably crowded assembly room in *Northanger Abbey*, her first novel; in *Persuasion*, her last, the Elliot sisters eschew the rooms altogether.

45. The Long Minuet was a new variation of the courtly dance which allowed more participants as well as a relaxed dress code

Bath's titular monarchy survived its creator by a little over fifteen years. The slow death of this imaginary autocracy proceeded from the very success of the spa that the office had been invented to foster. The worlds in which he was necessary – in which he was possible – had changed. While Nash was gone along with his office, however, his image was everywhere in Bath. In oil and stone, it occupied pride of place in the Pump Room, the Guildhall and in all three (after 1771) sets of assembly rooms. No artist, whether Thomas Rowlandson, Humphrey Repton or John Nixon, could depict any of these definitive Bath interiors without Nash's portrait presiding high above the heads of the crowd. In John Nixon's drawing of the Pump Room in 1790 (on the eve of its renovation and expansion), Prince Hoare's statue has shed the clumsiness that Goldsmith noted, so that an uncharacteristically slender, youthful and elegant Nash looks down from his niche on the motley assemblage shown awaiting the attention of the pumper. Established residents, those new Bathonians of the grand developments that now mounted the outlying hills and crossed the Avon, asserted

46. The Pump Room, by Thomas Rowlandson. Note Nash's statue, from the studio of Prince Hoare

their seniority among new arrivals by speaking of 'Mr Nash' as if they had just spotted him in Milsom Street, and wondering what 'Mr Nash' would think of banyans, or the long minuet, or John Wilkes, or the Duchess of Devonshire.

Bath tour guides – the ones who tell of Juliana Popjoy returning to Nash to nurse him in his old age, before moving into her tree – will have it that Bath declined after his death. There is anecdotal evidence to suggest that it became less aristocratic (whatever that means) after the middle of the century, but it would be a mistake to equate this development with 'decline'. In any case, Nash has lost his centrality in Bath to Jane Austen, as the Austenmania of the past decade has given St Jane pride of place in the touristic pilgrimage itinerary. In one sense, this development is only appropriate, given that it was Bath's transition into Austen's town of retired 'rears and vices' that unravelled Nash's republic of pleasure. Furthermore, our own deeper knowledge of the forces that drove Bath's development in the years that Nash lived there raises questions about the nature of his contribution, which to the

47. North Parade

archivally adapted eye appears insubstantial and insignificant compared to those of Ralph Allen, the two John Woods, physicians like Cheyne and Oliver, and the Wiltshire family. Enough of his contemporaries, however, including some of those named, believed Nash to be Bath's 'worthy benefactor' and felt that no one who knew Nash could doubt it. They selected him as the spa's emissary to the King, they credited him in stone with raising the General Hospital, while he, as well as the architect, the original governors and major donors, still lived, and they heralded his annual return to Bath in outsized capital letters above all of the other arrivals, dukes, duchesses and archbishops included. In an age obsessed with presentation of the self, and management of interactions with others, Nash demonstrated for those who came into his orbit, for many of whom this public culture was a new, unfamiliar and frightening world, the power locked within themselves.

Notes

Introduction

1. *Bath Anecdotes and Characters: By the Genius Loci* (London: John Dodsley and Edward and Charles Dilly, 1782), 20–21.
2. Peter Borsay, *The Image of Georgian Bath* (Oxford: Oxford University Press, 2000).
3. [R. Whatley], *Characters at the Hot-Well, Bristol, and at Bath, in October, 1723* (London: James Lacy, 1724), xviii–xix, xx–xxi, xxv, xxvii.
4. I owe this observation to Dr Peter Borsay.
5. I am indebted to Dr David Carnegie for this information.
6. Whatley, *Characters,* vi.
7. A thorough discussion of the current literature on politeness is found in Philip Carter, *Men and the Emergence of Polite Society* (London: Longman, 2001), 15–52.
8. Lorna Weatherill, *Consumer Behaviour and Material Culture in Britain 1660–1760* (London: Routledge, 1996), 26–7.
9. *The Works of Oliver Goldsmith,* ed. Arthur Friedman (Oxford: Oxford University Press, 1966), 3: 288–9.
10. Peter Briggs, 'The Importance of Beau Nash', *Studies in Eighteenth-Century Culture,* 22 (1992): 212.
11. Ibid., 226.
12. John Wood, *Essay Toward a Description of Bath* (London: W. Bathoe and T. Lowndes, 1765. Facsimile edition Bath: Kingsmead Reprints, 1969); *The Jests of Beau Nash, Late Master of the Ceremonies at Bath* (London: W. Bristow, 1763).
13. 'Lewis Melville' [Lewis S. Benjamin], *Bath under Beau Nash* (London: Eveleigh Nash, 1907); Edith Sitwell, *Bath* (London: Faber and Faber, 1932); John Walters, *Splendour and Scandal: The Reign of Beau Nash* (London: Jarrold's Publishers, 1968).
14. David Gadd, *Georgian Summer: Bath in the Eighteenth Century* (Bath: Adams and Dart, 1971), vii.
15. Alfred Barbeau, *Life and Letters at Bath in the Eighteenth Century* (London: William Heinemann, 1904); Willard Connelly, *Beau Nash: Monarch of Bath and Tunbridge Wells* (London: Werner Laurie, 1955).
16. See, for example, Peach's *Life and Times of Ralph Allen* (London: D. Nutt, 1895), 214–224.
17. Sarah Scott to Elizabeth Montagu, 17 November 1754, Montagu Papers MO 5245, Huntington Library.

18. Goldsmith, *Works,* 3: 322, 345; Barbeau, *Life and Letters at Bath,* 23–4n; George Scott to Philip Trahern, 27 December 1762, Egerton Manuscripts 3738, f36, British Library.
19. Briggs, 'The Importance of Beau Nash,' 212.
20. Elizabeth Montagu to Edward Montagu, 13 August 1753, Montagu Papers MO 2292.

1 *Bath and Its Kings (800 BC–AD 1705)*

1. Goldsmith, *Works,* 3:291–2.
2. Connelly, *Beau Nash,* 4–5.
3. Inventory of Richard Nash, deceased, of Camrose, 1699, Probate Records, Archdeaconry of St David's SD/1699/16, National Library of Wales.
4. Last Will and Testament of Elizabeth Nash of Camrose, 1727, Probate Records, Archdeaconry of St David's, SD 1727/18.
5. Graham Midgley, *University Life in Eighteenth-Century Oxford* (New Haven: Yale University Press, 1996), 1–15.
6. Connelly, 2–6, 8–10.
7. Goldsmith, *Works,* 3: 296.
8. George Scott to Richard Nash Young, 29 October 1763, Egerton MSS 3739, f98.
9. Goldsmith, *Works,* 3:294.
10. *The Diaries of Thomas Wilson, D. D. 1731–37 and 1750,* ed. C. L. S. Linnell (London: SPCK, 1964), 165.
11. Historical Manuscripts Commission, *Diary of John Perceval, First Earl of Egmont* (London: HMSO, 1920), 1: 343, 2: 254.
12. [Francis Fleming], *The Life and Adventures of Timothy Ginnadrake* (Bath: R. Crutwell, 1771), 3: 19.
13. Goldsmith, *Works,* 3:295.
14. Goldsmith, *Works,* 3:296–7, 334; Arthur Sherbo, 'A Manufactured Anecdote in Goldsmith's *Life of Richard Nash,' Modern Language Notes* 70 (January 1955): 20–21.
15. Thomas Guidott, *A Discourse of Bathe, and the Hot Waters There* (London: Henry Buome, 1676), 59–60.
16. Wood, *Description of Bath,* 71–6.
17. Guidott, *A Discourse of Bathe,* 55.
18. The following discussion of prehistoric, Roman and Anglo-Saxon Bath has been gleaned largely from Barry Cunliffe, *The City of Bath* (New Haven: Yale University Press, 1987), 5, 14–15, 18, 24–6, 38, 42, 54.
19. Phyllis Hembry, *The English Spa* (London: Athlone Press, 1990), 1–2, 26–7, 33.
20. Sylvia McIntyre, 'Bath: The Rise of a Resort Town, 1660–1800,' in Peter Clark, ed., *Country Towns in Pre-Industrial England* (Leicester: Leicester University Press, 1981), 201–2.
21. Jean Manco, 'The Cross Bath', *Bath History* 2 (1988): 63; *The Journeys of Celia Fiennes,* ed. John Hillaby (London: Macdonald, 1983), 265; [John Macky], *A Journey*

through England in Familiar Letters for a Gentleman Here, to His Friend Abroad (London: J. Pemberton, 1722), 2:130–31.

22. *News from Bath* (London: R. Baldwin, 1689); *The Loyalty and Glory of the City of BATH* (London: A. Milbourn, 1689).
23. Hedges to Nottingham, 2 September 1702; Godolphin to Nottingham 3 September 1702, Additional Manuscripts 29, 588, ff 172–3, British Library.
24. Thomas Ken, *Prayers for the Use of All Persons Who Come to the Baths for Cure* (London: Charles Brome, 1692), 3–5.
25. Thomas Guidott, *The Register of Bath* (London: F. Leach and Randal Taylor, 1694), 6–7, 59, 143–8.
26. Robert Pierce, *Bath Memoirs, or, Observations in Three and Forty Years Practice at the Bath* (Bristol: H. Hammond, 1697), n.p., 398.
27. William Oliver, *A Practical Essay on Fevers...To Which is Annex'd, A Dissertation on the Bath-Waters* (London: T. Goodwin, 1704), 241–251.
28. *A Letter from a Citizen of Bath, to his Excellency Dr R[adcliffe] at Tunbridge* (n.p., 1705), 7.
29. Richard Wendorf, *The Elements of Life: Biography and Portrait-Painting in Stuart and Georgian England* (Oxford: Oxford University Press, 1990), 211.
30. Goldsmith, *Works,* 3:300–301.

2 *The Stewards of the Feast*

1. J. Twistleton to Thomas Jervoise, 24 May 1710, Jervoise of Herriard Collection 44M69/F6/8/22, Hampshire Record Office.
2. Alexander Pope to Martha Blount, 6 October 1714, *Correspondence of Alexander Pope,* ed. George Sherburn (Oxford: Oxford University Press, 1956), 1: 260.
3. *The Diary of Dudley Ryder 1715–1716,* ed. William Matthews (London: Methuen, 1939), 240.
4. [Thomas Baker], *Tunbridge-Walks, or, The Yeoman of Kent* (London: Bernard Lintot, 1703), 21, 29–30, 59–60.
5. Alexander Sutherland, *Attempts to Revive Ancient Medical Doctrines* (London: Andrew Millar, 1763), 1:112.
6. *The Journeys of Celia Fiennes,* ed. John Hillaby. (London: Macdonald, 1983), 35.
7. Wood, *Description,* 226; Twistleton to Thomas Jervoise, 24 May 1710, Jervoise of Herriard Collection 44M69/F6/8/22, Hampshire Record Office.
8. *The Diary of Samuel Pepys,* ed. Robert Latham and William Mathews (Berkeley: University of California Press, 2000), 9: 240.
9. D'Urfey, *The Bath,* 1.
10. Elizabeth Verney to John Verney 8 September 1703, John Verney to Elizabeth Adams 29 September 1704, Verney Family Papers 52/260, 575, Claydon House Trust.
11. Wood, *Description,* 244.
12. *Bath Journal* 233 (8 August 1748). Italics in original.

13. Countess of Strafford to Earl of Strafford, 4 December 1711, *The Wentworth Papers 1705–1739,* ed. James J. Cartwright (London: Wyman and Sons, 1883), 219.
14. A. Ragisade to the Duke of Kent, 8 May 1706, Wrest Park Manuscripts L30/8/54/2, Bedford and Luton Archives. Author's translation from French.
15. *A Step to the Bath, with a Character of the Place* (London: J. How, 1700), 15.
16. Francis Fleming, *Timothy Ginnadrake,* 3:16.
17. Hembry, 115.
18. Goldsmith, *Works,* 3:299–300.
19. A. Ragisade to the Duke of Kent, 18, 22 May 1706, Wrest Park MSS L30/8/45/5, 54/1. Author's translation from French.
20. Hembry, 92.
21. Anne Nicholas to John Verney 7 June 1693, 14 June 1695, Verney Family Papers 46/520, 48/298.
22. Roger Townshend to Viscount Townshend of Raynham, 1 September [1698], MC 1601/78/862x8, Norfolk Record Office.
23. Peter Le Neve to Oliver Le Neve, September, 22 November 1701, MC 1639/4/815x1,1/40–59/386x5, Norfolk R.O.
24. *Tatler,* ed. Donald F. Bond (Oxford: Oxford University Press, 1987), 1:132; *The Spectator,* ed. Donald F. Bond (Oxford: Oxford University Press, 1965), 2:104.
25. J. Twistleton to Thomas Jervoise, 24 May 1710, Jervoise of Herriard Collection, 44M69/F6/8/22, Hampshire R.O.
26. Countess of Strafford to Earl of Strafford, 4 December 1711, *The Wentworth Papers 1705–1739,* ed. James J. Cartwright (London: Wyman and Sons, 1883), 219; John Gay to Thomas Parnell, 18 March 1715, *The Letters of John Gay,* ed. C. F. Burgess (Oxford: Oxford University Press, 1966), 21.
27. *Pepys Diary,* 9: 239–40.
28. Jean Manco, 'The Cross Bath,' *Bath History* 2 (1988): 61.
29. D'Urfey, *The Bath,* 1, 5, 19–20; Richard Steele, *Tatler,* ed. Donald Bond, 1:188. This appeared in *Tatler* number 24, 4 June 1709.
30. *A Step to the Bath, with a Character of the Place* (London: J. How, 1700), 13.
31. Samuel Gale, 'A Tour through Several Parts of England,' in John Nichols, ed., *Bibliotheca Topographica Britannica* (London: John Nichols, 1790; Facsimile edition New York: AMS Press, 1968), 3: 22.
32. Fiennes, *Journeys,* 36.
33. Thomas D'Urfey, *The Bath, or, The Western Lass* (London: Peter Buck, 1701), 1.
34. Wood, *Description,* 438.
35. 'On the Promiscuous Mixture of Company, and the Various Humours of Persons in the Hot Baths, at Bath in Somersetshire,' *The Lover's Miscellany: Or, Poems on Several Occasions, Amorous and Gallant* (London: J. Roberts, 1719), 27.
36. Thomas D'Urfey, *Wit and Mirth, or, Pills to Purge Melancholy* (London: Jacob Tonson, 1719), 2: 175.
37. *Ryder Diary,* 240; Anonymous Manuscript 'Diary of a Tour,' 1725, MS 38.43: 116, Bath Central Library.

38. Council Book 4:71–72, Bath City Archives.
39. [Mary Chandler], *A Description of Bath* (London: J. Gray, 1734), 11.
40. Wood, *Description*, 438.
41. Swift, 'The Progress of Marriage,' *Complete Poems*, 246.
42. Council Book 5: 322, 7: 53, BCA.
43. Manco, 'The Cross Bath,' 66–7.
44. Alexander Pope to Teresa Blount, September 1714, *Pope Correspondence*, 1: 257.
45. Council Book, 3: 545, 560; 4: 132.

3 *Regulator of the Diversions*

1. *London Magazine* 6 (December 1737): 684.
2. James Thomson to Mrs Robinson, 27 November 1742, Osborn Files 17858, Beinecke Library, Yale University.
3. Ibid.
4. Mrs Delany to Mrs Dewes, 4 September 1757, *The Autobiography and Correspondence of Mary Granville, Mrs Delany* (London: Richard Bentley, 1861. Facsimile edition New York: AMS Press, 1974), 3: 467.
5. Francis Fleming, *Timothy Ginnadrake*, 3: 27, 31–2.
6. Pope to John Caryll, 25 September 1714, *Pope Correspondence*, 1:256.
7. [Thomas Goulding], *An Essay Against Too Much Reading, with the Whole Lives and Proceedings of Sancho and Peepo, at Aix la Chapelle in Germany* (London: A. Moore, 1728), 22.
8. John Verney to Peter Lupart 18 August 1701, Verney Family Papers, 51/539.
9. *Bath Journal*, 405 (9 September 1751).
10. George Scott to John Allen, 15 October 1754, Egerton MSS 3728, ff15–17.
11. Peter Borsay, *The English Urban Renaissance: Culture and Society in the Provincial Town, 1660–1770* (Oxford: Oxford University Press, 1989), 272.
12. Hembry, 154.
13. Penelope J. Corfield, *The Impact of English Towns 1700–1800* (Oxford: Oxford University Press, 1982), 54–55.
14. Wood, *Description*, 417.
15. John Penrose, *Letters from Bath*, ed. Brigitte Mitchell and Hubert Penrose (Gloucester: Alan Sutton, 1983), 26.
16. Karl Ludwig von Pöllnitz, *Les Amusements de Spa: or, The Gallantries of Spaw in Germany*, tr. Hans de Veil (London: Ward and Chandler, 1737), 9–10.
17. [Thomas Goulding], *The Fortune-Hunter, or, The Gamester Reclaim'd* (Bath: privately printed, 1736), 5.
18. John, fifth Earl of Orrery, to Counsellor Kempe, 16 October 1731, *The Orrery Papers*, ed. Countess of Cork and Orrery (London: Duckworth, 1903), 1:99.
19. Daniel Defoe, *A Tour through the Whole Island of Great Britain* (2nd ed. London: J. Osborn, S. Birt, D. Browne, A. Millar, F. Cogan, J. Whiston, and J. Robinson, 1738), 2:241–2.

20. Elizabeth, Lady Anson to Marchioness Grey, 23 September, 4 November 1749, Wrest Park MSS L30/9/3/14–15.
21. *Orrery Papers,* 1: 99.
22. Whatley,*Characters,* 80–81; Wood, *Description,* 412–413; Goldsmith, *Works,* 3: 303.
23. Lady Hervey to Henrietta Howard, 7 June 1725, Additional MSS 22,628, f13.
24. Penrose, *Letters,* 29; Thomson to Robinson, 27 November 1742, Osborn MSS 17858.
25. Hembry, 154–155.
26. Mercy Doddridge to Philip Doddridge, Saturday 27 November 1742, *The Correspondence and Diary of Philip Doddridge,* ed. John Doddridge Humphreys (London: Henry Colburn and Richard Bentley, 1829), 4: 152.
27. Wood, *Description,* 442.
28. *The Diseases of Bath: A Satire Without a Frontispiece* (London: J. Roberts, 1737), 15, 20.
29. Wood, *Description,* 442.
30. Penrose, *Letters,* 36–7, 54.
31. Wood, *Description,* 416–417.
32. [Philip Thicknesse], *The New Prose Bath Guide for the Year 1778,* 2d ed. (London: Richard and John Dodsley, 1780), 90.
33. Tobias Smollett, *The Adventures of Peregrine Pickle,* ed. James L. Clifford (Oxford: Oxford University Press, 1964), 376–8; Thicknesse, *New Prose Bath Guide,* 88.
34. 'On the Game of Whisk', *The Bath Miscellany for the Year 1740* (Bath: W. Jones, 1741), 8.
35. Elizabeth Robinson [Montagu] to Margaret Cavendish Bentinck, Duchess of Portland, 15 December 1739, Montagu Papers MO 286.
36. George Lucy to Philippa Hayes, 6 January 1754, Lucy MSS L6/1432; same to same, 27 March 1751, L6/1426; 26 November 1753, L6/1430; 29 December 1758, L6/1452; 23 February 1760, L6/1454; 2 March 1760, L6/1455, Warwickshire Record Office.
37. Richard Seymour, *The Court Gamester* (London: Edmund Curll, 1719), iii, v–vi.
38. David Parlett, *The Oxford Dictionary of Card Games* (Oxford: Oxford University Press, 1992), 124.
39. *London Magazine* 6 (December 1737): 684.
40. George Lucy to Philippa Hayes, 29 December 1758, Lucy MSS L6/1452; Haywood, *Bath Intrigues,* 28–9.
41. *A Narrative of What Passed at Bath, Upon Account of the late Earthquake, Which Happened There on the 18th of March Last, in a Letter from a Gentleman at Bath, to his Friend at London* (London: W. Owen, 1750), 10–11.
42. James Brydges, first Duke of Chandos to Colonel Bladen, Bath, 23 October 1726, Stowe Manuscripts ST 57/29: 41, Huntington Library.
43. Chandos to the Marquis of Carnarvon, 11 September 1729, Stowe MSS ST 57/33: 246.
44. Mary Chamber to Henrietta Howard, 17 August 1730, Additional MSS 22, 627, f99.

45. George Lucy to Philippa Hayes, 2 March 1760, Lucy MSS L6/1455; Same to same 5 April 1760, L6/1457.
46. Mary Chamber to Henrietta Howard, 17 August 1730, Additional MSS 22,627, f100; Countess of Bristol to Earl of Bristol, 30 August 1721, *Letter Books of John Hervey, First Earl of Bristol*, ed. Sydenham Hervey (Wells: Ernest Jackson, 1894), 2:176.
47. *The Diseases of Bath: A Satire, Unadorn'd with a Frontispiece* (London: J. Roberts, 1737), 18.
48. *Orrery Papers*, 1: 99.
49. Christopher Anstey, *The New Bath Guide: Or, Memoirs of the B–r–d Family, in a Series of Poetical Epistles*, ed. Gavin Turner (Bristol: Broadcast Books, 1994), 85.
50. Countess of Bristol to Earl of Bristol, 29 May 1723, *Hervey Letters* 2: 303.
51. Elizabeth Montagu to Edward Montagu, July 1753, Montagu Papers MO 2285.
52. Amabel Campbell Grey, Lady Glenorchy, to Henry Grey, Duke of Kent, 21 November 1726, Wrest Park MSS L30/8/8/51.
53. Philip Carter, *Men and the Emergence of Polite Society, Britain 1660–1800* (London: Longman, 2001), 166–7.
54. P. Rameau, *The Dancing-Master, or, The Whole Art and Mystery of Dancing Explained*, tr. John Essex (2nd ed London: J. Brotherton, 1731), 2–12, 14–17, 24–6.
55. Goldsmith, *Works*, 3: 305–6.
56. Pope, *Epistle to a Lady*, ll.193–4.
57. *Letters from Lady Jane Coke to Her Friend Mrs Eyre*, ed. Florence Rathbone (London: Swan Sonnenschein, 1899), 8.
58. Neale, *Bath*, 26.
59. [John Playford], *The Dancing Schoole: Directions for Dancing Country Dances, with the Tunes to Each Dance, for the Treble Violin* (London: W. Pearson, 1716), 3.
60. Countess of Bristol to Earl of Bristol, 11 May 1723, *Hervey Letters* 2: 287–8.
61. 'The Arrival of the Storks: Or, the Overthrow of Two Monarchies. Written at Bath', in *A New Miscellany, being a Collection of Pieces of Poetry, from Bath, Tunbridge, Oxford, Epsom, and Other Places, in the Year 1725* (London: T. Warner, 1725), 48.
62. Goulding, *The Fortune Hunter*, 24–5.
63. Wood, *Description*, 351; Thomas Cox, *Magna Britannia et Hibernia, Antiqua et Nova, or, A New Survey of Great Britain* (London: E. and R. Nutt, 1720–1731), 4: 733.
64. Lawrence Stone, *Uncertain Unions and Broken Lives: Marriage and Divorce in England 1660–1857* (Oxford: Oxford University Press, 1995), 88–95.
65. Sir Thomas Cave to John Verney, Viscount Fermanagh, 17 September 1709, Verney Family Papers 54/123.
66. Countess of Bristol to Earl of Bristol, 16 September 1723, *Hervey Letters* 2: 331.
67. Hembry, 154.
68. Goulding, *The Fortune Hunter*, 102.
69. Goulding, *Essay*, 21.
70. Goulding, *The Fortune Hunter*, 38.
71. Ragisade to the Duchess of Kent 3 November 1713, Wrest Park MSS L30/8/54/3.

72. Pope to Martha Blount, 6 October 1714, *Pope Correspondence,* 1: 260.
73. J. Anthony Williams, ed., *Post-Reformation Catholicism in Bath* (London: Catholic Record Society, 1975), 1: 45.
74. Sir Gustavus Hume to Lord Polwarth, 30 November 1716, HMC Polwarth 1: 141.
75. *Ryder Diary,* 245.
76. 'Diary of Thomas Smith, Esq., of Shaw House,' *Wiltshire Archaeological and Natural History Magazine*, 11 (February 1869): 312.
77. *A True Account and Design of the Proceedings this Last Year in so Many Processions at Bath* (London: A. Moore, 1728), 5.
78. *Farley's Bristol Newspaper* 132 (11 November 1727); 161 (1 June 1728); 181 (19 October 1728); Goulding, *The Fortune Hunter,* 97.
79. Hembry, 117–18.
80. *Bath Journal* 59 (8 April 1745); Wood, *Description,* 439.
81. Goldsmith, *Works,* 3: 344.
82. 'On Mr Nash's present of his own Picture at full Length, fixt between the Busto's of Mr Pope, and Sir Is. Newton, in the Long Room at Bath', *Gentleman's Magazine* 11 (February 1741): 102.

4 *Overseer of the Marriage Market*

1. 'The Travels through England of Dr Richard Pococke,' ed. James Joel Cartwright, *Camden Society* 2nd series 44 (1889): 32.
2. Alexander Sutherland, *Attempts to Revive Ancient Medical Doctrines,*1: 124
3. Elizabeth Verney, Viscountess Fermanagh, to A. Tregea, 6 January 1706; John Verney, Viscount Fermanagh, to Peter Baxter, 14 January 1706, Verney Family Papers 53/147, 152.
4. George Lucy to Philippa Hayes, 10 January 1759, Lucy MSS L6/1451.
5. Chandos to Sir Charles Lloyd, 19 October 1726, Stowe Collection ST57/29: 36, Huntington Library.
6. Chandos to Henry Brydges, 23 October 1726, 2 February 1727, ST 57/29: 42–43, 170.
7. Chandos to Lloyd, 7 February 1727, ST 57/29: 184.
8. Samuel Johnson to Hester Thrale, 25 May 1780, *The Letters of Samuel Johnson,* ed. Bruce Redford (Princeton: Princeton University Press, 1992), 3: 262.
9. George Lucy to Philippa Hayes, 10 January 1759, Lucy MSS L6/1451.
10. Ingrid Tague, 'Love, Honor, and Obedience: Fashionable Women and the Discourse of Marriage in the Early Eighteenth Century,' *Journal of British Studies* 40 (January 2001): 76–81.
11. Letterbook of Cassandra, Duchess of Chandos (photocopy), Stowe Collection, STB Box 2, f 127, Huntington Library.
12. Elizabeth Robinson [Montagu] to Margaret, Duchess of Portland, 25 January 1740, Montagu Papers MO 290.
13. Susan Whyman, *Sociability and Power in Late Stuart England: The Cultural Worlds of the Verneys 1660–1720* (Oxford: Oxford University Press, 1999), 130.

14. Amanda Vickery, *The Gentleman's Daughter: Women's Lives in Georgian England* (New Haven: Yale University Press, 1998), 265–6.
15. Elizabeth, Lady Anson to Marchioness Grey, 9 Aug 1749, Wrest Park MSS L30/9/3/11.
16. Elizabeth Montagu to Margaret, Duchess of Portland, 18 April 1748, Montagu Papers MO 429.
17. *Ryder Diary*, 239.
18. Macky, *Journey through England*, 1722, 2: 132.
19. *Farley's Bristol Newspaper* 91 (28 January 1727).
20. Henry Penruddocke Wyndham to Tristram Huddleston Jervoise, 20 April 1762, Jervoise of Herriard Collection 44M69/F8/15/5.
21. Penrose, *Letters*, 103.
22. Macky, 2: 132.
23. *Ryder Diary*, 240.
24. [John Oldmixon], *Court Tales, or, A History of the Amours of the Present Nobility* (London: J. Roberts, 1717), 93.
25. Macky, 2: 128
26. Oldmixon, *Court Tales*, 93–6.
27. *Jests of Beau Nash*, 47–8.
28. *Memoirs of the Celebrated Miss Fanny M[urray]* (2nd ed. London: J. Scott and M. Thrush, 1759), 2–5, 24–34, 40–43, 47.
29. Melville, *Bath under Beau Nash*, 266.
30. George Scott to Dr Thomas Wilson, 11 June 1761, Egerton MSS 3736, f139.
31. Richard Nash to Charles Seymour, sixth Duke of Somerset, 17 August 1725, Petworth House Archives 16, West Sussex Record Office.
32. Same to same, 12 September 1725, PHA 16, West Sussex RO.
33. Goldsmith, *Works*, 3: 353, 356.
34. *Pope Correspondence*, 1: 260.
35. *Wilson Diaries*, 165.
36. Goldsmith, *Works*, 3: 321.
37. Sutherland, 1: 124.
38. Wood, *Description*, 412–13.
39. David M. Turner, *Fashioning Adultery: Gender, Sex and Civility in England, 1660–1740* (Cambridge: Cambridge University Press, 2002), 164.
40. Goldsmith, *Works*, 3: 331.
41. [Eliza Haywood], *Bath Intrigues: In Four Letters to a Friend in London* (London: J. Roberts, 1725. Facsimile edition Los Angeles: William Andrews Clark Memorial Library, 1986), 16, 25–6.
42. Whyman, *Sociability and Power*, 96.
43. Charlotte Lennox, *The Female Quixote, or, The Adventures of Arabella*, ed. Margaret Dalziel (Oxford: Oxford University Press, 1970), 274–6.
44. Whyman, *Sociability and Power*, 110, 142.
45. Lucy to Philippa Hayes, 2 March 1760, Lucy MSS 16/1455.

46. Wood, *Description,* 319–20.
47. [Richard Steele], 'A Description of the Bath, By Nestor Ironside, Esq.', in *The Tunbridge and Bath Miscellany for the Year 1714* (London: Edmund Curll, 1714), 20.
48. MS Commonplace Book of Gabriel Lepipre 1733–1753, Osborn Shelves c360/1: 17–31, Beinecke Library, Yale University.
49. Lepipre Commonplace Book, 1:256–7, 263.
50. Pope to John Caryll, 25 September 1714; Pope to Martha Blount, 6 October 1714, *Correspondence of Alexander Pope,* ed. George Sherburn (Oxford: Oxford University Press, 1956), 1: 255, 260.
51. MS Verses 'On Mrs Carrington & Miss Southwell desiring Mr Jones to Lampoon at Tunbridge Wells, 1745,' Lepipre Commonplace Book, 2: 36.
52. *Bath Journal* 353 (26 November 1750).
53. *Bath Miscellany 1740,* 43.
54. Abbé Le Blanc, *Letters on the English and French Nations*, translator unknown (London: J. Brindley, 1741), 2:373–7.
55. Jonathan Swift, 'The Progress of Marriage,' in *Jonathan Swift: Complete Poems,* ed. Pat Rogers (New Haven: Yale University Press, 1983), 246.
56. 'On Mr. and Mrs B–gs,' *Bath Miscellany 1740,* 1.
57. 'Corydon's Advice to Julia. On Mrs B–,' *A New Miscellany, being a Collection of Pieces of Poetry, from Bath, Tunbridge, Oxford, Epsom, and Other Places, in the Year 1725* (London: T. Warner, 1725), 63–4.
58. *Bath Miscellany 1740,* 16.
59. Goldsmith, *Works,* 3: 331.

5 Moderator of Disputes at Play

1. Anstey, *New Bath Guide,* 70.
2. Paul Langford, *A Polite and Commercial People: England 1727–1783* (Oxford: Oxford University Press, 1989), 572–4.
3. Gerda Reith, *The Age of Chance: Gambling in Western Culture* (London: Routledge, 1999), 1.
4. *New York Times* 3 May 2003, 6 May 2003.
5. Chandos to Colonel Bladen, 23 October 1726, ST 57/29: 41.
6. There is an example in the Lewis Walpole Library in Farmington, CT.
7. George Scott to John Newbery, 22 May 1762, Egerton MSS 3737, f176.
8. Goldsmith, *Works,* 3: 357.
9. Chesterfield to the Countess of Suffolk, 2 November 1734, *Letters to and from Henrietta, Countess of Suffolk, and her Second Husband, the Hon. George Berkeley* (London: John Murray, 1824), 2: 116–17.
10. Countess of Bristol to Earl of Bristol, 18 September 1723, *Hervey Letters,* 2: 333.
11. Fleming, *Timothy Ginnadrake,* 3: 22.
12. *Wilson Diary,* 165.
13. Goldsmith, *Works,* 3: 312 and note.

14. Letitia Cornwallis to Cassandra Duchess of Chandos, 23, 30 August 1730, Stowe Collection STB 1(27–8).
15. Goldsmith, *Works,* 3: 312–13.
16. Goulding, *The Fortune Hunter,* 77.
17. *Memoirs of the Celebrated Miss Fanny M[urray]* (2nd ed. London: J. Scott and M. Thrush, 1759), 5–6, 12.
18. See, for example, Lynn Hunt, ed., *The Invention of Pornography: Obscenity and the Origins of Modernity, 1500–1800* (New York: Zone Books, 1993).
19. Most notably Thomas Kavanagh, in *Enlightenment and the Shadows of Chance* (Baltimore: Johns Hopkins University Press, 1993).
20. Theophilus Lucas, *Lives of the Gamesters* (London: Jonas Brown, 1714), reprinted in Cyril Hughes Hartmann, ed., *Games and Gamesters of the Restoration* (London: George Routledge, 1930), 271.
21. Reith, *Age of Chance,* 72.
22. Thomas D'Urfey, *The Bath, or, The Western Lass* (London: Peter Buck, 1701), 29.
23. Quoted in Thomas Kavanagh, 'Gambling, Chance, and the Discourse of Power in *Ancien Regime* France,' *Renaissance and Modern Studies* 37 (1994): 35.
24. Chandos to Bladen, 23 October 1726, Huntington MSS ST 57/29: 41.
25. Countess of Bristol to Earl of Bristol, 20 September 1721, *Hervey Letter Books* 2:203; Chesterfield to Countess of Suffolk, 2 November 1734, *Letters to and from Henrietta, Countess of Suffolk, and her Second Husband, the Hon. George Berkeley* (London: John Murray, 1824), 2: 116; Richard Nash to Lady Jerningham, n.d., MS AL 658, Bath Central Library.
26. A. Ragisade to the Duke of Kent 18, 27 May 1706, Wrest Park MSS L30/8/54/1, 12. Author's translation from French.
27. Wood, *Description,* 225.
28. Mrs Francis Vaughan to John Sommerset, 23 November 1722, MS AL 987, Bath Central Library.
29. Eliza Haywood, *Bath Intrigues*, 39.
30. Diary of a Tour, 1725, MS 38.43, ff117–18, Bath Central Library.
31. Goulding, *Essay Against Too Much Reading,* 19–22.
32. Amanda Foreman, *Georgianna, Duchess of Devonshire* (New York: Random House, 1998), 35.
33. Kavanagh, *Enlightenment and the Shadows of Chance*, 30.
34. Lucas, *Lives of the Gamesters,* 275.
35. John Ashton, *The History of Gambling in England* (London: Duckworth, 1898), 136.
36. Charles Cotton, *The Compleat Gamester* (London: R. Cutler and Henry Brome, 1674) reprinted in Cyril Hughes Hartmann, ed., *Games and Gamesters of the Restoration* (London: George Routledge, 1930), 82, 84.
37. Anstey, *New Bath Guide,* 102.
38. Sarah Scott to Elizabeth Montagu, 27 October 1754, Montagu Papers MO 5244.
39. Quoted in Lewis Melville, *Bath under Beau Nash,* 184.

40. [John Macky], *A Journey through England in Familiar Letters for a Gentleman Here, to His Friend Abroad* (London: J. Roberts, 1714), 58.
41. Lucas, 27–28, 114–15.
42. Jeremy Collier, *An Essay upon Gaming, in a Dialogue between Callimachus and Dolomedes* (London: John Morphew, 1713. Reprint edition Edinburgh: Edmund Goldsmid, 1885), 30.
43. *Bath Anecdotes,* 32–3.
44. Goldsmith, *Works,* 3: 350.
45. *Bath Anecdotes,* 97.
46. Goldsmith, *Works,* 3: 389.
47. Letitia Cornwallis to Cassandra Duchess of Chandos, 23 August 1730, Stowe Collection STB 1(27).
48. Elizabeth, Countess of Bristol to John, Earl of Bristol, 30 August, 20 September 1721, *Hervey Letter Books,* 2: 176, 203.
49. Mary Chamber to Henrietta Howard, 27 July 1730, Additional MSS 22, 627, f98.
50. *Guardian* 174 (30 September 1713), in John Calhoun Stephens, ed., *The Guardian,* (Lexington: University Press of Kentucky, 1982), 567–8.
51. Collier, *Essay upon Gaming,* 19.
52. G. Odingsells, *The Bath Unmask'd: A Comedy* (London: J. Walthoe, 1725), 64, 76.
53. Peter Borsay, *The English Urban Renaissance* (Oxford: Oxford University Press, 1989) 250.
54. *Lord Hervey and His Friends,* ed. Earl of Ilchester (London: John Murray, 1950), 94.
55. *Gentleman's Magazine* 1 (September 1731): 397; Wood, *Description,* 448.
56. Wood, *Description,* 447–9, 452.
57. Horace Walpole to Horace Mann, 21 August 1755, *Correspondence of Horace Walpole,* ed. W. S. Lewis et al (New Haven: Yale University Press) 20: 492. Emphasis in original.
58. [Lydia Grainger], *Modern Amours, or, A Secret History of the Adventures of Some Personages of the First Rank* (London: n.p., 1733), 23.
59. Goldsmith, *Works,* 3: 325–7; Wood, *Description,* 448.
60. Letitia Cornwallis to Cassandra, Duchess of Chandos, 23 and 30 August 1730, Stowe Collection STB 1(27–8).
61. *London Magazine* 14 (July 1745): 345. Piece reprinted from *Universal Spectator* 875 (13 July 1745).

6 *A Duke, an Architect and a Landlady*

1. Borsay, *Image of Bath,* 300.
2. Wood, *Description,* n.p.
3. Chandos to Anne Phillips, 9, 16 November, 4 December 1727, Chandos Letterbooks, Stowe Collection ST 57/31: 4, 13–14, 33, Huntington Library.
4. Sylvia McIntyre, 'Bath: The Rise of a Resort Town, 1660–1800,' in Peter Clark, ed, *Country Towns in Pre-Industrial England* (Leicester: Leicester University Press, 1981), 202.

5. Wood, *Description*, 225–6, 231.
6. Much of the following discussion of John Wood the Elder is taken from Tim Mowl and Brian Earnshaw, *John Wood: Architect of Obsession* (Bath: Millstream, 1988).
7. Wood, *Description*, 225, 242.
8. Council Book 4: 396, Bath City Archive.
9. Wood, *Description*, 248, 381.
10. McIntyre, in Clark, ed., *Country Towns*, 219.
11. Sutherland, 1: 112.
12. Wood, *Description*, 244.
13. Neale, 39, 41.
14. [Claver Morris], *The Diary of a West Country Physician 1684–1726*, ed. Edmund Hobhouse (London: Simpkin Marshall, 1934), 64.
15. Penrose, *Letters from Bath*, 24–7.
16. Elizabeth, Lady Anson to Marchioness Grey, 30 August 1749, Wrest Park MSS L30/9/3/12.
17. William Brydges to James Brydges, 19 September 1711, Stowe Collection ST 58/9: 174–5.
18. Cassandra Brydges, Countess of Carnarvon, to Catherine Bourchier, September 1715, Stowe Collection STB 2: 8.
19. Chandos to Colonel Horsey, 25 April 1726, ST 57/28: 80.
20. Francis Brydges to William Brydges, 16 August 1726, Brydges Papers K12/44, Herefordshire Record Office.
21. Neale, 134.
22. Chandos to James Theobald, 4 April 1728, ST57/31: 75.
23. Chandos to Wood, 19 August 1727, ST 57/30: 231; Chandos Accounts, ST 12/4: 46.
24. Chandos to Anne Phillips, 16 May 1727, 5 July 1729, Chandos to Wood, 5 July 1729, ST 57/30: 11, 33: 178–9.
25. Chandos to Wood, 16, 27 December 1727, ST 57/31: 49, 58–9.
26. Chandos to Wood, 24 September 1728, ST 57/32: 172.
27. Chandos to Wood, 16 April 1728, ST57/31: 203–4.
28. Chandos to Anne Phillips, 15 August 1728, ST 57/32: 123.
29. James Farquharson to Wood, 19 December 1734, ST57/45: 225.
30. Chandos to Harris, 10 October 1730, ST 57/36: 47.
31. Neale, 119.
32. Chandos to Anne Phillips, 8 December 1726, ST 57/29: 110.
33. Chandos to Anne Phillips, 6 February 1727, ST 57/29: 178–9.
34. Chandos to Anne Phillips, 6 April 1727, ST 57/29: 290.
35. Chandos to Anne Phillips, 23 March, 24 April, 4 May 1727, ST 57/29: 254, 313, 332.
36. Chandos to Anne Phillips, 23 May, 10 July 1727, ST 57/30: 24, 116.
37. Chandos to Anne Phillips, 25 July 1727, ST 57/30: 153.
38. Chandos Accounts, ST 12/4: 155–9.

39. Neale, 141.
40. Chandos Accounts, ST 12/4: 284–93.
41. Neale, 55.
42. Chandos to Anne Phillips, 14 February 1727, ST 57/29: 199.
43. Chandos to Jane Degge, 25 June, 5, 16 July 1730, ST 57/35: 99, 161, 185–6.
44. Chandos to Jane Degge, 5 January 1731, ST 57/36: 336; James Farquharson to Jane Degge, 10 February 1731, ST 57/37: 58.
45. Chandos to John Ferguson, 12 November 1741, ST 57/55: 290.
46. Jane Austen, *Northanger Abbey and Persuasion,* ed. John Davies and James Kinsley (Oxford: Oxford University Press, 1971), 367, 262.

7 *Stone, Bricks, Mortar and Wood*

1. Wood, *Description,* 290, 320.
2. The standard biography of Allen, from which much of the material below comes, is Benjamin Boyce's *The Benevolent Man: A Life of Ralph Allen of Bath* (Cambridge: Harvard University Press, 1967).
3. Pope to Justice Fortescue, 23 January 1740, *Pope Correspondence* 4: 221–2.
4. James Ayres, *Building the Georgian City* (New Haven: Yale University Press, 1998), 71.
5. MS Autobiography of Richard Jones, Bath Reference Library, quoted in Mowl and Earnshaw, 43.
6. Boyce, 100; Walter Ison, *The Georgian Buildings of Bath* (London: Faber and Faber, 1948; reprint edition Bath: Kingsmead, 1969), 137.
7. Elizabeth Anson to Thomas Anson, 1 November 1749, D615/P(S)/1/3/10, Staffordshire Record Office.
8. The map is reproduced in Ison, *Georgian Buildings of Bath,* plate 2.
9. Pope to William Warburton, 12 November 1741, *Pope Correspondence,* 4: 370.
10. *Bath Journal* 271 (1 May 1749).
11. Much of this paragraph is adapted from Ayres, *Building the Georgian City,* 19–21, 23.
12. Mowl and Earnshaw, 39.
13. Simon Varey, *Space and the Eighteenth-Century Novel* (Cambridge: Cambridge University Press, 1990), 89.
14. Peter Gay, *The Enlightenment: The Rise of Modern Paganism* (New York: W.W. Norton, 1977), 39–71.
15. Mowl and Earnshaw, 24–5.
16. Christopher Woodward, '"O Lord! Bath is Undone; 'Tis Undone; 'Tis Undone!": Bath and the Pre-History of Architectural Conservation,' *Bath History* 7 (1998): 16.
17. Neale, 166.
18. Mowl and Earnshaw, 65.
19. Plans of these houses are reproduced in Ison, *The Georgian Buildings of Bath,* 106.
20. Mowl and Earnshaw, 66, 69.
21. Wood, *Description,* 347.
22. Mowl and Earnshaw, 136–7,139–40.

23. Wood, *Description,* 350–51.
24. Tobias Smollett, *An Essay on the External Use of Water* (London: M. Cooper, 1752), 38–9.
25. Wood, *Description,* 320.
26. Council Book 7: 53; Smollett, *Essay,* 34, 44.
27. Mowl and Earnshaw, 149.
28. Elizabeth, Lady Anson to Amabel, Marchioness Grey, 25 November 1755, Wrest Park MSS L30/9/3/54.
29. Sutherland, 1: 123–4, 128 .
30. Ibid., 1: 126.
31. Briggs, 'Importance of Beau Nash,' 219.
32. Sutherland 1:126–7, 129.

8 Libertines and Methodists in Sickness and in Health

1. *Bath Journal*, 268 (10 April 1749).
2. *Bath Journal*, 269 (17 April 1749).
3. Wood, *Description*, 442.
4. *The Letters of the Reverend John Wesley* (London: Epworth, 1931), 1: 319.
5. Edwin Welch, *Spiritual Pilgrim: A Reassessment of the Life of the Countess of Huntingdon* (Cardiff: University of Wales Press, 1995), 69.
6. *The Works of the Late Reverend James Hervey* (Edinburgh: John Reid, 1769), 5: 248.
7. Philip Doddridge to Mercy Doddridge, 3 April 1743, London New College MSS L1/1/46, Dr Williams's Library.
8. A. C. H. Seymour, *The Life and Times of Selina Countess of Huntingdon* (London: William Edward Painter, 1844), 1: 27, 443.
9. Boyd Stanley Schlenther, *Queen of the Methodists: The Countess of Huntingdon and the Eighteenth-Century Crisis of Faith and Society* (Bishop Auckland: Durham Academic Press, 1997), 24; Barbeau, *Life and Letters in Bath*, 160.
10. Welch, *Spiritual Pilgrim*, 2.
11. Ibid., 5, 53, 60–61
12. Philip Doddridge to Mercy Doddridge, 11 September 1746, New College MSS L1/1/91 (emphasis added); Elizabeth Rappit to Philip Doddridge, 17 February 1743, New College MSS L1/8/113; Mercy Doddridge to Philip Doddridge, 27 November 1742, *The Correspondence and Diary of Philip Doddridge,* ed. John Doddridge Humphreys (London: Henry Colburn and Richard Bentley, 1829), 4: 151–2; Philip Doddridge to Mercy Doddridge, 8 December 1742, New College MSS L1/1/39, Dr Williams's Library, London.
13. *Wilson Diaries*, 165.
14. John Brown, *On the Pursuit of False Pleasure, and the Mischiefs of Immoderate Gaming* (Bath: James Leake, 1750); *Bath Journal* 323 (30 April 1750).
15. Wood, *Description*, 312.

16. Daniel Defoe, Samuel Richardson, and others, *A Tour through the Whole Island of Great Britain* (2nd ed. London: J. Osborn, S. Birt, D. Browne, A. Millar, F. Cogan, J. Whiston, and J. Robinson, 1738), 2: 242.
17. *Bath Miscellany* 1740, 9.
18. J. Anthony Williams, *Post-Reformation Catholicism in Bath* (London: Catholic Record Society, 1975), 1: 50–53.
19. Alexander Pope to Martha Blount, 17 September 1734, *Pope Correspondence*, 3: 435.
20. Williams, *Catholicism in Bath*, 1: 61, *Penrose Letters*, 82.
21. [Mary Barber], *Poems on Several Occasions* (London: C. Rivington, 1734), 142.
22. Ken, *Bath Prayers*, 42–3.
23. Goulding, *The Fortune Hunter*, 23.
24. Anita Guerrini, *Obesity and Depression in the Enlightenment: The Life and Times of George Cheyne* (Norman: University of Oklahoma Press, 2000), 114.
25. Wood, *Description*, 279.
26. Mowl and Earnshaw, 141.
27. Penrose, *Letters*, 59.
28. Anne Borsay, *Medicine and Charity in Georgian Bath: A Social History of the General Infirmary, c. 1739–1830* (Aldershot: Ashgate, 1999), 192, 194–5.
29. *Bath Journal* 542 (6 May 1754).
30. Goldsmith, *Works*, 3: 340.
31. Elizabeth Robinson [Montagu] to Margaret, Duchess of Portland, 4 January 1740, Montagu Papers MO 288.
32. Steele, 'A Description of the Bath', *Tunbridge and Bath Miscellany*, 23.
33. Sir Justinian Isham to Justinian Isham, 6 June 1726, Isham Correspondence 1880, Northamptonshire Record Office.
34. George Cheyne, *The English Malady* (London: George Strahan, 1733), 277.
35. *Bath Journal* 274 (22 May 1749), 275 (29 May 1749).
36. *Journeys of Celia Fiennes*, 37.
37. George Grenville to Richard Temple Grenville, second Earl Temple, 25 December 1738, Stowe Collection STG 192 (7), Huntington Library.
38. William Oliver, *A Practical Essay on Fevers ... To Which is Annex'd, A Dissertation on the Bath-Waters* (London: T. Goodwin, 1704), 226–7.
39. Varey, *Space and the Novel*, 73.
40. Cheyne to Selina, Countess of Huntingdon, 18 January 1734, *The Letters of Dr George Cheyne to the Countess of Huntingdon,* ed. Charles F. Mullett (San Marino: Huntington Library, 1940), 35.
41. Smollett, *Essay*, 34.
42. Elizabeth Montagu to Sarah Robinson [Scott], 11 October 1743, Montagu Papers MO 5636.
43. Goldsmith, *Works*, 3: 357.
44. Cheyne to Countess of Huntingdon, 3 August 1734, *Cheyne Huntingdon Letters*, 42.
45. Sarah Scott to Elizabeth Montagu, 24 February, 16 March 1753; Elizabeth Montagu to Sarah Scott, March 1753, Montagu Papers MO 5233–4, 5732.

46. George Cheyne, *An Essay of Health and Long Life* (London: George Strahan, 1724), 1–2.
47. Guerrini, *Obesity and Depression*, 121–2, 127.
48. Cheyne, *English Malady*, 52, 156.
49. *The Letters of Doctor George Cheyne to Samuel Richardson (1733–1743)*, ed. Charles F. Mullett (Columbia: University of Missouri Press, 1943), 76.
50. Roy Porter and G.S. Rousseau, *Gout: The Patrician Malady* (New Haven: Yale University Press, 1998).
51. Goldsmith, *Works*, 3: 364–5, 391.
52. George Cheyne, *Observations Concerning the Nature and Due Method of Treating the Gout* (London: George Strahan, 1720), 14.
53. Cheyne, *Observations*, iv, 17, 42.
54. Cheyne, *English Malady*, 210.
55. Cheyne, *Essay*, 7–8.
56. Cheyne, *Essay*, 106–8.
57. Cheyne, *English Malady*, 182.
58. Smollett, *Essay*, 34, 38.
59. Elizabeth Montagu to Sarah Robinson [Scott], 2 July 1749, Montagu Papers MO 2210.
60. Cheyne, *Observations*, 57–8.
61. John Ambrose to unidentified, 25 November 1768, Jervoise of Herriard Collection 44M69/F19/2/22.
62. Quoted in Borsay, *Image of Bath*, 256.

9 Old Beaux Knash

1. 'On the Ancient City of Bath. Written on the Finishing the Circus,' in *Water Poetry: A Collection of Verses Written at Several Public Places* (London: G. Pearch, 1775), 31.
2. Sutherland, 1: 123–4.
3. *A Narrative of ... the Late Earthquake,* 4.
4. Trevor Fawcett, *Bath Entertain'd: Amusements, Recreations and Gambling at the Eighteenth-Century Spa* (Bath: Ruton, 1998), 46.
5. *Bath Anecdotes and Characters,* 23–31.
6. *Reflexions on Gaming, and Observations on the Laws Relating Thereto* (London: Henry Woodfall and William Strahan, 1750), 10–13, 42–43.
7. *Memoirs of Dr Charles Burney 1726–1769,* ed. Slava Klima, Gary Bowers, and Kerry S. Grant (Lincoln: University of Nebraska Press, 1988), 75.
8. *Reflexions on Gaming,* 36, 43–44.
9. Fawcett, *Bath Entertain'd,* 37.
10. Elizabeth Montagu to Edward Montagu, 21 July 1751, Montagu Papers MO 2233.
11. *Bath Journal* 350 (5 November 1750).
12. *Bath Journal* 360 (14 January 1751).
13. Sarah Scott to Elizabeth Montagu, 27 October 1754, Montagu Papers MO 5244.

14. *Bath Epistles, that have Pass'd between Miss Hazard, Lady Motherly, … &c. Highly Proper to be Read by Those who Frequent Bath, Tunbridge-Wells, &c.* (London: J. Smyth, 1757).
15. *Bath Journal* 350 (5 November 1750).
16. John Brown, *On the Pursuit of False Pleasure, and the Mischiefs of Immoderate Gaming* (Bath: James Leake, 1750); *Bath Journal* 323 (30 April 1750).
17. *Bath Journal* 218 (25 April 1748)
18. *Bath Journal* 421 (30 December 1751).
19. Bill of Complaint in *Richard Nash* v. *John Wiltshire*, 16 May 1757, Public Record Office, Chancery Proceedings, Six Clerks Series, PRO C12/492/19.
20. Answer of Charles Simpson in *Nash* v. *Simpson*, 11 January 1757, PRO C12/492/20; Answers of John, Walter, and William Wiltshire in *Nash* v. *Wiltshire*, 4 April and 15 July 1758, PRO C12/492/19.
21. Anonymous lampoon, quoted in *Notes and Queries*, second series 6 (24 July 1858): 75.
22. Quoted in Barbeau, 46, note 1.
23. Wapole to Sir Horace Mann, 21 March 1755, *The Letters of Horace Walpole,* ed. Peter Cunningham (Edinburgh: John Grant, 1906), 2: 480–481.
24. Elizabeth Montagu to Edward Montagu, 13 August 1753, Montagu Papers, MO 2292.
25. George Scott to John Allen, 13 March 1754, Egerton MSS 3727 ff 40–41.
26. George Scott to Thomas Wilson, 18 March 1760, Egerton MSS 3735, f109.
27. George Scott to William Jackson, 25 October 1760, Egerton MSS 3735, f120; Mary Granville Pendarves Delany to Mrs Dewes, 28 October 1760, *The Autobiography and Correspondence of Mary Granville, Mrs Delany* (London: Richard Bentley, 1861. Facsimile edition New York: AMS Press, 1974), 3: 606.
28. Sarah Scott to Elizabeth Montagu, 17 November 1754, Montagu Papers MO 5245.
29. John Archer to Susannah Archer, 27 February 1754, Monson 28B/7/2/34, Lincolnshire Archive.
30. Goldsmith, *Works,* 3: 359–360.
31. Deposition of James Quin in *Nash* v. *Wiltshire*, PRO C12/1486/13.
32. *Bath Chronicle* (12 March 1761).
33. Penrose, *Letters,* 82.
34. *Bath Journal* 911 (16 February 1761).
35. George Lucy to Philippa Hayes, 4 April 1762, Lucy MSS L6/1466.

10 The King is Dead; Long Live the King

1. *Bath Journal* 911 (16 February 1761).
2. Lady Caroline Brydges to James Brydges, Marquis of Carnarvon, 13 August 1751, Stowe Collection STB 11(2).
3. *Bath Journal* 494 (4 June 1753), 495 (11 June 1753), 496 (18 June 1753).
4. *The Life of Mr James Quin* (London: S. Bladon, 1766), 97.
5. George Scott to Philip Allen, 5 February 1763, Egerton MSS 3738, f75.

6. Friedrich Graf von Kielmansegge, *Diary of a Journey to England in the Years 1761–1762,* tr. Philippa Sidney Grafin von Kielmansegge (London: Longmans, 1902), 116–7.
7. George Scott to William Jackson, 18 May 1761; George Scott to Richard Crabbe, 27 May 1761, Egerton MSS 3736, ff114, 126.
8. Francis Fleming, *Timothy Ginnadrake,* 3: 126.
9. George Scott to Charles Moore, 19 December 1761; George Scott to Elizabeth Jones, 6 February 1762, Egerton MSS 3737, ff72, 96; George Scott to Philip Allen, 5 February 1763, Egerton MSS 3738, f74.
10. James Boswell, *London Journal 1762–1763*, ed. Frederick A. Pottle (New Haven: Yale University Press, 1992), 228, 327.
11. James Boswell, *Life of Samuel Johnson*, ed. George Birbeck Hill and L. F. Powell (Oxford: Oxford University Press, 1934–50), 1: 385, 456.
12. *Life of Quin*, 101.
13. Thomas Butler to Thomas Matthew, 10 August 1761, Thomas Wilson to Samuel Derrick, 7 February, 6 March 1762, Forster MSS 146/16, 33–4, National Art Library, Victoria and Albert Museum.
14. Tobias Smollett, *The Expedition of Humphry Clinker*, ed. Lewis Knapp (Oxford: Oxford University Press, 1966), 63.
15. *Boswell's London Journal*, 327.
16. Samuel Derrick, *Letters* (London: L. Davis and C. Reymers, 1767), 2: 83–4, 87.
17. *Life of Quin*, 105–6.
18. Francis Fleming, *Timothy Ginnadrake*, 3: 129.
19. George Scott to Wadham Wyndham, 1 June 1763, Egerton MSS 3738, f161.
20. Edmund Baker to Samuel Derrick, 27 September 1763, St. Leger to Samuel Derrick, 31 October 1763, Thomas Wilson to Samuel Derrick, 6 March 1764, Thomas Harvie to Samuel Derrick, 3 March 1765, Forster MSS 146/18–20, 30.
21. *Life of Quin,* 101–5.
22. *A Serious and Earnest Address, to the Subscribers to the Balls, and Other Persons Frequenting the Rooms at Bath; Concerning the Present Situation of Affairs* (Bath: C. Pope, 1767), 12–16.
23. Smollett, *Humphry Clinker*, 39, 62.
24. *Derrick's Jests; or, The Wits Chronicle* (London: I. Fell, 1769), 4, 14, 35.
25. Derrick, *Letters*, 2: 83, 103–4.
26. Smollett, *Humphry Clinker*, 49.
27. Penrose, *Letters from Bath*, 135–6.
28. *Life of Quin,* 97.
29. Fleming, 3: 128.
30. Derrick, *Letters,* 2: 89.
31. Penrose, *Letters from Bath*, 174.
32. George Scott to Elizabeth Jones, 18 December 1762, Egerton MSS 3738, ff 29–30.
33. 'The Two Kings of Bath', *The Bath Contest* (Bath: Archer and Cruttwell, 1769), 44.
34. *Bath Contest*, 11, 40.
35. *Bath Contest*, 3.

36. *Bath Contest*, 8.
37. *Bath Contest*, 19–20.
38. Entry for 31 March 1769, Anonymous Diary, January–August 1769, Huntington Library MSS 62593.
39. *Bath Contest*, 15–16.
40. *Bath Contest*, 9–10, 18, 25, 46.
41. Entry for 3 April 1769, Anonymous Diary, Huntington Library MSS 62593.
42. *Bath Contest*, 21, 57–8.
43. *Bath Contest*, 37, 44.
44. Entry for 12 April 1769, Anonymous Diary, Huntington Library MSS 62593; *Bath Chronicle* 443 (13 April 1769).
45. 'The BATH RIOT Described,' in *The Conciliade, being a Supplement to the Bath Contest* (Bath: Archer and Crutwell, 1769), 12–13.
46. *Bath Journal* 1335 (10 April 1769).

List of Illustrations

Picture credits

Bath Central Library: 22, 42; Bath Preservation Trust: 31; British Museum: Department of Prints and Drawings: 27; Christie's: 40; Huntington Library, San Marino, California: 6; National Portrait Gallery, London: 2, 18, 20, 30; private collection/www.bridgeman.co.uk: 10; Royal National Hospital for Rheumatic Diseases: 38; Tate Gallery: 41; Tunbridge Wells Museum: 16; Victoria Art Gallery, Bath and North East Council: 28, 35, 37, 44; Victoria Art Gallery, Bath and North East Council/www.bridgeman.co.uk: 1, 47

While every effort has been made to contact copyright-holders of illustrations, the author and publishers would be grateful for information about any illustrations where they have been unable to trace them, and would be glad to make amendments in further editions.

Select Bibliography

Manuscript sources

Bath Central Library:

Diary of a Tour, 1725

Richard Jones, 'The Life of Richard Jones,' n.d.

Sydenham Collection

Bath City Archives, Bath and Northeast Somerset Record Office:

Council Books

Bedfordshire and Luton Archives:

Wrest Park Manuscripts

British Library:

Letter Books of George Scott, Egerton Manuscripts 3727–3739

Frances Sheridan, 'A Journey to Bath,' 1749, Additional MSS 25,975

Hampshire Record Office:

Jervoise of Herriard Collection

Huntington Library:

Anonymous Diary, January–August 1769, MSS 62593

Chandos Letterbooks, MSS ST 57–58

Montagu Papers, MSS MO

Northamptonshire Record Office:

Isham Papers

John Scattergood Diary

Public Record Office:

Richard Nash v. *John Wiltshire*, PRO C12/492/19–21

Staffordshire Record Office:

Anson Letters
Victoria and Albert Museum:
Papers of Samuel Derrick, Forster MSS
Warwickshire Record Office:
Lucy Manuscripts

Periodicals

Bath Advertiser
Bath Chronicle
Bath Journal
Farley's Bristol Journal
Gentleman's Magazine
London Magazine

Printed sources

Advice to Mr L[ogga]n, the Fan-Painter, at Tunbridge-Wells (London: H. Carpenter, 1748).
Bath Anecdotes and Characters: By the Genius Loci (London: John Dodsley and Edward and Charles Dilly, 1782).
Bath: A Poem (London: Longman and Shewell; Bath: James Leake, 1748).
The Bath, Bristol, Tunbridge and Epsom Miscellany (London: T. Dormer, 1735).
The Bath Contest (Bath: Archer and Cruttwell, 1769).
The Bath Miscellany for the Year 1740 (Bath: W. Jones, 1741).
The Bath Toasts, for the Year 1715. Inscrib'd to Mr. Pope (London: Edmund Curll, 1715).
The Conciliade, being a Supplement to the Bath Contest (Bath: Archer and Crutwell, 1769).
Derrick's Jests; or, The Wits Chronicle (London: I. Fell, 1769).
The Difference between Keeping and Marriage (London: W. Webb, 1743).
The Diseases of Bath: A Satire Without a Frontispiece (London: J. Roberts, 1737).

A Dream, or, The Force of Fancy: A Poem, Containing Characters of the Company Now at Bath (London: Edmund Curll, 1710).
The Jests of Beau Nash, Late Master of the Ceremonies at Bath (London: W. Bristow, 1763).
A Journey to Bath and Bristol: An Heroi-Comic-Historic-, and Geographical Poem (London: J. Roberts, [1717]).
A Letter from a Citizen of Bath, to his Excellency Dr. R[adcliffe] at Tunbridge (N.p., 1705).
A Letter from the Facetious Doctor Andrew Tripe, at Bath, to the Venerable Nestor Ironside (London: John Morphew, 1713).
A Letter to Dr. Oliver, Desiring Him to Reconcile some few of the Assertions in his Essay on Feavers (London: A. Baldwin, 1704).
The Life of Mr. James Quin (London: S. Bladon, 1766).
The Lover's Miscellany: Or, Poems on Several Occasions, Amorous and Gallant (London: J. Roberts, 1719).
The Loyalty and Glory of the City of BATH (London: A. Milbourn, 1689).
Memoirs of the Celebrated Miss Fanny M[urray] (2d ed. London: J. Scott and M. Thrush, 1759). *A Narrative of What Passed at Bath, Upon Account of the late Earthquake, Which Happened There on the 18th of March Last, in a Letter from a Gentleman at Bath, to his Friend at London* (London: W. Owen, 1750).
A New Miscellany, being a Collection of Pieces of Poetry, from Bath, Tunbridge, Oxford, Epsom, and Other Places, in the Year 1725 (London: T. Warner, 1725).
News from Bath (London: R. Baldwin, 1689).
Origines Bathenses: or, The Origin of Bath, a Burlesque (London: T. Cooper, 1736).
The Pleasures of the Bath: With the First and Second Part of the Tipling Philosophers (Bristol: S. Farley, 1721).
The Rival Ball Rooms (Bath: R. Crutwell, 1774).
A Serious and Earnest Address, to the Subscribers to the Balls, and Other Persons Frequenting the Rooms at Bath; Concerning the Present Situation of Affairs (Bath: C. Pope, 1767).

A Step to the Bath, with a Character of the Place (London: J. How, 1700).

The Tunbridge and Bath Miscellany for the Year 1714 (London: Edmund Curll, 1714).

Tunbrigialia: or Tunbridge Miscellanies of the Year 1730 (London: T.B., 1730).

Tunbrigalia, or, The Tunbridge Miscellany, for the Years 1737, 1738, 1739 (London: T. Webb, 1740).

Water Poetry: A Collection of Verses Written at Several Public Places. (London: G. Pearch, 1775).

Addison, Joseph, and Richard Steele. *The Spectator*, edited by Donald F. Bond (Oxford: Oxford University Press, 1965).

Anstey, Christopher. *The New Bath Guide: Or, Memoirs of the B-- r--d Family, in a Series of Poetical Epistles,* edited by Gavin Turner (Bristol: Broadcast Books, 1994).

Baillie, Grisell. *The Household Book of Lady Grisell Baillie 1692–1733,* edited by Robert Scott Moncrieff (Edinburgh: Scottish Historical Society, 1911).

[Baker, Thomas]. *Tunbridge-Walks, or, The Yeoman of Kent* (London: Bernard Lintot, 1703).

[Barber, Mary]. *Poems on Several Occasions* (London: C. Rivington, 1734).

Brown, John. *On the Pursuit of False Pleasure, and the Mischiefs of Immoderate Gaming* (Bath: James Leake, 1750).

Burney, Charles. *Memoirs of Dr. Charles Burney 1726–1769,* edited by Slava Klima, Gary Bowers, and Kerry S. Grant (Lincoln: University of Nebraska Press, 1988).

Burr, Thomas Benge. *The History of Tunbridge Wells*. London: M. Hingeston, J. Dodsley, T. Caslon (Tunbridge Wells: E. Baker, 1766).

[Burton, John]. *Epistolae Altera Peregrinantis, Altera Rusticantis* (Oxford: J. Fletcher, 1748).

[Chandler, Mary]. *A Description of Bath, a Poem, Humbly Inscribed to Her Royal Highness the Princess Amelia* (London: J. Gray, 1734).

Cheyne, George. *The English Malady* (London: George Strahan, 1733).

— *An Essay of Health and Long Life* (London: George Strahan, 1724).

— *The Letters of Dr. George Cheyne to the Countess of Huntingdon,* edited by Charles F. Mullett (San Marino: Huntington Library, 1940).

— *The Letters of Doctor George Cheyne to Samuel Richardson (1733–1743),* edited by Charles F. Mullett (Columbia: University of Missouri Press, 1943).

— *Observations Concerning the Nature and Due Method of Treating the Gout* (London: George Strahan, 1720).

Coke, Jane. *Letters from Lady Jane Coke to Her Friend Mrs. Eyre,* edited by Florence Rathbone (London: Swan Sonnenschein, 1899).

Collier, Jeremy. *An Essay upon Gaming, in a Dialogue between Callimachus and Dolomedes* (London: John Morphew, 1713. Reprint edition Edinburgh: Edmund Goldsmid, 1885).

Cowper, Mary. *Diary of Mary, Countess Cowper, Lady of the Bedchamber to the Princess of Wales, 1714–1720* (London: John Murray, 1864).

Cox, Thomas. *Magna Britannia et Hibernia, Antiqua et Nova, or, A New Survey of Great Britain* (London: E. and R. Nutt, 1720-1731).

Defoe, Daniel. *The Fortunes and Misfortunes of the Famous Moll Flanders* (Oxford: Oxford University Press, 1971).

— *A Review of the State of the British Nation* (Facsimile edition New York: Columbia University Press, 1938).

— *A Tour Thro' the Whole Island of Great Britain* (London: George Strahan, 1724).

— *A Tour through the Whole Island of Great Britain* (Second edition London: J. Osborn, S. Birt, D. Browne, A. Millar, F. Cogan, J. Whiston, and J. Robinson, 1738.

Delany, Mary Granville Pendarves. *The Autobiography and Correspondence of Mary Granville, Mrs. Delany* (London: Richard Bentley, 1861. Facsimile edition New York: AMS Press, 1974).

Derrick, Samuel. *Letters* (London: L. Davis and C. Reymers, 1767).

Doddridge, Philip. *The Correspondence and Diary of Philip Doddridge*, edited by John Doddridge Humphreys (London: Henry Colburn and Richard Bentley, 1829).

Dodsley, Robert. *The Correspondence of Robert Dodsley 1733–1764*, edited by James E. Tierney (Cambridge: Cambridge University Press, 1988).

[Draper, Joseph]. *A Brief Description of Bath, in a Letter to a Friend* (N.p., 1747).

D'Urfey, Thomas. *The Bath, or, The Western Lass* (London: Peter Buck, 1701).

— *Wit and Mirth, or, Pills to Purge Melancholy* (London: Jacob Tonson, 1719).

Fielding, Henry. *The History of Tom Jones*, edited by Martin C. Battestin (Middletown: Wesleyan University Press, 1975).

Fielding, Henry and Sarah. *The Correspondence of Henry and Sarah Fielding*, edited by Martin Battestin and Clive T. Probyn (Oxford: Oxford University Press, 1993).

Fiennes, Celia. *The Journeys of Celia Fiennes*, edited by John Hillaby (London: Macdonald, 1983).

Fleming, Francis. *The Life and Adventures of Timothy Ginnadrake* (Bath: R. Cruttwell, 1771).

Gainsborough, Thomas. *The Letters of Thomas Gainsborough*, edited by John Hayes (New Haven: Yale University Press, 2001).

Gale, Samuel. 'A Tour through Several Parts of England,' in John Nichols, editor, *Bibliotheca Topographica* (London: John Nichols, 1790. Facsimile edition New York: AMS Press, 1968).

Gay, John. *The Letters of John Gay*, edited by C.F. Burgess (Oxford: Oxford University Press, 1966).

Goldsmith, Oliver. *The Works of Oliver Goldsmith*, edited by Arthur Friedman (Oxford: Oxford University Press, 1966).

Goulding, Thomas. *An Essay Against Too Much Reading, with the Whole Lives and Proceedings of Sancho and Peepo, at Aix la Chapelle in Germany* (London: A. Moore, 1728).

— *A True Account and Design of the Proceedings this Last Year in so Many Processions at Bath* (London: A. Moore, 1728).
— *The Fortune-Hunter, or, The Gamester Reclaim'd* (Bath: Privately Printed, 1736).
[Grainger, Lydia]. *Modern Amours, or, A Secret History of the Adventures of Some Personages of the First Rank* (London: n.p., 1733).
Guidott, Thomas. *A Discourse of Bathe, and the Hot Waters There* (London: Henry Brome, 1676).
— *The Register of Bath* (London: F. Leach and Randal Taylor, 1694).
[Haywood, Eliza]. *Bath Intrigues: In Four Letters to a Friend in London.* (London: J. Roberts, 1725. Facsimile edition Los Angeles: William Andrews Clark Memorial Library, 1986).
Hervey, John. *Letter Books of John Hervey, First Earl of Bristol*, edited by Sydenham Hervey (Wells: Ernest Jackson, 1894).
Historical Manuscripts Commission Reports:
11th Report
15th Report
Astley MSS
Bath MSS
Dropmore MSS
Egmont Diary
Hastings MSS
Polwarth MSS
Portland MSS
Howard, Henrietta. *Letters to and from Henrietta, Countess of Suffolk, and her Second Husband, the Hon. George Berkeley* (London: John Murray, 1824).
Johnson, Samuel. *The Letters of Samuel Johnson,* edited by Bruce Redford (Princeton: Princeton University Press, 1992).
Ken, Thomas. *Prayers for the Use of All Persons Who Come to the Baths for Cure* (London: Charles Brome, 1692).

Kielmansegge, Friedrich Graf von. *Diary of a Journey to England in the Years 1761–1762,* translated by Phillipa Sidney, Grafin von Kielmansegge (London: Longmans, 1902).

Le Blanc, Abbé. *Letters on the English and French Nations*, translator unknown (London: J. Brindley, 1741).

Lennox, Charlotte. *The Female Quixote, or the Adventures of Arabella,* edited by Margaret Dalziel (Oxford: Oxford University Press, 1970).

Lucas, Theophilus. *Memoirs of the Lives, Intrigues, and Comical Adventures of the Most Famous Gamesters and Celebrated Sharpers in the Reigns of Charles II, James II, William III, and Queen Anne* (London: James Brown, 1714).

[Macky, John]. *A Journey through England in Familiar Letters for a Gentleman Here, to His Friend Abroad* (London: J. Roberts, 1714).

[Macky, John]. *A Journey through England in Familiar Letters for a Gentleman Here, to His Friend Abroad* (London: J. Pemberton, 1722).

[Miège, Guy]. *The Present State of Great Britain.* (London: J. Nicholson, A. Bell, R. Smith, and J. Round, 1707).

— *A New Present State of England* (London: R. Baldwin, 1750).

[Morris, Claver]. *The Diary of a West Country Physician 1684–1726,* edited by Edmund Hobhouse (London: Simpkin Marshall, 1934).

Odingsells, G. *The Bath Unmask'd: A Comedy* (London: J. Walthoe, 1725).

[Oldmixon, John]. *Court Tales, or, A History of the Amours of the Present Nobility* (London: J. Roberts, 1717).

Oliver, William. *A Practical Essay on Fevers . . . To Which is Annex'd, A Dissertation on the Bath-Waters* (London: T. Goodwin, 1704).

The Orrery Papers, ed. Countess of Cork and Orrery (London: Duckworth, 1903).

Osborn, Sarah Byng. *Letters of Sarah Byng Osborn 1721–1773,* edited by John McClelland (Stanford: Stanford University Press, 1930).

Penrose, John. *Letters from Bath,* edited by Brigitte Mitchell and Hubert Penrose (Gloucester: Alan Sutton, 1983).

Pierce, Robert. *Bath Memoirs, or, Observations in Three and Forty Years Practice at the Bath* (Bristol: H. Hammond, 1697).

[Playford, John]. *The Dancing Schoole: Directions for Dancing Country Dances, with the Tunes to Each Dance, for the Treble Violin* (London: W. Pearson, 1716).

Pococke, Richard. *The Travels through England of Dr. Richard Pococke,* edited by James Joel Cartwright (London: Camden Society, 1889).

Pöllnitz, Karl Ludwig von. *Les Amusemens de Spa: or, The Gallantries of Spaw in Germany,* translated by Hans de Veil (London: Ward and Chandler, 1737).

Pope, Alexander. *Correspondence of Alexander Pope,* edited by George Sherburn (Oxford: Oxford University Press, 1956).

Prévost, Antoine François (Abbé), et al, *Le Pour et Contre,* edited by Steve Larkin (Oxford: Oxford University Press, 1993).

Quinton, John. *A Treatise of Warm Bath Water, and of Cures Made Lately at Bath in Somersetshire* (Oxford: n.p., 1733).

Rameau, P. *The Dancing-Master, or, The Whole Art and Mystery of Dancing Explained,* translated by John Essex (Second edition London: J. Brotherton, 1731).

Ryder, Dudley. *The Diary of Dudley Ryder 1715–1716,* edited by William Matthews (London: Methuen, 1939).

Seymour, Richard. *The Court Gamester* (London: Edmund Curll, 1719).

Smith, Thomas. 'Diary of Thomas Smith, Esq., of Shaw House.' *Wiltshire Archaeological and Natural History Magazine* 11 (November 1867): 82–105; (May 1868): 204–17; (February1869): 308–315.

Smollett, Tobias. *An Essay on the External Use of Water* (London: M. Cooper, 1752).

— *The Adventures of Peregrine Pickle,* edited by James L. Clifford (Oxford: Oxford University Press, 1964).

— *The Adventures of Roderick Random* (Oxford: Oxford University Press, 1979).
— *The Expedition of Humphry Clinker,* edited by Lewis Knapp (Oxford: Oxford University Press, 1966).
Steele, Richard. *The Tatler,* edited by Donald Bond (Oxford : Oxford University Press, 1987).
Sutherland, Alexander. *Attempts to Revive Ancient Medical Doctrines* (London: Andrew Millar, 1763).
Swift, Jonathan. *Jonathan Swift: Complete Poems,* edited by Pat Rogers (New Haven: Yale University Press, 1983).
Thicknesse, Philip. *The New Prose Bath Guide for the Year 1778* (Second edition London: Dodsley, 1780).
— *The Valetudinarian's Bath Guide, or, The Means of Obtaining Long Life and Health* (London: Dodsley, 1780).
[Ward, Edward]. *The Insinuating Bawd and the Repenting Harlot, Written by a Whore at Tunbridge, and Dedicated to a Bawd at the Bath* (London: J. How and M. Fabian, 1700).
Warner, Richard. *The History of Bath* (Bath: R. Crutwell, 1801).
The Wentworth Papers 1705–1739, edited by James J. Cartwright (London: Wyman and Sons, 1883).
Wesley, John. *The Letters of the Reverend John Wesley* (London: Epworth, 1931).
Whatley, R. *Characters at the Hot-Well, Bristol, in September, and at Bath, in October, 1723* (London: James Lacy, 1724).
Wilson, Thomas. *The Diaries of Thomas Wilson, D.D. 1731-37 and 1750,* edited by C.L.S. Linnell (London: Society for the Propagation of Christian Knowledge, 1964).
Wood, John. *Essay Toward a Description of Bath*. London: W. Bathoe and T. Lowndes, 1765 (Facsimile edition Bath: Kingsmead Reprints, 1969).

Secondary sources

Ayres, James. *Building the Georgian City* (New Haven: Yale University Press, 1998).

Baker, C.H. Collins and Muriel I. *The Life and Circumstances of James Brydges, First Duke of Chandos* (Oxford: Oxford University Press, 1949).

Barbeau, Alfred. *Life and Letters at Bath in the Eighteenth Century* (London: William Heinemann, 1904).

Barker-Benfield, G.J. *The Culture of Sensibility: Sex and Society in Eighteenth-Century Britain* (Chicago: University of Chicago Press, 1992).

Barton, Margaret. *Tunbridge Wells* (London: Faber and Faber, 1937).

Bermingham, Ann, and John Brewer, editors. *The Consumption of Culture 1600–1800: Image, Object, Text* (London: Routledge, 1995).

Borsay, Anne. *Medicine and Charity in Georgian Bath: A Social History of the General Infirmary, c. 1739–1830* (Aldershot: Ashgate, 1999).

Borsay, Peter. *The English Urban Renaissance: Culture and Society in the Provincial Town* (Oxford: Oxford University Press, 1989).

— *The Image of Georgian Bath 1700–2000: Towns, Heritage, and History* (Oxford: Oxford University Press, 2000).

Briggs, Peter M. 'The Significance of Beau Nash.' *Studies in Eighteenth Century Culture* 22 (1992): 208–30.

Carter, Philip. *Men and the Emergence of Polite Society, Britain 1660–1800* (London: Longman, 2001).

Clark, Peter, Editor. *Country Towns in Pre-Industrial England* (Leicester: Leicester University Press, 1981).

Connelly, Willard. *Beau Nash: Monarch of Bath and Tunbridge Wells* (London: Werner Laurie, 1955).

Corfield, Penelope J. *The Impact of English Towns 1700-1800* (Oxford: Oxford University Press, 1982).

Cunliffe, Barry. *The City of Bath* (New Haven: Yale University Press, 1987).

Davis, Graham, and Penny Bonsall. *Bath: A New History* (Keele: Keele University Press, 1996).

Fawcett, Trevor. *Bath Entertain'd: Amusements, Recreations and Gambling at the Eighteenth-Century Spa* (Bath: Ruton, 1998).

— 'Dance and Teachers of Dance in Eighteenth-Century Bath.' *Bath History* 2 (1988): 27–48.

— 'Eighteenth-Century Shops and the Luxury Trade.' *Bath History* 3 (1990): 49–75.

Fawcett, Trevor, and Marta Inskip. 'The Making of Orange Grove.' *Bath History* 5 (1994): 24–50.

Ferguson, Oliver W. 'The Materials of History: Goldsmith's *Life of Nash*.' *PMLA* 80 (September 1965): 372–86.

Gadd, David. *Georgian Summer: Bath in the Eighteenth Century* (Bath: Adams and Dart, 1971).

Guerrini, Anita. *Obesity and Depression in the Enlightenment: The Life and Times of George Cheyne* (Norman: University of Oklahoma Press, 2000).

Hamilton, Meg. *Bath Before Beau Nash: A Guide Based on Gilmore's Map of Bath, 1692–4* (Bath: Kingsmead, 1978).

Handasyde, Elizabeth. *Granville the Polite: The Life of George Granville Lord Lansdowne, 1666–1735* (London: Humphrey Milford, 1933).

Hembry, Phyllis. *The English Spa 1560–1815: A Social Histor.* (London: Athlone Press, 1990).

Hill, Mary K. *Bath and the Eighteenth-Century Novel* (Bath: Bath University Press, 1989).

Hopkins, Robert H. *The True Genius of Oliver Goldsmith* (Baltimore: Johns Hopkins University Press, 1969).

Hoppit, Julian. *A Land of Liberty? England 1689–1727* (Oxford: Oxford University Press 2000).

Ilchester, Earl of. *Lord Hervey and His Friends* (London: John Murray, 1950).

Ison, Walter. *The Georgian Buildings of Bath* (London: Faber and Faber, 1948).

Langford, Paul. *A Polite and Commercial People: England 1727–1783* (Oxford: Oxford University Press, 1989).

MacDonald, Michael, and Terence R. Murphy. *Sleepless Souls: Suicide in Early Modern England* (Oxford: Oxford University Press, 1990).

Manco, Jean. 'The Cross Bath.' *Bath History* 2(1988): 49–84.

Melville, Lewis. *Bath under Beau Nash* (London: Eveleigh Nash, 1907).

Monod, Paul Kléber. *Jacobitism and the English People, 1688–1788* (Cambridge: Cambridge University Press, 1989).

Mowl, Tim, and Brian Earnshaw. *John Wood: Architect of Obsession* (Bath: Millstream Books, 1988).

Neale, Ronald S. *Bath 1680–1850: A Social History* (London: Routledge, 1981).

Parlett, David. *A History of Card Games* (Oxford: Oxford University Press, 1991).

Peach, Robert E. M. *The Life and Times of Ralph Allen* (London: D. Nutt, 1895).

Petrie, Charles. *The Jacobite Movement* (London: Eyre and Spottiswoode, 1959).

Sitwell, Edith. *Bath* (London: Faber and Faber, 1932).

Sloman, Susan. *Gainsborough in Bath* (New Haven: Yale University Press, 2002).

— 'The Immaculate Captain Wade': 'Arbiter Elegantiae." *Gainsborough's House Review* 1993/1994 (1994): 46–62.

Stone, Lawrence. *Uncertain Unions and Broken Lives: Marriage and Divorce in England 1660–1857* (Oxford: Oxford University Press, 1995).

Taylor, Richard. *Goldsmith as Journalist* (Rutherford: Fairleigh-Dickinson University Press, 1993).

Turner, David M. *Fashioning Adultery: Gender, Sex and Civility in England, 1660–1740* (Cambridge: Cambridge University Press, 2002).

Tyte, William. *Bath in the Eighteenth Century: Its Progress and Life Described.* (Bath: G. and F. Pickering, 1903).

Varey, Simon. *Space and the Eighteetnh-Century Novel* (Cambridge: Cambridge University Press, 1990).

Vickery, Amanda. *The Gentleman's Daughter: Women's Lives in Georgian England* (New Haven: Yale University Press, 1998).

Walters, John. *Splendour and Scandal: The Reign of Beau Nash* (London: Jarrold's Publishers, 1968).

Weatherill, Lorna. *Consumer Behaviour and Material Culture in Britain 1660–1760* (London: Routledge, 1996).

Wendorf, Richard. *The Elements of Life: Biography and Portrait-Painting in Stuart and Georgian England* (Oxford: Oxford University Press, 1990).

Williams, J. Anthony. *Post-Reformation Catholicism in Bath* (London: Catholic Record Society, 1975).

Williams, Marjorie. *Lady Luxborough Goes to Bath.* (Oxford: Basil Blackwell, 1946).

Woodward, Christopher. ''O Lord! Bath is Undone; 'Tis Undone; 'Tis Undone!' Bath and the Pre-History of Architectural Conservation.' *Bath History* 7 (1998): 7–26.

Index

C